英汉对照典藏版

轻松走进
剑桥大学

陆路平
陈　柳　编著
[英] Anthony Powell

中国宇航出版社
·北京·

图书在版编目（CIP）数据

轻松走进剑桥大学/陆路平等编著．—北京：中国宇航出版社，2010.8

（轻松走进世界名校系列）

ISBN 978-7-80218-766-5

Ⅰ.①轻… Ⅱ.①陆… Ⅲ.①英语-阅读教学-自学参考资料 Ⅳ.①H319.4

中国版本图书馆 CIP 数据核字（2010）第 118234 号

策划编辑 李士振　　装帧设计 03工舍
责任编辑 李士振　　责任校对 裴燕娜

出版发行 中国宇航出版社
社 址 北京市阜成路 8 号　　邮 编 100830
(010)68768548
网 址 www.caphbook.com/www.caphbook.com.cn
经 销 新华书店
发行部 (010)68371900　　(010)88530478（传真）
(010)68768541　　(010)68767294（传真）
零售店 读者服务部　　北京宇航文苑
(010)68371105　　(010)62529336
承 印 三河市君旺印装厂
版 次 2010 年 8 月第 1 版　　2010 年 8 月第 1 次印刷
规 格 787×960　　开 本 1/16
印 张 18　　字 数 341 千字
书 号 ISBN 978-7-80218-766-5
定 价 29.80 元（附赠全文 MP3 光盘）

本书如有印装质量问题，可与发行部联系调换

前言 Preface

剑桥，是一幅历经800年沧桑造就的精神地图。12世纪，平坦、潮湿的沼泽地上来了三位修士，圣芳济修士、黑袍修士和卡莫修士，他们在这里创立了剑桥古镇。100多年后，为了抗议法庭对两名教师的诬告，牛津大学的教师们停止授课，纷纷离去。其中一部分人打算重建学校，他们来到了剑桥古镇，剑桥大学便由此诞生。剑桥大学先后获得了英王亨利三世和教皇格雷戈尔九世的特许，在此后整整600年，与牛津大学一起成为英国仅有的大学。至今，剑桥大学和牛津大学仍然是英国最优秀的两所大学，合称为“牛桥”(Oxbridge)。

在《泰晤士报高等教育增刊》最新的大学排行榜上，剑桥大学名列全球第二，在刚刚宣布的诺贝尔奖得主名单上，一位学者又为这所古老的大学增添了一项殊荣。然而，对于一个大学的神话来说，它最令人着迷的地方还是小说家福斯特描述得最为恰当:“精神和肉体，理智和情感，工作和玩乐，建筑和风景，欢笑和严肃，生活和艺术，这些对应物在别处是对立的，在这里却融为一体。人与书籍互相支持，智慧与情感携手并行，思索成为一种热情，辩论因痴迷而意味深长。”

你心中的剑桥大学是什么样的？本书试图以一种轻松的心态为基点，集故事性、趣味性为一体，通过解读13世纪以来剑桥大学的历史，发掘剑桥的古老建筑和街巷，庭院和绿地，感受剑桥师生在学习生活中的疯狂与浪漫，欣赏这里丰富的文化艺术及其独特的个性，追踪那些曾经生活在这里的著名的以及平凡的人物，为大家构建一个了解、熟悉剑桥大学的崭新视角，让你轻松走进剑桥。此外，在人们眼中，剑桥大学和牛津大学总是密不可分的，本书还会展示这两所大学间的合作与竞争。近年来越来越多的中国学子远赴英国留学，剑桥大学自然是他们梦寐以求的，本书也会对剑桥的留学生活加以介绍。

本书共分为10个单元，每个单元包括4篇文章。每篇文章分为3个部分，包括焦点对话、难点解析和主题延伸。焦点对话针对口语，让您在了解剑桥大学的同时，又能扩大词汇量，提高口语表达能力。难点解析针对语法，让您轻松记单词、快乐学语法。主题延伸针对文化，让您进一步了解剑桥精神和文化。此外，本书还配有由北京外国语大学专家配音录制的MP3光盘，您在学习的时候可以模仿诵读，对口语和听力的提高都有很大帮助。

编者

2010年夏于北京外国语大学

目录 CONTENTS

Unit 1 History and Legends 烟波何处寻

Unit 2 Architectures & Landscapes 诗意栖息地

Unit 3 Life & Study 青春舞飞扬

目录 CONTENTS

Unit 4 Literature & Art 浪漫芳草园

Unit 5 Science & Technology 行行出状元

Unit 6 Celebrities & Alumni 桃李满天下

Unit 7 Chinese in Cambridge 剑桥中国心

Unit 8 Women in Cambridge 巾帼胜须眉

Unit 9 Competitor and Partner 牛桥恩仇录

目录 CONTENTS

Unit 10 Overseas Study 领略英伦风情

Unit 1 History and Legends
烟波何处寻

1 Established in 1209
追溯剑桥

Kerry and Tom are going to school toghther.

T: Tom　　K: Kerry

T: Morning, Kerry! You have shadows under your eyes. It seems that you didn't sleep well last night. What's the matter?

K: Oh, I did have a sleepless night after having watched a piece of news about the University of Cambridge. It sent shivers down my spine.

T: Now you have really hooked my curiosity. As far as I know, the University of Cambridge is consistently ranked in the world's top five universities and the leading university in Europe by numerous media and academic rankings. How can it **terrify**[①] you?

K: Yes, you are quite right. This is a university with over 800 years history, thus, it provides a platform for those myths and legends.

T: 800 years? Are you sure? That's quite a long time!

K: Of course. The year of 2009 marked its 800th anniversary.

T: So what myth or legend have you heard about?

K: On the evening news last night, the ghost in the university has become the talk of the town....

T: You are kidding, aren't you? There is no such a thing existing in the world.

① terrify *v.* 使某人受惊，惊吓某人

K: No, I'm serious. In the video shot by a tourist at the campus, we can see a **blurred**① white shadow go through the wall and enter the castle of a college.

T: A ghost? Even though the university manages to maintain its **medieval**② appearance since its foundation, with those lawn, rivers, castles, it cannot be a place of ghost.

K: Students of this university believe that's **Crowell**③'s spirit. People had the head of this **beheaded**④ revolutionist buried somewhere at the campus. As the alumni, he may sometimes feel like returning to his old dormitory.

T: This story completely makes no sense. It must be made up to boom the local tourism. Don't be mocked.

K: All right. Maybe I shouldn't trouble trouble until trouble troubles me. By the way, do you know the relationship between Oxford and Cambridge?

T: A little. I find some materials online that tell me they are both friends and rivals.

K: Oh, in my eyes, they have much cultural and practical association as a historic part of British society. You see, both of them are ranked the top five universities in the world; they both locate in the British Island, and Cambridge is founded by scholars leaving Oxford after a dispute with the **townsfolk**⑤ there.

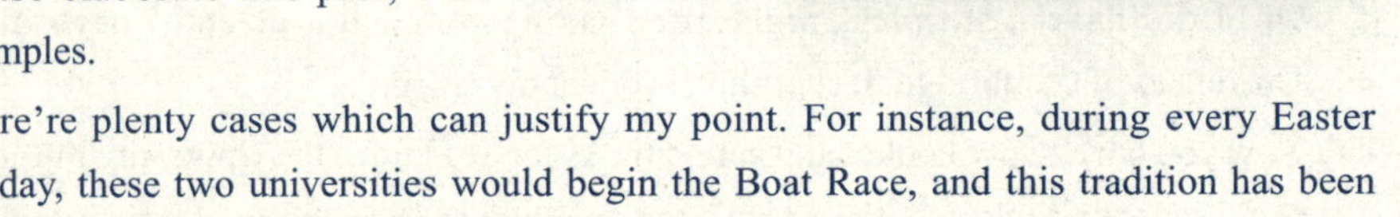

T: However, on the other hand, they are in a long competition since then.

K: Please elaborate this part, OK? I'd like more examples.

T: There're plenty cases which can justify my point. For instance, during every Easter holiday, these two universities would begin the Boat Race, and this tradition has been maintained since the 19th century!

K: Boat Race? Why?

T: Because they cannot tell which one is better academically, and sports is one of the most reasonable ways to pick out a winner.

K: Oh, I remember that the Boat Race is a rowing race in England between the Oxford University Boat Club and the Cambridge University Boat Club. The first race was in

---

① blurred *adj.* 模糊不清的

② medieval *adj.* 中世纪的

③ Crowell 克伦威尔，英国政治家、军事家、宗教领袖。17 世纪英国资产阶级革命中，资产阶级新贵族集团的代表人物、独立派的首领。

④ behead *v.* 斩首，砍头

⑤ townsfolk *n.* 城里人，市民

1829 and it has been held annually since 1856, each spring on the Thames in London with the exception of the two world wars.

T: This event is very popular. About a quarter of a million people watch the race live from the banks of the river, around seven to nine million people on TV in the UK.

T: 早上好！凯瑞！你有黑眼圈，昨晚没睡好吧。出什么事儿了吗？

K: 我昨晚的确失眠了，就是因为看了电视上一则有关英国剑桥大学的新闻。真让我毛骨悚然。

T: 你现在激起我的好奇心了。据我所知，剑桥大学稳居世界大学排名的前五名，还被众多媒体和学术机构评为欧洲最好的大学。关于这样一所大学的消息怎么会吓到你呢？

K: 你说得对。这是一所有着 800 多年历史的大学，所以它也为众多奇谈和传说提供了素材。

T: 800 年？真的吗？这真是一段漫长的时光！

K: 是的。2009 年剑桥大学迎来了 800 周年校庆。

T: 那么你从新闻里听到了什么样的奇谈或是传说呢？

K: 在昨晚的晚间新闻里，剑桥大学里的鬼影已经成了街头巷尾的话题……

T: 你在开玩笑吧？世界上根本没有这种东西。

K: 不，我是说真的。有位游客在校园里拍了一段视频，上面有个模糊的白色影子直接穿过了城墙，进入了一个学院的古堡里。

T: 鬼？即使剑桥竭力保持了自其创始以来的中世纪风貌，有草坪、河流、古堡等等，那也不代表它就成了座鬼城呀。

K: 剑桥大学的学生认为那是克伦威尔的鬼魂。听说这位被斩首的革命家就是被埋在了剑桥大学里。作为校友，克伦威尔可能有时候想要回自己原来的宿舍看看。

T: 这些故事都是毫无根据的。它们是被编出来刺激当地旅游业发展的。你可别上当了。

K: 你说得对。也许我不该自寻烦恼。对了，你了解牛津大学和剑桥大学之间的关系吗？

T: 知道一点儿。根据我在网上查到的资料，他们既是朋友，又是对手。

K: 噢，在我眼中，它们之间有着众多文化和实践的结合，都是英国社会历史的一部分。你瞧，它们都是世界排名前五的大学，都位于大不列颠岛上，而且剑桥是在一群牛津的学者们为了躲避与当地人的争斗，离开了牛津之后建立起来的。

T: 但是从另一方面来看，剑桥自创立的那一天起，就和牛津展开了漫长的竞争。

K: 你能详细说说吗？我想听听。

T: 例子可多着呢。比如，在每年的复活节放假期间，这两所大学就会举办“牛津剑桥划艇比赛”，这一传统可是从 19 世纪就已经流传下来的！

K: “划艇比赛”？为什么是比这个项目呢?

T: 因为它们没法决出哪所学校在学术上更为出色，而体育运动就是能够合情合理地挑选出赢家的最好方式之一。

K: 哦，我想起来了，这个划艇比赛是在英格兰举行的剑桥大学划艇俱乐部和牛津大学划艇俱乐部之间的比赛。第一次比赛是在 1829 年，除了在两次世界大战期间暂停过以外，自 1856 年以来每年都在伦敦的泰晤士河举行。

T: 这个比赛很受欢迎。在英国，大约有 25 万人在泰晤士河河岸现场观看比赛，有 700 万到 900 万人通过电视收看。

1 Oh, I did have a sleepless night after having watched a piece of news about the University of Cambridge. **It sent shivers down my spine.**

It sent shivers down my spine. 意为“令人毛骨悚然”。

➢ The story was so terrible that it sent shivers down my spine.
这故事太可怕，它使我毛骨悚然。

2 On the evening news last night, the ghost in the university has become **the talk of the town.**

talk of the town 意为“街谈巷议、街头巷尾的话题、众人口中的谈资”。

➢ The modern sculpture outside the new library is the talk of the town.
新图书馆外面的那尊现代雕塑成了街谈巷议的话题。

3 Maybe I shouldn't **trouble trouble until trouble troubles me**.

Never trouble trouble until trouble troubles you. 这是句谚语，意为“不要自寻烦恼”，也可以说成 Don't meet trouble halfway。

➢ You will pass the exam and don't meet trouble halfway.
你会通过考试的，不要自寻烦恼。

4 Cambridge is consistently ranked in the world's top five universities and the leading university in Europe by **numerous** media and academic rankings.

numerous 意为“数目众多的，数量大的”，注意与 numerable 相区别，后者意为可数的，可计算的。

➢ The Earth is only one of the **numerous** planets in the universe.
地球只是宇宙中众多星球中的一个。

➢ He explained that this is because China faces both **numerable** favorable conditions and restrictive factors during this period.
他认为原因是这一阶段中国经济既具备许多有利条件同时又面临许多制约因素。

Established in 1209

The University of Cambridge (informally Cambridge University, or simply Cambridge) is the second oldest university in England. The university was formed, early records suggest, in 1209 by scholars leaving Oxford after a **dispute**[1] with the townsfolks there. The two "ancient universities" have many common features and are often jointly referred to as **Oxbridge**[2]. In addition to cultural and practical associations as a historic part of British society, the two universities also have a long history of **rivalry**[3] with each other.

Academically[4], Cambridge is consistently ranked in the world's top five universities and the leading university in Europe by numerous media and academic rankings. The University's **alumni**[5] include 85 Nobel Laureates as of 2009.The University is a member of **the Russell Group**[6] of research-led British universities. The history of the University of Cambridge could trace its origin to a crime committed in 1209. Although not always a reliable source, the detail given in **contemporane-**

① dispute *n.* 争论，争吵
② Oxbridge *n.* 牛津大学与剑桥大学的合称
③ rivalry *n.* 敌对关系，对手关系
④ academically *adv.* 学术地，学术上而言
⑤ alumni *n.* 校友
⑥ The Russell Group 罗素大学集团，英国一名校大学联盟，成立于 1994 年，由 19 所英国研究型的大学组成，被称为英国的常春藤联盟，代表着英国的优秀大学。

ous① writings lends them credence.

Two Oxford scholars were convicted of the murder or **manslaughter**② of a woman and were hanged by the town authorities with the assent of King John. In protest at the hanging, the University of Oxford went into voluntary **suspension**③, and scholars **migrated**④ to a number of other locations, including the pre-existing school at Cambridge (Cambridge had been recorded as a "school" rather than as a university when John Grim held the office of Master there in 1201). These exiled Oxford scholars (post-graduate researchers by present day **terminology**⑤) started Cambridge's life as a university in 1209.

Cambridge is a **collegiat**⑥ university, meaning that it is made up of self-governing and independent colleges, each with its own property and income. Most colleges bring together academics and students from a broad range of disciplines.

Sustaining a world-class university demands investment in new facilities, new areas of study, and most importantly, in people; continued **fundraising**⑦ efforts and innovative partnerships will be vital. The University celebrated its 800th anniversary in 2009, marking the legacy of eight centuries and determined to remain among the world's greatest universities.

追溯剑桥

剑桥大学（有时被简称为剑桥）是除了牛津大学以外，英国历史最悠久的大学。根据记载，剑桥大学成立于 1209 年，最早是由一批为躲避殴斗而从牛津大学逃离出来的学者们建立的。剑桥大学和牛津大学（University of Oxford）这两所历史悠久的大学因为具有许多共同特点，常常被合称为“牛桥”。作为英国社会历史的一部分，剑桥大学和牛津大学在文化以及实践方面有着许多合作，但除此之外，这两所学校之间同样存在着旷日持久的竞争。

从学术成就上来说，在众多媒体和

① contemporaneous *adj.* 同时期的，同时代的
② manslaughter *n.* 过失杀人
③ suspension *n.* 暂停，停止
④ migrate *v.* 移居，移民
⑤ terminology *n.* 用词，术语
⑥ collegiate *adj.* 学院的
⑦ fundraising *n.* 募集资金，募捐

学术机构的排名中，剑桥大学稳居全球排名前五位，同时它也是欧洲各所大学的领头羊。截止至 2009 年，剑桥大学一共培养了 85 位诺贝尔奖得主。剑桥大学还是英国名校联盟“罗素大学集团”（Russell Group）的成员。

剑桥大学的历史可追溯到1209年的一起刑事案件上。尽管信息来源并不十分可靠，但从相关资料来看，这一说法还是有一定可信度的。

牛津大学的两名学者因被控蓄意谋杀一名妇女，在获得当时的国王约翰的许可后，被牛津当局处以绞刑。为了抗议这一行为，牛津大学开始了罢课，许多学者开始移居其他地方，其中就包括了剑桥学校(即剑桥大学的前身。1201 年约翰·格林担任校长时，剑桥仅仅被称为一所“学校”，而非“大学”)。这些流亡的牛津学者，在 1209 年将剑桥学校变成了剑桥大学，赋予了其新的生命力。用今天的标准来看，他们就是一批硕士研究生。

这所学校是一所学院式大学，由独立管理和独立发展的学院构成，每所学院都拥有自己独立的财产和收入，招收来自各专业的学生。

要想维持世界一流大学的水准，需要不断地对设备、研究领域，特别是人力资源方面进行投资。因此，持续为剑桥大学募集资金，开拓新的合作关系就变得尤为重要了。2009 年是剑桥大学建校 800 周年，在向世界展示了它在 8 个世纪里所取得的成就之后，剑桥大学决心继续为保持世界一流大学水平而不断努力。

2 Town and Gown
城市与大学

焦点对话

Anna is reading a book, and Zac walks towards her.

Z: Zac	A: Anna

Z: What are you reading?

A: Oh, a book about the history of Cambridge. I'm reading the part named "Town and Gown".

Z: What does this phrase mean?

A: "Town" and "gown" are referring to the two **distinct**[①] communities of a university town: "town" being the non-academic population and "gown" **metonymically**[②] being the university community.

Z: I see. Just like some ancient seats of learning such as Oxford, Cambridge and St. Andrews.

A: You're right. Sometimes, the term is also used to describe modern university towns.

Z: Perhaps this term came into being when the oldest universities in the world began to form. I guess it was in **the Middle Ages**[③]?

A: Yes. During that time, students admitted to the European universities often held minor

---

① distinct *adj.* 清楚的，明显的，特别的

② metonymically *adv.* 转喻地

③ the Middle Age 中世纪，是欧洲历史上的一个时代（主要是西欧），由西罗马帝国灭亡（公元 476 年）数百年后，在世界范围内，封建制度占统治地位的时期，直到文艺复兴时期（公元 1453 年）之后，资本主义抬头的时期为止。

clerical[①] status and **donned**[②] garb similar to that worn by the clergy. These **vestments**[③] evolved into the academic long black gown, worn along with **hood**[④] and cap.

Z: We can see that the hood nowadays is often adorned with different colors; maybe that is the way to **designate**[⑤] from which college the young scholars come from.

A: Besides, by their distinctive clothing, the students were set apart and distinguished from the citizens of the town; hence the phrase "town and gown".

Z: Now that kind of gown has become a tradition in the universities. University students all over the world wear gowns like that at special occasions, for example, the degree ceremony and so on.

A: That's true. Now you understand this phrase, and do you want to know more about it?

Z: I'd like to. Tell me more about it!

A: OK. The town and gown **rivalry**[⑥] is mentioned in the book, too.

Z: Rivalry? You mean they do not get along well with each other?

A: Yes. Conflict was **inevitable**[⑦] in the medieval university towns where two separately governed bodies with different priorities and loyalties shared the same restricted space.

Z: Sounds reasonable. Moreover, violence was **commonplace**[⑧] in medieval life, not only between scholars and townsmen but among ordinary citizens.

A: It also happened between scholars from different regions of Europe who attended the universities. Violent confrontations between town and gown erupted on a recurring basis.

Z: I heard that The University of Cambridge was originally set-up after a fight between the townspeople of Oxford and scholars from the University of Oxford forced many scholars to flee to a new location.

A: That is mentioned in the book. That was in 1209, and several decades later, the tension between the scholars at Cambridge and the towns people forced the King to grant special privileges and protection to Cambridge University.

Z: As urban universities increase in size and complexity, the conflict between them may become more and more severe.

---

① clerical *adj.* 牧师的，办事员的，神职人员的
② don *vt.* 穿上
③ vestment *n.* 法衣，官服，礼服
④ hood *n.*（修道士袍服上的）兜帽，大学制服后的垂布
⑤ designate *vt.* 标出，指定
⑥ rivalry *n.* 竞争，竞赛
⑦ inevitable *adj.* 必然的，不可避免的
⑧ commonplace *n.* 老生常谈，司空见惯的事

A: That's for sure. To a large extent, "town versus gown" disputes have moved from the streets into the courts and city hall.

Z: Did they ever pay regard to the town-gown connection?

A: No idea. Universities boast that their existence is the **backbone**① of the town economy, while the towns counter with claims that the institution is "robbing" them of tax revenue.

Z: The same thing may happen today, however the situation is much better than before since violence seldom happened.

Z: 你在读什么呢，安娜?

A: 我在看一本关于剑桥历史的书，正读到"市镇与学袍"的部分。

Z: 这是什么意思?

A: 市镇与学袍是指大学城里面截然不同的两个群体。"市镇"指的不搞学术研究的普通市民，而"学袍"当然是指大学了。

Z: 我明白了。一些古老的大学所在地就是这样的大学城，比如牛津、剑桥和圣安德鲁斯等等。

A: 你说的对。有时候，这个也用来指代现在的大学城。

Z: 也许这个词是伴随着世界上最古老的几所大学的成立而产生的吧，是中世纪时期?

A: 是的。那时候，欧洲的大学生们常常会被安排一个无关紧要的神职，他们经常穿着和神职人员相似的衣服。那种衣服经过长时间的演变，就渐渐变成了长长的黑色学士袍，外加上垂布和一顶帽子。

Z: 现在的垂布经常会用不同的颜色来装饰，也许这就是用来分辨那些年轻的学者分别来自哪个学院的一种方法吧。

A: 此外，因为这种特别的服装，学生们就和市民们区别开了。所以才有了"市镇和学袍"这个说法。

Z: 现在，这种服装已经成为了大学里的一项传统。世界各地的大学生在特殊的场合都会穿这种学袍，比如说在毕业典礼上。

① backbone *n.* 支柱，脊椎

A: 对啊。现在你知道这个说法的意思了吧，想不想了解更多关于“市镇和学袍”的事情啊?

Z: 快讲讲吧。

A: 好的。书里面还提到了市镇和大学之间的对立。

Z: 对立? 你是说他们之间的关系不好吗?

A: 对。 中世纪的大学城里，这两个独立团体身处同一片土地，却有着不同权益和信仰，免不了会发生冲突。

Z: 说的有道理。再说，暴力事件在中世纪十分普遍，不仅仅是在学者与市民之间，市民之间也常常会发生。

A: 来自欧洲不同地区的学者之间也会起冲突。市镇与大学之间的冲突更是会反复发生。

Z: 我听说，剑桥大学就起源于牛津市民和牛津大学之间的一场争端，许多牛津的学者不得不逃到一个新的地方。

A: 书里面也提到了这一点。那是在 1209 年了。几十年后，剑桥学者和市民之间的矛盾又激化了，国王不得不亲自出面授予大学一些特权，对其进行保护。

Z: 随着大学的面积不断扩大，结构越来越复杂，他们之间的冲突就越来越激烈。

A: 这是肯定的。 有时候，市镇和大学之间的纷争甚至会从大街上转移到法院和市政厅。

Z: 他们难道从来都不考虑市镇和大学之间的紧密联系吗?

A: 我也不知道。大学会说自己是城市经济的支柱，而城市反而会指责大学抢走了他们的一部分税收。

Z: 这在今天也可能发生，可是情况已经比原来好多了，至少暴力事件很少出现。

1 During that time, students **admitted** to the European universities often held minor clerical status and donned garb similar to that worn by the clergy.

（1）与介词 to 搭配，或者直接接宾语，意为“承认（坏事)”。

➢ He admitted to the murder.
他承认犯了罪。

➢ She admitted having stolen the lipstick.
她承认偷了那支口红。

➢ He admitted that he has stolen the bicycle.
她承认偷了自行车。

（2）与介词 into, in 搭配，意为“允许入内”。

➢ He was admitted to hospital suffering from burns.
他由于烧伤，被送入医院治疗。

（3）作不及物动词，与 of 搭配，或者作及物动词，意为“容许有”。

➢ The facts admit (of) no other explanation.
这些事实不容许有别的解释。

2 We can see that the hood nowadays is often **adorned** with different colors; maybe that is the way to designate from which college the young scholars come from.

adorn 接双宾语，与介词 with 搭配，意为“装饰，使生色”。

➢ He adorned his story with all sorts of adventures that never happened.
他在故事里编造了各式各样的离奇情节，为其增色。

3 Universities boast that their existence is the backbone of the town economy, while the towns counter with claims that the institution is "**robbing**" them of tax revenue.

（1）rob 意为“抢劫，抢夺”，还可以用作比喻义。

➢ I've been robbed!
我被抢劫了！

➢ They planned to rob a bank.
他们计划去抢劫一家银行。

➢ They knocked him down and robbed him of his watch.
他们把他打倒在地，并抢走了他的手表。

➢ The silly ending robs the plot of any credibility.
这个愚蠢的结尾使整个情节变得一点不可信。

（2）俗语 rob Peter to pay Paul，意为“借东还西，剜肉补疮”。

Town and Gown

Unlike the universities in China, Cambridge University has no fence or gate at all, but with its colleges scattering around the Cambridge city. There is nothing to feel surprised about if you get to know how the **medieval**[1] universities came into existence.

Nearly all the medieval universities were founded without physical campuses. The masters simply rented lecture halls in the host cities. Early on there were few **identifiable**[2] campus buildings. Most students took **lodging**[3] in the university towns. The scholars often **congregated**[4] in identifiable areas of cities. Thus, the medieval institutions were more integrated into the cities than in the case of the Academy.

Over the centuries, the relationship between town and gown has remained **ambivalent**[5] and the University at Cambridge owes much to "town and gown" troubles at Oxford University. In 1209 scholars and masters escaping troubles between the university and townsfolk in Oxford began arriving in Cambridge. By 1226 the scholars had organized themselves, offered regular courses of study, and named a Chancellor to lead them.

The first great boost to the formation of a university came from Henry III, who gave the scholars his support as early as 1231. Henry decreed that only students studying under a recognized Master were allowed to remain in Cambridge.

Like Oxford, Cambridge experienced a fair share of trouble between townsfolk and scholars. Both sides were protective of their unique rights and privileges. Later, the tension between the scholars at Cambridge and the towns people forced the King to grant special privileges and protection to Cambridge University, which helped **enormously**[6] in the **survival**[7] and future success of the University. For example, The university had the right to enforce laws regulating the quality of bread and ale sold in the town, and to monitor rates charged for food, fuel, and candles.

In 1381 tension between the town and university **exploded**[8] into violence, with attacks on university property throughout Cambridge. The result was that even more civil authority was awarded to the University Chancellor. Late until early in the 21th Century, the Blair Government has taken the last privilege of Cambridge.

---

① medieval *adj.* 中世纪的
② identifiable *adj.* 可辨认的，可认明的
③ lodging *n.* 寄宿处，寄宿
④ congregate *vi.* 聚集
⑤ ambivalent *adj.* 矛盾的，好恶相克的
⑥ enormously *adv.* 巨大的，庞大的
⑦ survival *n.* 幸存，残存
⑧ explode *vi.* 爆发，爆炸，激增

Eight centries **elapsed**[①] in a flash, the relationship between town and gown in Cambridge has been closer and more **harmonious**[②] than ever.

城市与大学

与中国的大学不同，剑桥大学既没有围墙，也没有大门，它的各个学院零散地分布在剑桥市的各个角落。当你了解了中世纪时期大学的形成过程，你就不会感到奇怪了。

几乎所有的中世纪大学都没有固定的校园。教师们通常只是租用城市的厅堂来进行授课。早期属于学校的建筑寥寥无几，大多数学生都居住在大学所在的市镇里。学者们常常在城市某个特定地点集会。所以在中世纪时期，大学与城市结合得更加紧密，而不仅仅是一个作学问的高等学府。

几个世纪以来，市镇和大学的关系都比较紧张，剑桥大学的形成就是牛津大学城市镇和大学之间矛盾激化的结果。1209 年，一些牛津的学者和教师为了躲避纠纷，来到了剑桥。从 1226 年开始，这些学者们开始有组织地进行授课，还任命了一位校长来进行领导。

剑桥大学的第一次大发展要归功于亨利三世。早在 1231 年，他就表示了自己对学者们的支持。他还颁布法令，只有从师于剑桥正式导师的学生才可以留在剑桥。

和牛津一样，剑桥也经历过一段市民与学者的纷争。双方互不相让，都努力维护自己的利益和特权。之后，剑桥市的学者和民众之间的矛盾愈演愈烈，国王不得不亲自出面授予大学一些特权来保护它，所以日后才有了剑桥大学的繁荣和成就。例如，大学有权执行法令来限定麦芽酒的销售、规定面包的质量，监察食物、燃料和蜡烛的价格。

1381 年，市镇和大学的矛盾空前激化，发生了暴动，大学遭到袭击。结果，大学反而被赋予了更多的特权。直到 21 世纪初，布莱尔政府才取消了剑桥大学最后的特权。

转眼间，8 个世纪过去了，剑桥的市镇和大学之间的联系更加紧密，关系也愈加和谐。

---

① elapse *vi.* 时间过去，消逝

② harmonious *adj.* 和谐的，和睦的

3 Ancient Buildings
古老的建筑

焦点对话

Craig is taking pictures of some buildings around, and Lily comes over to him.

C: Craig　　　L: Lily

L: Hello, Craig! Let me have a look at your pictures!

C: OK, here you are.

L: Wow. They are really great. You are so skilled in taking pictures.

C: Thanks. These buildings are just beautiful in themselves. I like the **gothic**[①] hall very much.

L: I guess this one is King's College in Cambridge? I heard form Lucy that you went there last Weekend. How is your journey?

C: A little bit tired, but **it's paid off**[②]. How do you know that this is the King's College?

L: Are you kidding me? This is the Cambridge's **landmark**[③]! But I have no idea why it was called the King's College; does it have something to do with kings?

C: You're right. King's College was founded in 1441 by King Henry VI. His first design was modest, but by 1445 it was intended to be a magnificent display of royal **patronage**[④].

L: I heard that it has taken them 80 years to finish the building.

---

① gothic *adj.* 哥特式的

② It's paid off. 这也值了

③ landmark *n.* 地标性建筑

④ patronage *n.* 赞助，资助

C: Really? It was a huge project. Let me show you another picture. See, this is the **bronze**① statue of King Henry VI in the middle of the yard.

L: Having the king's support, this college must have some privileges in the past. There is no wonder that buildings here are so splendid.

C: That is true. The college was used to be granted a remarkable series of **feudal**② privileges, and all of this was supported by a **substantial**③ series of **endowments**④ from the King.

L: I heard that students in this college are more politically active than other colleges. That may have something to do with their traditions.

C: It has its own student unions both for undergraduates and for graduates. The student union has a long record of **activism**⑤.

L: Their activities must have exerted great influence on the college and the university.

C: That's for sure. *Time Magazine* published in 2000 a list of the most "influential and important" people of the twentieth century.

L: Are there any students or fellows from this college in the list?

C: That is what I'm going to say. In a list of one hundred names, King's was the only European institution that could claim two.

L: Where did you take this photo? Why there is only one small tree standing in the middle of the yard?

C: It is perhaps the world's most famous apple tree.

L: Oh, I see. Is it Newton's apple tree?

C: Yes, but it is not the original one. It is said that this tree is the **offspring**⑥ of the apple tree which led Newton to have discovered **the law of gravity**⑦.

L: That's interesting. So, these were taken in the famous Trinity College which produced **numerous**⑧ famous people like Newton, Bacon, **Byron**⑨ and so on?

---

① bronze *adj.* 青铜制的
② feudal *adj.* 封建制的
③ substantial *adj.* 大量的，实质的，内容充实的
④ endowment *n.* 捐助，捐赠
⑤ activism *n.* 行动主义，激进主义
⑥ offspring *n.* 后代，子孙
⑦ the law of gravity 万有引力定律
⑧ numerous *adj.* 大量的，许多的
⑨ Byron 乔治·戈登·拜伦，是英国 19 世纪初期伟大的浪漫主义诗人。其代表作品有《恰尔德·哈罗德游记》、《唐璜》等。在他的诗歌里塑造了一批“拜伦式英雄”。拜伦不仅是一位伟大的诗人，还是一个为理想战斗一生的勇士；他积极而勇敢地投身革命，参加了希腊民族解放运动，并成为领导人之一。

C: Yes, you're right. This one was also taken in the New Court, which was built in Tudor-Gothic style.

L: It's beautiful!

C: And this is a view of the Wren Library.

L: I wish I could spend my college years in this kind library. It must be an enjoyment.

C: This one is St. Catherine's. Its red brick buildings dating from the end of the seventeenth century, and its court, planted with **elms**①, opening to the street.

L: Lovely. This is the first time I see the pictures of it since it is not as famous as the King's, Trinity.

C: Actually, beside those buildings in colleges, there are many beautiful corners in Cambridge.

L: 你好，克雷格！让我看看你拍的照片好吗？

C: 好的，给你吧。

L: 哇，拍得真不错。你拍照的技术很好。

C: 谢谢夸奖。这些建筑本身就很漂亮。我非常喜欢这个哥特式的门厅。

L: 我猜这应该是剑桥的国王学院吧? 我听露西说，上周末你去了剑桥? 玩得怎么样啊?

C: 有点累，但是很值得。你怎么知道这里是国王学院的?

L: 你不是在跟我开玩笑吧? 这是剑桥的标志性建筑啊！不过，我不知道它为什么叫做“国王学院”，难道它真的和国王有关系?

C: 你说对了。国王学院是 1441 年由亨利六世主持建造的。刚开始的设计并没有这么华丽，但到了 1445 年，就决定把它建造得更加宏伟壮丽，以展示皇家权威。

L: 我听说整个建筑花了 80 年才完成。

C: 真的吗? 这真是个巨大的工程。我给你看看另外一张照片。看，草坪中间就是亨利六世的纪念铜像。

L: 有了国王的支持，这个学院过去肯定享有不少特权吧。难怪这个学院的建筑这么宏伟。

C: 对啊。这个学院曾经拥有过不少封建特权呢，而且这些都由国王连续不断地捐赠

---

① elm *n.* 榆树

来支持。

L: 听说，这个学院的学生要比其他学院的学生都活跃。这肯定和他们的传统有关系。

C: 它有自己的本科生学生会和研究生学生会，学生会一向很活跃。

L: 他们的活动肯定对学院，乃至整个剑桥大学都产生了重大影响。

C: 也许吧。2000 年的《时代周刊》报道过 20 世纪全球最有影响力的人物名单。

L: 里面有这所学院的人吗?

C: 这正是我要说的。在这 100 个名字当中，国王学院是唯一拥有两位入选人的欧洲机构。

L: 你这些照片是在哪里拍的。为什么庭院中间只有一棵这样的小树啊?

C: 这恐怕是世界上最为著名的苹果树了。

L: 哦，我知道了。这是牛顿的苹果树吗?

C: 是的，但这不是原来那棵。据说，这棵树是那棵让牛顿发现万有引力定律的苹果树的后代。

L: 真有意思。所以这些照片就是在鼎鼎有名的三一学院拍的啰? 很多名人都出自那里，像牛顿、培根、拜伦等。

C: 你说的对。这张也是在新庭拍的，它是都铎时代的哥特式风格的建筑。

L: 太漂亮啦!

C: 这张是莱恩图书馆。

L: 真希望我也能在这样的图书馆里度过自己的大学时光，这绝对是种享受。

C: 这张是圣凯瑟琳学院，建成于 17 世纪，楼体都用红色的砖块盖成，庭院里种满了榆树。

L: 真漂亮。这是我第一次看到它的照片，它并不像国王学院和三一学院那么有名气。

C: 实际上，除了这些建筑，剑桥还有很多漂亮的地方。

难点解析

1 Their activities must have **exerted** great influence on the college and the university.

（1）运用（力量，技巧等以达到某预期的结果）

➢ She couldn't open the door, even by exerting all her strength.
她即使竭尽全力也无法把门打开。

（2）exert oneself 意为“努力，尽力”。

➢ She can run 100 metres in 13 seconds without unduly exerting herself.
她无需过分努力就能在 13 秒内跑完 100 米。

2 In a list of one hundred names, King's was the only European institution that could **claim** two.

（1）认领，对……提出要求，索取，声称有……权利

➢ Did you claim on the insurance after your car accident?
你出车祸后有没有向保险公司索取赔偿?

（2）claim to do sth. 或者 claim that 后接宾语从句

➢ They claim to have discovered/claim that they discovered a cure for the disease, but this has not yet been proved.
他们声称已经发现了治疗此病的一种药物，但此事尚未得到证实。

（3）值得，需要

➢ This problem claims our undivided attention.
这个问题值得我们密切注意。

Ancient Buildings

It is a commonplace remark that Cambridge as a town contrasts **unfavorably**[1] with Oxford, and an **acute**[2] American writer, himself an alumnus of Trinity College, **has gone so far as to**[3] describe it as, of all English provincial towns, the most insignificant, the dullest, and the ugliest.

The street architecture is mean, dingy yellow brick being the chief material of the houses, and the site, is as dreary and uninteresting as anything in England. But the glory of Cambridge is of course its group of colleges, whose varied beauty is rivaled only by Oxford; and the **Cantab**[4] will not easily allow that anything at Oxford is finer than Trinity, King's, or the Fitz William Museum. Of the university buildings, the last-named, founded by Viscount

① unfavorably *adv.* 不适宜的，不利的
② acute *adj.* 严重的，急性的，激烈的，尖锐的
③ has gone so far as to 过分地做某事
④ Cantab *n.* 英国剑桥大学的学生或者毕业生，剑桥市市民

FitzWilliam, who died in 1816, is one of the noblest classical buildings in England, and contains valuable books, paintings, prints, and sculpture. The Senate-house, opened in 1730, is a building of **admirable**① proportions, with a richly-decorated **interior**②.

Among the colleges, Trinity holds the premier place as the largest. Its great court covers more than two acres of ground, and the chapel, dating from **Queen Mary's**③ reign, has been restored and elaborately decorated. King's College, founded by Henry VI, in connection with his famous school at Eton, is celebrated for its chapel, unquestionably the finest building in Cambridge. It was finished in 1536, and ranks with St. George's Chapel, Windsor, among the most perfect existing specimens of **perpendicular**④ architecture.

Third in architectural importance is St. John's, with its four courts. The picturesque buildings are mostly Tudor or Jacobean. In size and wealth, St. John's ranks next to Trinity, and it has produced many famous scholars.

In addition, we have St. Catherine's, its red brick buildings dating from the end of the seventeenth century, and its court, planted with elms, opening to the street. Many noted **ecclesiastics**⑤ and **theologians**⑥ have been educated here. Magdalene is the only college on the north side of the river Cam. Not much remains of the ancient buildings, the finest part of the college being the Pepysian library containing the books of the famous diarist, and many black letter volumes. St. Peter's or Peterhouse, the oldest college in Cambridge, preserves some of its ancient buildings, has pretty gardens and a small deer-park, and a library rich in medieval theology. All of those buildings are scenic pictures which should not be missed in Cambridge.

古老的建筑

常听人说，剑桥市根本就不能和牛津市相比。一位激进的美国作家甚至过分地说，在英格兰所有的市镇中，剑桥是最无足轻重、枯燥乏味和不堪入目的，而这位作家自己就曾经是三一学院的一员。

街道旁的建筑十分简陋，暗红色的砖块是建造房屋的主要材料，这样的场景在英格兰随处可见，令人感到压抑、无趣。当然了，剑桥也有它的亮点，坐落在市区各个地方的学院，其变换多姿的美景恐怕只有牛津才可与之媲美。剑桥人也绝不会同意，

① admirable *adj.* 令人钦佩的，值得赞扬的

② interior *adj.* 内部的，国内的，本质的

③ Queen Mary 玛丽女王一世。英国伊丽莎白一世女王的姐姐，亨利八世的长女，人称“血腥玛丽”。1553～1558 年在位，成长于欧洲宗教改革的汹涌大潮之中。

④ perpendicular *adj.* 垂直的，直立的

⑤ ecclesiastic *adj.* 教会的，神职的

⑥ theologian *n.* 神学者

牛津有什么能比得过三一学院、国王学院和菲茨威廉博物馆的建筑。所有大学的建筑中，这所菲茨威廉博物馆是英格兰古建筑中最有名气的，里面有着大量的藏书、图画、报刊和雕塑。建造这个博物馆的菲茨威廉伯爵已经在1816年去世。1730年开放的议会大楼十分宽敞，内部装潢也甚为华丽。

三一学院是所有学院中面积最大的，其庭院超过了两英亩。还有可以追溯到玛丽女王统治时期的小教堂，后来被整修一新并精心装饰了一番。亨利六世主持建造的国王学院在1536年建成，与伊顿学院毗邻，并和圣乔治教堂，温莎教堂一起被视为为现存的垂直式建筑的典型代表。

第三重要的建筑是圣约翰学院，它共有4个庭院。这些别致的建筑大多是都铎时期或者是詹姆士一世时期建造的，无论从规模还是从财力上来说，圣约翰学院都仅次于三一学院。这里也走出了许多的著名学者。

此外，还有圣凯瑟琳学院，其典型的红砖建筑建成于17世纪末期，敞开的庭院里种满了榆树，许多著名的牧师和神学家都曾在此就读。莫德林学院是唯一一所坐落在康河北岸的学院，它并没有太多的古建筑。学院中最漂亮的应该算是佩皮斯图书馆了，里面有很多佩皮斯这位著名日记作家的书和黑体字卷册。剑桥大学历史最悠久的学院——圣彼得学院里保留有很多古建筑，它的花园小巧可爱，还拥有一所小型的鹿园，图书馆里拥有很多中世纪神学方面的典藏。所有的这些建筑都是剑桥大学里不可错过的风景。

4 Map of 800 Years' Spirit
800 年的精神地图

Charles and Nancy are talking about the 800th Anniversary Ceremony of Cambridge University.

C: Charles　　N: Nancy

C: Have you come out to see the light show last night?

N: Yes, of course. It was really **spectacular**①. I heard that it was designed by a **world-renowned**② light artist Ross Ashton.

C: This year has been a very special one for the University of Cambridge, as we have celebrated 800 years since our foundation.

N: True. The 800th Anniversary has been **commemorated**③ in a wide variety of events throughout the year, and now the time has come to bring the celebrations to a close.

C: Do you still remember that exactly twelve months from the start of the Anniversary Year, when more than 10,000 people crowded into central Cambridge to witness a spectacular light show on the Senate House and Old Schools?

N: Yes. But it is a pity that I haven't witnessed the show because of some personal affairs. When I got know that this show would last for 3 days and was even bigger than that of last year, I felt so happy and decided to go out and see it every night.

---

① spectacular *adj.* 壮观的，惊人的

② world-renowned *adj.* 世界知名的

③ commemorate *vt.* 庆祝，纪念，成为……的纪念

C: Whereas last year's show focused on Cambridge's **illustrious**① history, this year's show will focus on the **transformative**② research taking place at Cambridge.

N: **Stunning**③ images will showcase the breadth of work happening today.

C: This was the finale of the 800th anniversary and a truly perfect one. I like the name of the show "Transforming tomorrow".

N: I like it too. One committee member of the anniversary said that they were hoping to look forward and transforming tomorrow by recognizing how much our predecessors have done and current students and staff are doing in a way that we hope again will inspire the next generation to continue this for at least 800 years.

C: Besides the anniversary, there has also been the Darwin Festival to mark 200 years since the birth of Cambridge man Charles Darwin and 150 since the publication of his **ground-breaking**④ *Origin of Species*.

N: I saw a light show of Darwin last night. He was riding on a **turtle**⑤. Did you see it?

C: Yes. It was funny. The designer is a genius.

N: Comparing to the University, we are here just for a short time. We should cherish every moment of being here.

C: You're right. We're here to celebrate the accomplishments, the many accomplishments of our **predecessors**⑥ ,which have exerted great influence on the development of the society.

N: Do you know why they choose King's College to give the show?

C: King's is renowned for fine food and **immaculate**⑦ service so it was the perfect setting for the show. King's Hall is a spectacular venue full of **grandeur**⑧, but is also a **flexible**⑨ space which made it ideal for this prominent event.

N: Sounds good. Have you attended other events or lectures during the year, for example, the exhibition in Cambridge University Library which lasts for 6 months?

C: Yes. It was a great exhibition named "Advancing by degrees" which explores themes of governance, membership, scholarship and outreach across the centuries to ask what

---

① illustrious *adj.* 辉煌的，著名的，杰出的
② transformative *adj.* 变化的，变形的，有改革能力的
③ stunning *adj.* 极好的，震耳欲聋的
④ ground-breaking *adj.* 独创的，开拓性的
⑤ turtle *n.* 海龟，龟，甲鱼
⑥ predecessor *n.* 前任，前辈
⑦ immaculate *adj.* 完美的，无瑕疵的
⑧ grandeur *n.* 庄严，壮丽，宏伟
⑨ flexible *adj.* 灵活的，柔韧的

makes Cambridge.

N: I am sure everyone who came to the exhibition has already found the answer. Physical growth and development of Cambridge have not obscured the fact that the university's enduring staple is its people and ideas.

C: 你昨晚去看光影秀了吗?

N: 当然去了，真是太精彩了。我听说这是由世界著名的光影艺术家罗斯·阿什顿设计的。

C: 去年对剑桥来说真是非同寻常的一年，它都成立800周年了。

N: 对啊。为了庆祝建校800周年，学校在去年一整年间举办了各种各样的活动，现在到了结束庆典的时候了。

C: 你还记得吗，在周年庆典前一年，有上万人挤进剑桥市中心，想在参议院大楼和老学堂一睹迷人的光影秀。

N: 记得。但是很可惜，我因为别的事情耽搁而没看成那场秀。当我知道这次的光影秀会连续举办3天，而且会比上次的规模还大时，我特别高兴，决定每晚都要出来看。

C: 去年的光影秀主要展示了剑桥的辉煌历史，今年的就主要展示剑桥有改革意义的成果。

N: 这些精美绝伦的图影，向人们展示了当今科学成就的巨幅图景。

C: 这次光影秀大概是800年庆典的终曲了。它真的十分完美，我很喜欢它的名字“改变明天”。

N: 我也很喜欢。一位庆典活动的负责人说，他们希望通过认识先辈们的贡献和目前师生们的付出，来展望未来，改变明天。并且表示，这将会激励下一代人，从而使这种盛况再延续至少800年。

C: 除了周年庆典，还举办了达尔文节以纪念查尔斯·达尔文诞辰200周年和《物种起源》发表150周年。

N: 我昨晚就看到了达尔文的光影秀，他骑在一个乌龟上。你看见了吗?

C: 看见了，特别有趣。设计师真是个天才。

N: 和剑桥相比，我们只是这里的匆匆过客，真应该珍惜在这里的每一分钟。

C: 你说的对。我们在这里为先辈们所取得的成就而庆贺，这些成就对社会的发展产生了重要的影响。

N: 你知道他们为什么会选择国王学院来作这次光影秀吗?

C: 国王学院精致的食物和周到的服务很有名气，是作展示的理想场所。它的门厅气势恢宏，又不失张力，用来作这个重要展示十分完美。

N: 有道理。在这一年中，你还参加过别的展览或者讲座吗，比如剑桥大学图书馆里举办的为期6个月的特展?

C: 去了。那个展览也相当不错，名字叫做“逐步发展”，它探讨了学校在各个时期的管理、录取、奖学金制度等问题，并且让人思考究竟是什么成就了剑桥。

N: 我敢肯定每位去看过展览的观众都已经找到了答案。剑桥大学物质上的增长和发展揭露了这样一个事实——人材和思想才是大学最重要的组成部分。

1 Whereas last year's show focused on Cambridge's illustrious history, this year's show will **focus on** the transformative research taking place at Cambridge.

（1）（使）聚焦，（使）集中

➢ The beams of light moved across the sky and focused on the aircraft.
一道道光线射过天空，焦点集中在飞机上。

（2）（使）集中（注意力）于

➢ We're going to focus on the question of homeless people.
今天我们要集中讨论露宿者的问题。

（3）调节……的焦距

➢ The astronomer focused his telescope on the moon.
这位天文学家（对准月亮）调节望远镜的焦距。

2 **Comparing** to the University, we are here just for a short time. We should cherish every moment of being here.

（1）与介词 to, with 搭配，意为“比较、对照”。

➢ The report compares the different types of home computer currently available.
报告比较了目前在市面出售的各种型号的家用电脑。

（2）比较（两者）之间的相同之处

➢ It's impossible to compare London and New York.
伦敦与纽约是无法比较的。

（3）作不及物动词，与介词 with 搭配，意为“比得上”。

➢ Last year was an excellent year for wine.I'm afraid this year's doesn't compare.
去年是葡萄酒的好年成，恐怕今年是比不上啦。

3 It was a great exhibition named "Advancing by degrees" which **explores** themes of governance, membership, scholarship and outreach across the centuries to ask what makes Cambridge.

（1）探险，探测

➢ Her dream is to explore the Amazon jungle one day.
她的梦想就是有朝一日能够去亚马逊丛林探险。

（2）仔细检查，研究，探讨

➢ We must explore all the possibilities.
我们必须探讨所有的可能性。

Map of 800 Years'Spirit

In 2009, the University of Cambridge reaches a special **milestone**① — 800 years of people, ideas and achievements that continue to transform and benefit the world. **Myriad**② achievements and world-changing ideas were born within the walls of Cambridge, from the establishment of the fundamentals of physics to the discovery of the structure of DNA; from the transformative thinking of great Cambridge philosophers, poets and artists; to the groundbreaking work of its many Nobel Prize winners.

As claimed by the university itself, its mission is to contribute to society through the pursuit of education, learning, and research at the highest international levels of **excellence**③. The core values of it are: freedom of thought and expression and freedom from discrimination. Questioning spirit, close inter-relationship between teaching, scholarship and research are often encouraged in Cambridge.

It is one of the world's leading research universities. Cambridge affiliates have won more than 80 Nobel Prizes, more than any other institution in the world. Some of the most

① .milestone *n.* 里程碑，划时代的事件
② myriad *adj.* 无数的，种种的
③ excellence *n.* 优秀，长处，美德

famous scientific minds in history have studied, researched or taught here. This is the home of Newton and Darwin, Crick and Watson, Babbage and Hawking. However, it is also the place where the first fully 3D computer game was written, where the **precursor**① to the modern **webcam**② was invented, and where some of today's best-known **entertainers**③ began their careers.

Cambridge is a **collegiate**④ university, meaning that it is made up of self-governing and independent colleges, each with its own property and income. Most colleges bring together academics and students from a broad range of disciplines, and within each **faculty**⑤, school or department within the university, academics from many different colleges will be found. The University of Cambridge currently has 31 colleges, of which three, Murray Edwards, Newnham and Lucy Cavendish, admit only women. The other colleges are now mixed, though most were originally all-male.

Cambridge provides an **unparalleled**⑥ learning experience for the students, who come here from across the globe. The teaching staff are world leaders in their fields, working towards the discoveries and innovations that will transform lives now and in the years to come.

During the eight centuries, colleges have been found one after another with the constructions of distinctive buildings; numerous scientists, writers, artists and politicians spent wonderful days either studying or teaching in Cambridge. Though some buildings decayed in the 800 years, the spirit and charm of Cambridge is still thriving. May Cambridge enjoy a more brilliant future!

800 年的精神地图

2009 年，剑桥迎来了一个特殊的里程碑——800 年的人文思想和成就仍然在改变和造福这个世界。从物理学的奠基到 DNA 结构的发现；从剑桥哲人，诗人和艺术家改变世界的思想，到诸多诺贝尔奖获得者的突出贡献，人类历史上大量的成就和改变

① precursor *n.* 先驱，先导
② webcam *n.* 摄像头
③ entertainer *n.* 演艺人员，表演者
④ collegiate *adj.* 学院制的，大学的
⑤ faculty *n.* 科，系
⑥ unparalleled *adj.* 空前未有的，无比的，无双的

世界的理念都出自剑桥大学。

剑桥宣称，自己的使命就在于通过追求教育、学习和研究的最高水准而对社会作出贡献。其核心价值观为“思想和表达的自由”和“零歧视”。剑桥大力提倡质疑的精神，以及教、学、研紧密结合。

剑桥是世界上一流的研究型大学之一，诺贝尔奖获得者多达80余人，比世界上其他任何机构都要多。历史上很多著名的科学家都曾经在剑桥学习、做研究或授课。牛顿、达尔文、克里克、沃森、巴贝其还有霍金都来自剑桥；世界上第一个真正意义上的3D游戏，第一代调制解调器网络摄像头都出自剑桥；同时，剑桥也是许多著名演艺界人士初展拳脚的地方。

剑桥大学是一所学院制的大学，由许多高度自治的独立学院组成，每所学院财务独立、自主经营、自负盈亏、多数学院里都有不同学科的学生，在大学里的每个科、院和系几乎都可以找到来自不同学院的学生。剑桥大学共有31所学院，其中默里爱德华兹学院，纽纳姆学院和露西·卡文迪什学院都只招收女生，尽管其他学院原来都只招收男生，现在都变成了男女统招。

剑桥大学为来自世界各地的学子提供了一个绝佳的学习机会。这里的教职工都是其所在研究领域的领头羊，致力于用科学发现和创新来改变人类现状和创造美好未来。

800年来，各个学院相继设立，一座座颇具特色的古楼拔地而起，数不清的科学家、作家、艺术家和政治家在这里度过了他们人生中最丰富多彩的时光。经历了800年的风风雨雨，尽管那些古老的建筑都已失去了往日的风采，但是剑桥的恢弘气势和魅力依然催人向上。期待剑桥的明天会更美好。

Unit 2 Architectures & Landscapes 诗意栖息地

5 The Gentle Waves of River Cam

剑河的柔波

Jane and Anthony are reading ***Farewell Again to Cambridge***①, which is written by Xu Zhimo.

J: Jane　　A: Anthony

J: Xu Zhimo is one of my favorite Chinese poets. His poems are full of romance.

A: I like his poems, too. And among his poems, *Farewell Again to Cambridge* is my all-time favorite.

J: I can memorize some **verses**② of this poem: The golden **willows**③ by the riverside; are young brides in the setting sun. Their reflections on the **shimmering**④ waves; always **linger**⑤ in the depth of my heart.

A: The river that Xu Zhimo mentioned is River Cam, isn't it?

J: Yes. River Cam is a lovely river that flows through the city and university of Cambridge, **Cambridgeshire**⑥ in eastern England.

A: As the river flows through Cambridge it drops through 3 levels, respectively known as

① *Farewell Again to Cambridge*《再别康桥》
② verse 诗节
③ willow *n.* 柳树
④ shimmering *adj.* 微微发光的
⑤ linger *v.* 逗留，徘徊
⑥ Cambridgeshire 剑桥郡

the Top, Middle and Lower River.

J: The 1.5km **stretch**① of the Middle River from **Queens' College**② to Magdalene College is known as the College Backs and it is one of the most beautiful stretches of river in England.

A: Set amongst spacious **lawns**③ and **intimate gardens**④ are some of Cambridge's grandest buildings, including King's College Chapel and the Wren Library.

J: More rural than the Backs, the Top River stretch winds through **woodland**⑤ and open **meadows**⑥ to Grantchester, once the beloved home of the poet Rupert Brooke.

A: The Cam is fed by springs rising from **chalk aquifers**⑦ south east of Cambridge. The water quality is good, so the river supports plenty of fish including **pike**⑧, carp and **eels**⑨. Ducks, geese and swans are common sights.

---

① stretch *n.* 水域
② Queens'College 女王学院
③ lawn *n.* 草坪
④ intimate garden 私人花园
⑤ woodland *n.* 林地
⑥ meadow *n.* 草地，牧场
⑦ chalk aquifers 白垩蓄水层
⑧ pike *n.* 梭鱼
⑨ eel *n.* 鳗鱼

J: And **punting**[①] on the River Cam is the most romantic and **exhilarating**[②] way to see this unique, historic town with its ancient university and bustling area.

A: Xu Zhimo mentioned punting in his poem, too. For instance: to seek a dream? Just to pole a boat upstream; to where the green grass is more **verdant**[③]. Or to have the boat fully loaded with **starlight**[④]; and sing aloud in the splendor of starlight.

J: His poem shows the popularity of punting. Punting is great fun once you get the hang of it and drifting along the River Cam gives you a different perspective of Cambridge's colleges.

A: King's College Chapel, the Wren Library and The Bridge of Sighs are just some of the famous Cambridge landmarks you'll see when you take to the river.

J: An article about the punts of Cambridge recorded that punts were developed in **medieval**[⑤] times to provide stable craft which could be used in areas of water too shallow for rowing conventional craft.

A: In such area like the Fens, which locates in north of Cambridge, punts were integral to local trades such as eel fishing and **reed-cutting**[⑥], until they died out in the late nineteenth century.

J: Punts were introduced to Cambridge as pleasure craft in **Edwardian times**[⑦]. One of the pioneers of punt hire on the River Cam was F. Scudamore, who founded his business in 1910, quickly establishing punting as Cambridge's favorite pastime.

J: 徐志摩是我最喜欢的中国作家之一，他的诗歌充满了浪漫气息。

A: 我也喜欢他的诗。在他所作的诗歌中，《再别康桥》是我最喜欢的。

J: 我还能背诵这首诗中的一些诗句：那河畔的金柳，是夕阳中的新娘，波光里的艳影，在我的心头荡漾。

A: 徐志摩在诗中提到的河就是剑河，对吗?

J: 是的，剑河是一条秀丽的河，它流经英格兰东部剑桥郡的剑桥大学城。

A: 当剑河流经剑桥时，由于落差的原因，它分成 3 个河段，分别被人称为上河段、中河段和下河段。

---

① punt *v.* 撑船
② exhilarating *adj.* 令人高兴的
③ verdant *adj.* 翠绿的
④ starlight *n.* 星光
⑤ medieval *adj.* 中世纪的
⑥ reed-cutting *n.* 割芦苇
⑦ Edwardian times 爱德华时代

J: 位于中河段，从女王学院到麦格达伦学院的一段1500米长的水域被称作“后园景观”，这是剑河在英格兰境内风景最漂亮的水域之一。

A: 剑桥大学宏伟的建筑，如国王学院教堂和雷恩图书馆坐落于宽敞的草坪和私人花园中。

J: 和后园景观相比，上河段流域的乡土气息更浓一些，它流经格兰切斯特的林地和开阔牧场，这里曾是诗人鲁伯特·布鲁克挚爱的家。

A: 剑河里满是剑桥东南部的白垩蓄水层冒出的泉水。剑河的水质很好，所以适合多种鱼类生存，包括梭鱼、鲤鱼和鳗鱼。鸭、鹅和天鹅也经常能在河里看到。

J: 剑桥风格独特、历史悠久，拥有古老的大学和繁华的商业地带。在剑河撑船是游览这个城镇最浪漫和最令人欣喜的方式。

A: 徐志摩在他的诗中也提到了撑船，比如：寻梦？撑一支长篙，向青草更青处漫溯，满载一船星辉，在星辉斑斓里放歌。

J: 他的诗歌向我们展示了撑船的流行。一旦你掌握了要领，撑船会带给你很多欢乐。撑船在剑河上漂流，你可以从一个不同的视角欣赏剑桥大学各学院。

A: 当你撑船在水里滑行时，你就会看到国王学院教堂、雷恩图书馆和叹息桥等著名剑桥地标。

J: 关于剑桥方头平底船的一篇文章记载道，这种船始创于中世纪。剑河的一些流域水太浅，划传统的大船不方便，所以人们改划较轻便的方头平底船。

A: 在剑桥北部的沼泽地带，方头平底船对于捕鳗鱼和割芦苇等当地贸易来说是必不可少的，直到那些贸易在19世纪晚期退出历史舞台。

J: 在爱德华七世的时代，方头平底船被作为娱乐工具引进剑桥。剑河租船业务的开创者之一是斯丘达莫尔。他在1910年创业，很快就把撑船发展为剑桥最受欢迎的娱乐方式。

难点解析

1 And among his poems, *Farewell Again to Cambridge* is my **all time favorite**.

（1）all-time 这个形容词可以用在很多地方，all-time high\low\best etc. 意为“前所未有（空前）的高 \ 低 \ 好等。

➢ The price of wheat reached an all-time low of 42cents in 1932.
1932 年小麦的价格降到了前所未有的低价——42 美分。

（2）all-time record\classic etc. 意为“已知最好的记录\经典（作品）等”。

➢ He's one of pro football's all-time great receivers.
他是职业橄榄球迄今最好的直传球接手之一。

2 More rural than the Backs, the Top River stretch **winds through** woodland and open meadows to Grantchester, once the beloved home of the poet Rupert Brooke.

wind through 意为“蜿蜒曲折穿过”。

➢ Wind a path through the mountains.
在山中沿小路蜿蜒前行。

3 And punting on the River Cam is the most romantic and exhilarating way to see this unique, historic town with its ancient university and **bustling** area.

bustling 意为“熙熙攘攘的，忙乱的，”它的动词形式是 bustle。

➢ Everyone was bustling in and out.
人人都在匆忙地进进出出。

➢ The street was bustling with Christmas shoppers.
街道上挤满了为欢度圣诞节购物的人群。

The Gentle Waves of River Cam

Cambridge is famous as the home of one of the two oldest English universities, but the city has a long and eventful history of its own. The Roman may be the first to bridge the River Cam in 43 AD. In 875 the **Anglo-Saxon Chronicle**① called it Grantabrycge - one of the earliest known uses of the word 'bridge' in the English Language, suggesting that the town was famous for its bridge.

In the Middle Ages the River Cam was used for transporting corns as far as **King's Lynn**②, and stones into the centre of Cambridge. However, by the 17th century the River was

① Anglo-Saxon Chronicle 盎格鲁－撒克逊编年史
② King's Lynn 金斯林，地名

badly **silted up**[①], and it took almost another century before a Parliament Act saw improvements to its condition.

The surrounding area of the Fens cover an area of some 800 square miles and are so low that the highest point is just 50m above sea level, with some parts having dropped below sea level entirely. As the river makes its way to the North Sea it **deposits**[②] huge amounts of silt over time which accounts for the ever-decreasing nature of the waters, makes of which today is actually reclaimed **marshland**[③].

This was not always the case, however. Records showed that during the 17th century the waters were plentiful here. Despite the Romans' attempts at draining the land, the area remained **swampland**[④] for many generations. From about 1500 until the mid-17th century, high ranking clergy, members of the **aristocracy**[⑤] and even royalty would attempt to drain the land, but it was only when the underlying peat **shrank**[⑥] over time and the levels were gradually **seeped**[⑦] off into new channels and waterways that the waters moved from being deep lakes into the **myriad**[⑧] of shallow channels as they are today.

Cambridge itself is steeped in history with an academic heritage dating back to as early as 1209. Some of the first colleges to be founded were built right on the banks of the river. On the riverside the colleges would benefit from the major trade route into the town of Cambridge. The result today is the "Backs", a one mile stretch of river that supports some of finest examples of architecture in England. Altogether there are 8 colleges and 9 bridges. These include Queens' College with the Mathematical Bridge, King's College with its famous chapel, and the Bridge of Sighs at St. John's College.

---

① silt up 淤泥充塞
② deposit *v.* 沉淀下
③ marshland *n.* 沼泽地
④ swampland *n.* 沼泽地
⑤ aristocracy *n.* 贵族
⑥ shrank *v.* 缩小
⑦ seep *v.* 渗透
⑧ myriad *n.* 无数

剑河的柔波

剑桥以拥有两所英国最古老的大学之一剑桥大学而闻名于世，而这座城市本身就历史悠久、历经沧桑。人们认为，早在公元 43 年，罗马人就在剑河上筑桥了。公元 875 年，盎格鲁－撒克逊编年史把在剑河上筑的桥称之为“格兰特桥”，这是英语语言中最早使用“桥”这一单词的用法，这暗示了这座城市是以桥而闻名的。

中世纪时期，剑河作为运输通道，可将玉米运至金斯林，将石头运至剑桥中心。但是到了 17 世纪，剑河就被淤泥堵塞。差不多过了一个世纪，议会法案的实施才使情况好转。

剑河的沼泽地带覆盖了约 800 平方英里流域，而且地势很低，最高点仅高于海平面 50 米，有些部分则完全低于海平面。由于入海口地势低，当剑河流入北海时，它会滞留大量淤泥。经年累月，河水不断减少，今天的大部分河段都变成沼泽地了。

但是，以前的情况并不是这样。据史料记载，17 世纪时这里水源充足。尽管罗马人试图把水排干，但是历经数代，这片地区仍然是沼泽地。从 1500 年到 17 世纪中期，高级牧师、贵族，甚至是皇室成员都试图把这块地段的水排空，但是只有当底层的泥炭随着时间推移而逐渐被侵蚀，河水流向新的渠道和航道，他们的目标才实现，因为这样一来，河水就不能聚积在一起形成深湖，而只能变成今天的无数浅水渠了。

剑桥本身有着丰富的学术传统，它的学术传统可以追溯到公元 1209 年。最早的一批学院是在剑河的右岸建立起来的。通往剑桥镇的贸易航道都要通过剑河，建于河边的学院受益于此，结果形成了今天的“后园景观”。在一英里的水域内，游客们可以看到英格兰最漂亮的一些建筑。总共有 8 个学院和 9 座桥位于“后园景观”内，这其中包括拥有数学桥的女王学院，著名教堂的所在地国王学院和以叹息桥闻名的圣约翰学院。

6 Bridge of Sighs 难道桥也会叹息

焦点对话

John and Clara are browsing **through**[1] a **photo album**[2] of University of Cambridge.

J: John　　C: Clara

J: The **erections**[3] of Cambridge are so beautiful and impressive.

C: Yeah. And I notice that there are plenty of bridges in Cambridge, for example, **Clare College Bridge**[4], the oldest of Cambridge's current bridges.

J: It survives as the oldest due to all its contemporaries being destroyed by the **Roundhead**[5] forces in the Civil War, to make the town of Cambridge more defensible.

C: But compared with Clare College Bridge, **Bridge of Sighs**[6] is more beautiful.

J: Bridge of sighs belongs to **St John's College**[7] and it has a long history.

C: But why such a lovely bridge is called Bridge of Sighs?

J: There are various versions about its special name. Some say that because of the strict

---

① browse through 浏览
② photo album 相册
③ erection *n.* 建筑物
④ Clare College Bridge 克莱尔学院桥
⑤ Roundhead 圆颅党，英国国会中的一知名党派。该党发迹与最盛时期约为英国内战时期。
⑥ Bridge of Sighs 叹息桥
⑦ St John's College 圣约翰学院，是剑桥大学第二大学院，在学生人数上仅次于三一学院。学院的创办人是王太后玛格丽特·博福特（Margaret Beaufort）女士。

graduate examination of the University of Cambridge, it's difficult for students who don't work hard to pass it.

C: Oh, I see! After **flunking**[①] the exam, they would stand on the bridge and sigh or **weep**[②] to express their regret. So the university named it Bridge of Sighs, to **alert**[③] the students to study **diligently**[④].

J: You are very smart and this version seems to stand up under scrutiny. But still there are different versions.

C: I'm curious about the other versions. Can you give me more details?

J: Others claim that the name of the bridge comes from the fact that students who break the university's rules have to stand on the bridge to reflect their mistakes as a punishment. When they think about their misbehaviors, they would have a sigh.

C: So many stories bring fame to this bridge. And that reminds me of a story that I heard many years ago. The story is that in Cambridge, students would sigh as they walked through this bridge, taking their last look at the city before taking the exams.

J: In fact, this bridge was named after Bridge of Sighs, Venice. The view from Bridge of Sighs was the last view of Venice that **convicts**[⑤] saw before their imprisonment.

C: You mean the **enclosed**[⑥] bridge made of white limestone and having windows with stone bars in Venice, which connected the old prisons to the **interrogation rooms**[⑦] in the **Doge's Palace**[⑧]?

J: Yes. The bridge name, given by Lord Byron in the 19th century, came from the suggestion that prisoners would sigh at their final view of beautiful Venice out the window before being taken down to their cells.

C: I can see the structural similarity between the bridge in Cambridge and its Venetian **namesake**[⑨]—they are both covered bridges.

J: And Bridge of Sighs in Cambridge has connection with Lord Byron, too.

C: Really? What connection?

---

① flunk *v.* 通不过（考试），不及格
② weep *v.* 哭泣
③ alert *v.* 使（某人）保持警觉，提醒（某人）注意
④ diligently *v.* 勤勉地
⑤ convict *n.* 囚犯
⑥ enclosed *adj.* 封闭的
⑦ interrogation room 审讯室
⑧ Doge's Palace 总督府
⑨ namesake *n.* 同名的人，同名物

J: When Lord Byron fell from grace of **Duchess of Bronte**[①], he jumped off the bridge to commit suicide, but was saved by a **passer-by**[②]. After that, the college sealed[③] the open bridge to a **gallery bridge**[④].

C: Lord Byron is too emotional, but his story adds romance to this bridge.

J: In the tourist guide of St. John's College, readers can find the description for the pictures of Bridge of Sighs emphasizes that the bridge has never brought any punishment for any students.

J: 剑桥的建筑真是漂亮，令人印象深刻。

J: 是啊。而且我注意到剑桥有很多桥，比如说，剑桥大学现存的桥中历史最悠久的是克莱尔学院桥。

J: 这是因为在英国内战期间，圆颅党武装力量为了增强剑桥镇的防御能力，把和克莱尔学院桥同时代的桥都毁了，所以克莱尔学院桥是现存的最古老的桥。

C: 但是和克莱尔学院桥相比，叹息桥更漂亮。

J: 叹息桥隶属于圣约翰学院，历史很悠久。

C: 但是人们为什么把这座赏心悦目的桥叫做叹息桥呢?

J: 关于它特殊名字的来源，有很多的版本。有些人说是因为剑桥大学的毕业考试十分严格，学习不够用功的学生很难通过这个考试。

C: 哦，我知道了！学生们考试失败后会站在桥上叹息或是哭泣以表达他们的悔恨。所以学校把这座桥命名为叹息桥，提醒学生们要刻苦学习。

J: 你很聪明，而且这个版本看起来是比较权威的。但是还有其他不同的版本。

C: 我对其他的版本很好奇。你能详细跟我说说吗?

J: 有些人说这座桥名字的来源是这样的：违反学校规定的学生必须接受惩罚，即站在桥上反思他们的错误。当想到自己的不当行为时，他们会发出一声叹息。

C: 这么多的故事给这座桥带来了名气。这又让我想起了多年前听到的一个故事。当

① Duchess of Bronte 勃伦特公爵夫人
② passer-by *n.* 路人
③ seal *v.* 密封，封闭
④ gallery bridge 廊桥

剑桥的学生们走过这座桥要去参加考试时，他们会叹息，站在桥上看风景是他们对剑桥镇的最后一瞥。

J: 事实上，这座桥是根据威尼斯的叹息桥而命名的。从叹息桥上看到的风景是囚犯们进入监狱之前对威尼斯的最后一瞥。

C: 你指的是威尼斯那座由白色石灰岩建造、带有窗户和石栏的封闭桥吗？就是连接旧监狱和总督府审讯室的那座吗？

J: 是的。拜仁勋爵在 19 世纪给威尼斯的这座桥取名为叹息桥。他是根据这样的联想取名的：犯人在被关进监狱之前走在这座桥上，当他们从窗户向外看美丽的威尼斯最后一眼时会发出叹息。

C: 我能看出剑桥的叹息桥和威尼斯的叹息桥在构造上有相似点，它们都是廊桥。

J: 剑桥的叹息桥也和拜伦勋爵有联系。

C: 真的吗？什么联系？

J: 当拜伦勋爵失宠于勃伦特公爵夫人时，他从桥上跳下来想自杀，但他被一个路人救了。从那以后，圣约翰学院就把原本是敞口式的桥梁封闭成廊桥了。

C: 拜伦勋爵太情绪化了，但是他的故事又为这座桥增添了传奇色彩。

J: 在圣约翰学院的旅游指南上，读者们可以看到在对叹息桥图片的描述上，校方强调从没有在桥上处罚过任何学生。

难点解析

1 You are very smart and this version seems to **stand up** under scrutiny. But still there are different versions.

stand up 意为“站起来，竖立，站得住脚，坚持，经得起，拥护，抵抗”。

- Always stand up for your friends.
  要永远维护朋友的利益。

- Stand up under close scrutiny.
  经得住仔细推敲。

2 I'm **curious about** the other versions.

curious about 意为“对……好奇的”。

- Don't be so curious about my affairs!
  不要老是打听我的事！

➢ I am most curious about the new invention.
我很想了解这项新发明。

3 And that **remind** me **of** a story that I heard many years ago.

remind of 意为"就……提醒（某人），使（某人）想起……"。

➢ Miss Lemon reminds her boss of two appointments.
莱蒙小姐提醒她的老板有两个约会。

➢ These photos remind me of my childhood.
这些照片使我想起了我的童年。

4 When Lord Byron **fell from grace** of Duchess of Bronte, he jumped off the bridge to commit suicide, but was saved by a passer-by.

fall from grace 意为"失宠"，grace 意为"恩惠、恩宠"。

➢ He had been the king's favourite, and his sudden fall from grace surprised everyone.
他本是国王的幸臣，一朝失宠众人无不感到意外.

Bridge of Sighs

Bridge of Sighs in Cambridge is a covered bridge belonging to St John's College of Cambridge University. It was built in 1831 and crosses the River Cam between the college's **Third Court**① and **New Court**②. The **architect**③ was Henry Hutchinson.

Bridge of Sighs is divided into three **layers**④: the upper layer, the middle layer, and the lower layer. The lower layer is the half-oval **arch**⑤, and the middle layer is a passage, also called "the gallery". Differ from other galleries, the floor of the gallery is not straight, but arched, which means the walkers-by have to cross the bridge on the **slope**⑥. The whole bridge is in light yellow.

Bridge of Sighs came into being because the building of New Court made necessary a

① Third Court 第三庭院
② New Court 新庭院
③ architect *n.* 建筑师，设计师
④ layer *n.* 层
⑤ arch *n.* 拱门，拱形物
⑥ slope *n.* 斜坡，斜面

second crossing of the river between it and Third Court, and New Court's architect seized the opportunity for some more charming and **allusive**① romanticism. Today it is part of the main **thoroughfare**② through the College and used daily by those who live and work here.

On two separate occasions, students have pulled the **prank**③ of **dangling**④ a car under the bridge. In the first incident, a 1928 **Austin 7**⑤ was punted down the river using four punts that had been **lashed together**⑥, and then **hoisted**⑦ up under the bridge using ropes. In the second incident, a Reliant Regal three-wheeler car was dangled under the bridge. In neither case was the bridge damaged.

Now the bridge is one of Cambridge's main tourist attractions and Queen Victoria is said to have loved it more than any other spots in the city.

Interestingly, there is also a bridge called bridge of sighs in the University of Oxford, because of its similarity to the famous Bridge of Sighs in Venice. The bridge was originally named as Hertford Bridge, because it located in Hertford College.

And Hertford Bridge is never intended to be a **replica**⑧ of the Venetian bridge, and indeed it bears a closer resemblance to the Rialto Bridge in the same city.

There is a false legend saying that many decades ago, a survey of the health of students was taken, and as Hertford College's students were the heaviest, the college closed off the bridge to force them to take the stairs, giving them extra exercise.

难道桥也会叹息

剑桥大学的叹息桥是一座封闭的桥，隶属于剑桥大学圣约翰学院。这座桥建于1831年，横跨剑河，连接圣约翰学院的第三庭院和新庭院。该桥的设计师是亨利·哈钦森。

叹息桥被分成三层：顶层、中层和底层。它的底层是一个半椭圆形的桥拱，中层是一个通道，也叫做“长廊”。与其他的长廊不同的是，长廊的通道不是平直的，而是拱形的，意味着路人过桥要上下坡。整座桥是浅黄色的。

---

① allusive *adj.* 暗指的，隐喻的
② thoroughfare *n.* 通道
③ prank *n.* 恶作剧
④ dangle *v.* 悬吊
⑤ Austin 7 奥斯汀 7，奥斯汀车是英国著名的品牌车。
⑥ lash together 将一物和令一物牢系在一起
⑦ hoist *v.* 把……吊起，升起
⑧ replica *n.* 复制品

新庭院的建立使得它和第三庭院之间必须要有第二条通道过河，所以人们才修建了叹息桥。而新庭院的建筑师也抓住这个机会修桥，他想把桥建得更迷人，并让这座桥散发出神秘的气息。今天这座桥是通往圣约翰学院的主要通道，生活和工作在那里的人们每天都从那走过。

学生们把车悬吊在桥底，在不同的时段玩起了相似的恶作剧。在第一次恶作剧中，一辆1928年生产的奥斯汀车被托在四艘连在一起的方头平底船上，然后学生们再用绳索把船吊到桥底。在第二次恶作剧中，一辆“罗宾”牌三轮车被吊到了桥底下。两次恶作剧都没有对桥造成损害。

现在叹息桥是剑桥市主要的旅游景点之一。据说在剑桥市的所有景点中，维多利亚女王最喜欢的就是叹息桥。

有意思的是，在牛津大学也有一座桥叫做叹息桥，名字的来源也是因为它和著名的威尼斯叹息桥有相似之处。牛津的叹息桥起初叫做赫特福德桥，因为它位于赫特福德学院。

赫特福德桥并不想成为威尼斯叹息桥的复制品，事实上，它和位于威尼斯的里亚托桥更相似。

还有一个错误的传说认为是几十年前，牛津大学进行了一次学生健康状况调查，鉴于赫特福德学院的学生是全校学生中体重最重的，赫特福德学院就把桥的通道关上，迫使学生们走楼梯，让他们多运动。

7 The Mathematical Bridge
没有铆钉的数学桥

焦点对话

Sam and Poly are visiting the Mathematical Bridge in Cambridge together.

S: Sam　　P: Poly

S: The style of this Mathematical Bridge is quite unusual in what do you think?

P: Yes, this bridge is built in sort of Chinese style. It's **delicate**[①] and elegant.

S: I heard that William Etheridge, the designer of Mathematical Bridge, had visited China.

P: Actually, it's not true. And there are plenty of **baseless**[②] stories told by some guides to **gullible**[③] tourists. For example, Mathematical Bridge was designed and built by Sir Isaac **Newton**[④].

S: But Sir Isaac Newton died in 1727, 22 years before the building of this bridge, and therefore he cannot possibly have had anything to do with this bridge.

P: Yes. The bridge was built in 1749 by James Essex the Younger to the design of William Etheridge. It had **subsequently**[⑤] been rebuilt to the same design in 1866 and 1905.

S: And the Mathematical Bridge is a wooden bridge across the River Cam, between two parts of Queens' College, Cambridge.

P: As the story goes, the **original**[⑥] bridge was built without **bolts**[⑦] ,but held together only by mathematical principles and a clever design.

S: And the story states that students of Queens' College were so curious about this bridge

---

① delicate *adj.* 精美的，雅致的
② baseless *adj.* 无根据的
③ gullible *adj.* 易受骗上当的
④ Sir Isaac Newton 艾萨克·牛顿爵士
⑤ subsequently *adv.* 随后地
⑥ original *adj.* 原来的，起初的
⑦ bolt *n.* 螺栓

that they took the bridge apart but then failed to put them back together.

P: But according to the records, the **joints**[1] of the original bridge are **fastened**[2] by **nuts**[3] and bolts. Only a **pedant**[4] could claim that the bridge was originally built without nails.

S: In reality, bolts are an inherent part of the design. When it was first built, **iron spikes**[5] were **driven into**[6] the joints from the outer side, where they could not be seen from the inside of the **parapets**[7], explaining why bolts were thought to be an addition to the original.

P: And anyone who believes that students could have **disassembled**[8] the bridge cannot have a serious grasp on reality, given the size and weight of the wooden material of the bridge.

S: The River Cam divides Queen's College into two sections, and this bridge is built to connect the two sides.

① joint *n.* 接合处
② fasten *v.* 系紧，拴住
③ nut *n.* 螺母
④ pedant *n.* 学究，夫子
⑤ iron spike 大铁钉
⑥ drive into 敲入
⑦ parapet *n.* 护栏
⑧ disassemble *v.* 拆卸

P: Queen's College is a **delightful**[①] college to **stroll around**[②], in particular the older section.

S: The famous places and **sights**[③] nearby Mathematical Bridge are Imperial War Museum Duxford, Great St Mary's Church and Museum of Archaeology.

P: As Britain's largest **aviation**[④] museum, Duxford houses nearly 200 aircraft, military vehicles, artillery and minor naval vessels in seven main exhibitions buildings.

S: And the site also provides **storage space**[⑤] for the museum's other collections of material such as films, photographs, documents, books and artefacts.

P: Based on the historic Duxford Aerodrome, the site was originally operated by the Royal Air Force (RAF) during the First World War.

S: During the Second World War Duxford played a prominent role during the Battle of Britain and was later used by United States Army Air Forces fighter units in support of the daylight bombing of Germany.

S: 这座数学桥的风格不太常见，你认为呢?

P: 是的，这座桥有点像中国建筑，很雅致。

S: 我听说数学桥的设计师威廉·埃斯里奇曾到过中国。

P: 其实这个说法是不对的。关于数学桥，还有很多没有事实依据的故事呢，是由一些导游告诉游客的，那些游客太容易上当了。举个例子，有人说数学桥是由艾萨克·牛顿爵士设计并建造的。

S: 但是艾萨克·牛顿爵士1727年就去世了，22年后这座桥才建起来。因此，他不可能和这座桥有任何联系。

P: 是啊，这座桥是由詹姆斯·小埃塞克斯根据威廉·埃斯里奇的设计在1749年建造的。后来根据原设计，人们又在1866年和1905年重建了这座桥。

S: 数学桥是横跨剑河的一座木桥，连接了剑桥大学女王学院的两部分。

P: 传说最初的桥是没有螺栓的，整座桥是依靠数学原理和绝妙的设计搭建起来的。

---

① delightful *adj.* 令人高兴的，讨人喜欢的
② stroll around 漫步，散步，逛
③ sight *n.* 景观，风景名胜
④ aviation *n.* 航空
⑤ storage space 储藏室，收藏室

S: 还有一个传说，女王学院的学生对这座桥很好奇，以至于他们想把这座桥拆开一探究竟，但后来却恢复不了原状了。

P: 但是根据史料记载，原桥的联接处是用螺母和螺栓拴住的。只有一个学者声称原桥是没有铆钉的。

S: 事实上，铆钉是这座桥设计的一个内在部分。开始建桥时，大铁钉是从外部敲入联接处的，所以从护栏内看不到铁钉。这也就解释了为什么人们觉得铁钉是后来才加上的原因。

P: 考虑到这座桥的木质材料的大小和重量，如果谁相信学生们能够把桥拆开，谁就没有认真地考虑实际情况。

S: 剑河把女王学院分成两部分，而数学桥的建立就是为了连接这两部分。

P: 当你漫步女王学院，特别是漫步于历史较悠久的校区时，你会感到无比惬意。

S: 数学桥附近的著名建筑和景观有帝国战争博物馆达克斯福德分馆、圣玛丽教堂和考古学博物馆。

P: 作为英国最大的航空博物馆，达克斯福德分馆收藏了近 200 架飞机、军用车、大炮和小型军舰，分布在 7 个主展馆中。

S: 该博物馆还设有收藏室专门收集其他材料，如电影、相片、文献、书籍和手工制品。

P: 该博物馆的原址是达克斯福德机场，是一战时英国皇家空军使用的机场。

S: 二战时，达克斯福德机场在伦敦保卫战中发挥了重要作用，随后被美国空军战斗机连借用，支持了对纳粹德国的日间轰炸。

1 **As the story goes**, the original bridge was built without bolts - held together only by mathematical principles and a clever design.

as the story goes 意为“正如传说所说”，经常用的还有 as the saying goes，意为“正如俗话所说、常言道”。

➢ One thing led to another as the saying goes.
常言道，环环相扣。

2 Only a pedant could **claim** that the bridge was originally built without nails.

claim 意为“声称、断言、主张”。

➢ Johnny claimed he'd been dining with friends at the time of the murder.
约翰尼声称，凶案发生时自己正和朋友们进餐。

claim 还可以做名词用。

➢ Dino denies claims that he is involved in a drugs ring.
迪诺否认自己与贩毒集团有关系的说法。

3 **In reality**, bolts are an inherent part of the design.

in reality 意为“事实上，实际上”。

➢ Henry always seems so confident, but in reality he's extremely shy.
亨利看起来总是很自信，实际上他极为腼腆。

4 And anyone who believes that students could have disassembled the bridge cannot have a serious grasp on reality, **given** the size and weight of the wooden material of the bridge.

given 意为“考虑到……”。

➢ Given the circumstances, you've coped well.
考虑到各种情况，你已经算是处理得很好了。

given 后还可以加 that。

➢ Given that there was so little time, I think they've done a good job.
考虑到没有多少时间，我认为他们算是做得不错了。

The Mathematical Bridge

The Mathematical Bridge was built in 1749 by James Essex the Younger to the design of William Etheridge. It had subsequently been rebuilt to the same design in 1866 and 1905.

The Queen's College still possesses an old model of the bridge, and we **assume**① that this is Etheridge's model of 1748. It is to be noted that even the model has **screws**② at the joints.

The design of the Mathematical Bridge **resembles**③ Etheridge's much greater Old Walton Bridge, a three-**arch**④ bridge over the Thames at Walton, built from1748 to 1750.

William Etheridge was one of a very long family line of **carpenters**⑤. His birth was not

① assume *v.* 假设
② screw *n.* 螺丝钉
③ resemble *v.* 像……，类似于
④ arch *n.* 拱，拱门
⑤ carpenter *n.* 木匠

recorded, but his **baptism**① took place on 3rd January 1708 at St Margaret's **parish church**②. His career as a master carpenter first **came to light**③ in 1738-1749 when he worked under James King in the building of the first bridge to cross the Thames at Westminster. From 1747-1750 he worked on the Walton Bridge and in 1748 produced the design and model for the Mathematical Bridge.

The Mathematical Bridge was the earliest recorded work of James Essex the Younger. He later constructed the Essex Building, which was intended to be part of a new building along the river, replacing the 1460s part of the President's Lodge.

By the 1860s, the original bridge of 1749 was badly **decayed**④. Photographs showed many **timbers**⑤ patched, and the sides of the bridge apparently leaning inwards. It was repaired in 1866.

There was one change of the design: the **pedestrian**⑥ decking was **sloped**⑦ instead of stepped on each side, making it possible today for wheeled trolleys to be used over the bridge. The use of the word repairing suggests that this was not a complete rebuilding, however, and maybe parts of the original bridge were retained and continued to decay, explaining why this version lasted less than 40 years.

In 1905 the bridge was completely rebuilt by local builder William Sindall. In this version of the bridge, the joints were fastened by nuts and bolts passing right through the joint, the bolt heads being on the internal **elevations**⑧ of the side arches, and therefore visible to people passing over the bridge.

Previous versions of the bridge had the joints fastened by iron pins or screws driven in from the outer elevation, which were therefore not visible to the casual passer-by on the bridge, as the screws did not penetrate as far as the inner elevation.

---

① baptism *n.*（基督教的）洗礼
② parish church 教区教堂
③ come to light 显露，为大家所熟知
④ decay *v.* 腐烂，腐蚀
⑤ timber *n.* 木材
⑥ pedestrian *n.* 步行者
⑦ slope *v.* 倾斜
⑧ elevation *n.*（建筑物的）正视图，立体图

没有铆钉的数学桥

数学桥是1749年詹姆斯·小埃塞克斯根据威廉·埃斯里奇的设计建造的，随后人们又在1866年和1905年根据同样的设计重建了这座桥。

女王学院还保留着这座桥的一个旧模型，我们假设这就是埃斯里奇1748年设计的模型，值得注意的是这座模型的联结处也有螺丝钉。

数学桥的设计和埃斯里奇设计的老沃尔顿桥相似，但是老沃尔顿桥比数学桥大得多，是一座建于1748～1750年间的横跨泰晤士河、位于沃尔顿的三门拱桥。

威廉·埃斯里奇的家族是历史悠久的木匠家族中的分支。埃斯里奇出生日期不详，但他是在1708年1月3号于玛格丽特教区教堂接受洗礼的。他作为职业木匠首次为大家所熟知是在1738～1749年间，当时他在詹姆斯国王指导下建造位于威斯敏斯特的第一座横跨泰晤士河的桥。从1747～1750年，他建造了沃尔顿桥，1748年他做出了数学桥的设计和模型。

数学桥是詹姆斯·小埃塞克斯有记载的最早作品。他后来建造了埃塞克斯大楼，想替代15世纪60年代建立的部分校长住所，让其成为剑河岸边一座新建筑的一部分。

到了19世纪60年代，1749年建的数学桥已经被严重腐蚀了。照片显示了很多修葺过的木材，而且桥栏很明显地向内倾斜。1866年，人们修复了这座桥。

在修复过程中，人们对原设计做了一个改动：人行道铺板改成斜面的，而不是在桥的两侧都铺设，这样轮椅就能在整座桥上使用。但是“修复”这个词说明这并不是完全的重建，可能部分原桥被保留了下来并继续被腐蚀，这就是为什么修复后的桥维持不到40年就又要重修了的原因吧。

1905年，该桥由当地建筑师威廉·辛德尔整体重建，在这座重建的桥中，联接处由螺母和螺栓拴住，并穿过了联接处。螺栓头突出于侧拱门的内侧，所以走过桥的人都能看得到。

前几个版本的数学桥的铁针或螺丝钉是从外部钉进联接处的，而螺丝钉并没有穿透到桥的内部，所以对于不仔细观察的过桥者来说是看不到的。

8 Newton's Apple Tree

牛顿的苹果树

焦点对话

Henry and Rachel are watching a **documentary film**① about Sir Isaac Newton.

H: Henry　　R: Rachel

H: As a mathematician and physicist, Sir Isaac Newton is one of the **foremost**② scientific intellects of all time.

R: I can't agree with you more. And Newton remains **influential**③ to scientists, as demonstrated by a 2005 survey of members of Britain's Royal Society.

H: Newton's study lays the groundwork for most of classical **mechanics**④. In one of his books, Newton described **universal gravitation**⑤ and the **three laws of motion**⑥ which **dominated**⑦ the physical world for the next three centuries.

R: Speaking of the universal gravitation, do you know how Newton comes up with this law?

H: Of course. Newton himself often told the story that he was **inspired**⑧ to **formulate**⑨ his theory of gravitation by watching the fall of an apple from a tree.

---

① documentary film 纪录片
② foremost *adj.* 最著名的
③ influential *adj.* 有影响的
④ classical mechanics 经典力学
⑤ universal gravitation 万有引力
⑥ three laws of motion 三大运动定律
⑦ dominate *v.* 主宰，支配
⑧ inspire *v.* 赋予某人灵感，启迪
⑨ formulate *v.* 构想出

R: Cartoons have gone further to suggest the apple actually hit Newton's head, and that its impact somehow made him aware of the force of gravity.

H: It is known from his notebooks that he was grappling in the late 1660s with the idea of **terrestrial**① gravity. However it took him two decades to develop the **full-fledged**② theory.

R: In the year 1666 Newton retired again from Cambridge to his hometown in Woolsthorpe, Lincolnshire. Observing a fully formed apple drop from the tree **prompted**③ Newton to ask the vital questions.

H: I heard that Newton asked himself: "Why should that apple always **descend**④ **perpendicularly**⑤ to the ground? Why should it not go **sideways**⑥ or upwards, but constantly to the earth's centre?"

R: In the popular myth we all grew up with, Newton was hit on the head by the apple, its impact suggestively knocking a moment of enlightened inspiration into him.

H: John Conduitt, Newton's assistant at the Royal Mint and husband of Newton's niece, described the event when he wrote about Newton's life.

R: John Conduitt's version is different from those stories we heard, right?

H: Yes. According to Conduitt, Newton was pensively **meandering**⑦ in a garden and it came into his thought that the power of gravity was not limited to a certain distance from earth, but that this power must extend much further than was usually thought.

R: Although there are many versions, the apple tree at Newton's home became well-known around the world.

H: It's true. And in the back garden of the Isaac Newton Institute for Mathematical Sciences in Cambridge is an apple tree. There is another in the University Botanic Gardens.

R: Each is said to be a **descendant**⑧ of the apple tree at Woolsthorpe Manor that inspired the founder of modern physics to **inquire into**⑨ the nature of gravitation and the laws of motion.

---

① terrestrial *adv.* 地球的，陆地的
② full-fledged *adj.* 全面的
③ prompt *v.* 促使
④ descend *v.* 下降
⑤ perpendicularly *adv.* 垂直地
⑥ sideways *adv.* 斜向一边的
⑦ meander *v.* 漫步，散步
⑧ descendant *n.* 后代
⑨ inquire into 调查

H: But some people said that a descendant of the original tree can be seen growing outside the main gate of Trinity College, Cambridge, below the room Newton lived in when he studied there.

R: Wow, it's really confusing. Any apple trees in Cambridge may be the descendant of the apple tree inspiring Newton in his hometown.

H: 作为一位数学家和物理学家，艾萨克·牛顿爵士是有史以来最著名的科学家之一。

R: 我非常同意你的观点。2005 年对英国皇家学会的调查显示，牛顿仍然对现在的科学家有一定的影响。

H: 牛顿的研究为经典力学的大部分内容打下了基础。在他的一本书中，牛顿描述了万有引力和三大运动定律，主宰了接下来三个世纪的物理世界。

R: 说到万有引力，你知道牛顿是怎么想到这个定律的吗?

H: 我当然知道。牛顿自己就经常说他是看到苹果从树上落下受到启发而构想出万有引力定律的。

R: 漫画还更夸张地暗示那个苹果其实是掉在牛顿的头上，被苹果砸到的牛顿开始注意到万有引力的存在。

H: 从牛顿的笔记中我们知道他是在 17 世纪 60 年代晚期提出“地球重力”这个概念的，但是他花了 20 多年时间才构建出一个成熟、全面的理论体系。

R: 1666 年，牛顿再次从剑桥大学“退休”回到他的家乡：林肯郡伍尔索坡。观察到一个成熟的苹果从树上落下，牛顿心中疑惑重重。

H: 我听说牛顿自问道:“为什么苹果会永远垂直地落到地上呢? 它为什么不斜向一边或是往上窜，而是朝着地心的方向坠落呢? ”

R: 在我们从小听到大的传说中，牛顿被苹果砸到，受到了极大的启发。

H: 约翰·孔杜伊特是牛顿在皇家铸币厂的助手，同时也是牛顿外甥女的丈夫。当他描述牛顿的生活时，提到了这一事件。

R: 约翰·孔杜伊特的版本和我们听到的那些故事不同，对吗?

H: 是的。根据孔杜伊特的描述，牛顿闷闷不乐地在花园里散步，他突然想到引力的作用并不是局限在一定的距离之内的，它的作用肯定比之前人们认为的要大。

R: 虽然有很多不同的版本，但牛顿家乡的苹果树已经闻名于世了。

H: 的确如此。在剑桥大学艾萨克·牛顿数学研究所的后花园就有一棵苹果树，另外在剑桥大学植物园也有一棵。

R: 正是受到位于家乡的伍尔索坡庄园的一棵苹果树启发，现代物理学之父牛顿开始对万有引力的本质和运动三大定律进行探索研究。据说剑桥的两棵苹果树之一就是那棵苹果树的后代。

H: 但是有些人说那棵苹果树的后代长在剑桥大学三一学院的主门外，上方就是牛顿当时住的房间。

R: 哇，这真令人感到困惑。牛顿家乡的苹果树给予了他灵感，剑桥大学的任何一棵苹果树都有可能是它的后代。

1 As a mathematician and physicist, Sir Isaac Newton is one of **the foremost** scientific intellects **of all time**.

the foremost\ best\biggest etc… of all time 意为"有史以来最著名的\最好的\最大的……"。

➢ This is the most successful movie of all time
这是有史以来最成功的一部电影。

2 Newton's study **lays the groundwork** for most of classical mechanics.

groundwork 意为"根基、基础"，lay the groundwork 意为"打下基础"。

➢ The groundwork for the peace summit was laid during last month's conference.
和平峰会的基础是在上个月那次会议期间打下的。

3 It is known from his notebooks that Newton was **grappling** in the late 1660s **with** the idea that terrestrial gravity.

grapple with 意为"尽力解决（某困难、问题）"。

➢ The government is grappling with major areas of social policy.
政府正努力处理社会政策主要领域中的问题。

➢ They grappled with their consciences
他们在与良知抗争。

➢ We should grapple with the political realities of our time.
我们应当与这个时代的政治现实抗争。

4 Newton was pensively meandering in a garden it **came into his thought** that the power of gravity was not limited to a certain distance from earth,...

come into sb's thought 意为"某人想到……", come into 本意为"卷入（某事）"。

➢ Mary, a minor character, doesn't come into the story much.
玛丽是个配角，在故事中没有她什么戏。

Newton's Apple Tree

Newton was an English physicist and mathematician, and the greatest scientist of his era.

Isaac Newton was born on 4 January 1643 in Woolsthorpe, Lincolnshire. His father was a **prosperous**[①] farmer, who died three months before Newton was born. His mother remarried and Newton was left in the care of his grandparents. In 1661, he went to Cambridge University where he became interested in mathematics, **optics**[②], physics and **astronomy**[③]. In October 1665, a **plague**[④] epidemic forced the university to close and Newton returned to Woolsthorpe. The two years he spent there were an extremely fruitful time during which he began to think about **gravity**[⑤]. He also devoted time to optics and mathematics, working out his ideas about **calculus**[⑥].

In 1667, Newton returned to Cambridge, where he became a fellow of Trinity College. Two years later he was appointed second **Lucasian professor of mathematics**[⑦]. It was Newton's **reflecting telescope**[⑧], made in 1668, that finally brought him to the

① prosperous *adj.* 繁荣的，富裕的
② optics *n.* 光学
③ astronomy *n.* 天文学
④ plague *n.* 瘟疫
⑤ gravity *n.* 万有引力
⑥ calculus *n.* 微积分
⑦ Lucasian professor of mathematics 卢卡斯数学教授，学术界中最负盛名的教授名衔。
⑧ reflecting telescope 反射望远镜

attention of the scientific community and in 1672 he was made a fellow of the Royal Society. From the mid-1660s, Newton conducted a series of experiments on the composition of light, discovering that white light is composed of the same system of colours that can be seen in a rainbow and establishing the modern study of optics. In 1704, Newton published *The Opticks* which dealt with light and colour. He also studied and published works on history, **theology**① and **alchemy**②.

In 1687, with the support of his friend the **astronomer**③ Edmond Halley, Newton published his single greatest work, the *Philosophiae Naturalis Principia Mathematica* (*Mathematical Principles of Natural Philosophy*). This showed how gravity, applied to all objects in all parts of the universe.

In 1689, Newton was elected member of parliament for Cambridge University. In 1696, Newton was appointed **warden**④ of the Royal Mint, settling in London. He took his duties at the Mint very seriously and campaigned **against**⑤ corruption and inefficiency within the organization. In 1703, he was elected president of the Royal Society, an office he held until his death. He was knighted in 1705.

Newton was a difficult man, prone to depression and often involved in bitter arguments with other scientists, but by the early 1700s he was the dominant figure in British and European science. He died on 31 March 1727 and was buried in Westminster Abbey.

牛顿的苹果树

牛顿是一位英国物理学家和数学家，也是他那个时代最卓越的科学家之一。

1643年1月4号，艾萨克·牛顿出生于林肯郡伍尔索坡。牛顿的父亲是一个富裕的农民，在牛顿出生前3个月就过世了。他的妈妈改嫁，而他则由祖父母养大成人。1661年，他进入剑桥大学学习，对数学、光学、物理学和天文学产生了兴趣。1665年10月，一场大瘟疫迫使剑桥大学暂时关闭，牛顿回到了伍尔索坡。在那两年中他收获颇丰，他开始思考重力问题，还致力于光学和数学研究，提出了“微

① theology *n.* 神学
② alchemy *n.* 炼金术
③ astronomer *n.* 天文学家
④ warden *n.* 监护人
⑤ campaign against 开展反……的运动

积分”的概念。

1667 年，牛顿回到剑桥大学，成为三一学院的研究员。两年后他被任命为第二任卢卡斯数学教授。1668 年牛顿发明的反射望远镜终于使他受到科学界的关注。1672 年，牛顿成为了英国皇家学会的会员。从 17 世纪 60 年代中期起，牛顿做了一系列关于光的构成的实验，发现了白光是由同一体系的不用颜色构成的，那些不同的颜色可以在彩虹中看到。他由此创立了现代光学。1704 年，牛顿出版了《光学》一书，阐述了光和颜色的有关原理。他还研究历史、神学和炼金术，并出版了相关著作。

1687 年，在他的朋友，天文学家埃德蒙·哈雷的帮助下，牛顿出版了他最伟大的专著《自然哲学的数学原理》。这本著作展示了万有引力是如何适用于宇宙中的万事万物的。

1689 年，牛顿当选为剑桥大学校委会委员。1696 年，他被任命为位于伦敦的皇家铸币厂的监管人。他在铸币厂尽心尽力工作，并在铸币厂内部发起反腐败和反低效率工作的运动。1703 年，牛顿被评选为英国皇家学会主席，并一直担任这个职务直到去世。1705 年，他被封为爵士。

牛顿不是个容易相处的人，他有抑郁倾向，经常陷入和其他科学家的激烈争论中。但是一直到 18 世纪早期，牛顿仍是英国乃至欧洲科学界的领军人物。1727 年 3 月 31 日，牛顿逝世，葬于威斯敏斯特教堂。

Unit 3 Life & Study 青春舞飞扬

9 Cambridge Union Society 唇枪舌剑

焦点对话

Victoria and Luke are discussing a piece of news on *Telegraph*.

V: Victoria　　　L: Luke

V: Wow, Cambridge students are going to receive **pole dancing**[1] classes to help combat summer exam stress.

L: It's unbelievable. But Francisco, who is responsible for arranging the pole dance classes, said that the classes are for fitness and **well-being**[2], and are not intended to be sexual.

V: And the report said that **Cambridge Union Society**[3] officers have **confirmed**[4] that.

L: Wait a minute, you mean Cambridge Union Society, the famous debating society in Cambridge?

V: Yes. And the lessons will take in the Blue Room of the Union building, more commonly used as the venue for debates among **venerable**[5] statesmen including Winston Churchill and former **Archbishop**[6] Desmond Tutu.

L: I'm curious about Cambridge Union Society. Since its founding in 1815, the Society has

---

① pole dancing 钢管舞
② well-being *n.* 健康
③ Cambridge Union Society 剑桥联合会，也称剑桥辩论会
④ confirm *v.* 证实
⑤ venerable *adj.* 受尊重的，受敬佩的
⑥ Archbishop *n.* 大主教

developed a worldwide reputation as a noted symbol of **free speech**[1] and open debate.

V: For almost two hundred years, the Cambridge Union Society has stood as a centre of debate and free speech in British intellectual life.

L: The Society is **fiercely**[2] independent and has often been at the centre of **controversy**[3]. Shortly after its founding in 1815 it was **temporarily**[4] closed down by the University for being too **contentious**[5].

V: But today with its own bar, library and cinema facilities, it has become an **integral part**[6] of student life in Cambridge.

L: Speaking of its origin, the exact origin of the Society remains steeped in legend, but as the story goes the Union was founded in 1815 at the conclusion of a drunken **brawl**[7] between three smaller College debating societies.

V: And the'union' of the three societies provided the basis for the name "The Cambridge Union Society."

L: The Union originally existed as a gentleman's club, the sole preserve of the rich and well connected and, using the Union as a model, a similar society was subsequently formed in Oxford.

V: This is in stark contrast to today, where all members of the University are welcomed amongst the **diverse**[8] **membership**[9].

① free speech 言论自由
② fiercely *adv.* 猛烈地
③ controversy *n.* 争议
④ temporarily *adv.* 临时
⑤ contentious *adj.* 容易引起争论的
⑥ integral part 主要的部分
⑦ brawl *n.* 争吵
⑧ diverse *adj.* 不同的，多种多样的
⑨ membership *n.* 会员制

L: The Union has debated all sorts of topics: crime, drugs, **prostitution**①, race, law, **abortion**②, gay rights and the media.

V: Topics like **asylum seekers**③, Europe, Iraq, pornography and tuition fees have all taken place over the last few years.

L: Debates on international affairs have often been the most **controversial**④. Following the attendance of the **Ambassador**⑤ of South Africa at a debate in the early 1980s there was a full-scale riot outside the building with **bricks**⑥ being hurled through the windows.

V: A debate on the **motion**⑦ "This house believes the Palestinians want too much and give too little" was so controversial that the President at the time received death threats, policemen **stood guard**⑧ outside the building.

L: In the past the Union had debated some of the most important events of the 20th Century. In 1938, the same year that Chamberlain visited the Union, conscription⑨ was debated.

V: Newspapers at that time said that the motion was passed with an overwhelming majority against conscription, causing much controversy and consternation

V: 哇，剑桥大学的学生准备接受钢管舞课程训练，以缓解盛夏期末考试的压力。

L: 真难以置信。但是负责安排钢管舞课的弗朗西斯科说安排这样的课只是为了健身和健康，不是为了性感。

V: 报道还说剑桥联合会的主管证实了此事。

L: 等一下，你说的剑桥联合会就是那个著名的剑桥辩论会吗？

V: 是的，而且钢管舞课还要在联合会大楼的“蓝厅”开课呢。蓝厅平时多用作德高望重的政治家们开展辩论的场所，包括英国前首相温斯顿·丘吉尔和前大主教德斯蒙德·图图等人都在此辩论过。

L: 我对剑桥联合会很好奇。自从1815年建立以来，联合会就作为言论自由和公开辩论的著名标志而享誉世界。

---

① prostitution *n.* 卖淫
② abortion *n.* 堕胎
③ asylum seekers 寻求正式避难者
④ controversial *adj.* 有争议的
⑤ ambassador *n.* 大使
⑥ brick *n.* 砖块
⑦ motion *n.* 动议
⑧ stand guard 站岗
⑨ conscription *n.* 征兵

V: 在其近200年的历史中，剑桥联合会一直是英国知识分子生活中辩论和言论自由的中心。

L: 联合会非常独立并经常处于争议之中。在1815年成立后不久，它就被剑桥大学临时关闭了，因为它太容易引起争论了。

V: 但是在今天，拥有自己的酒吧、图书馆和电影院设备的联合会已经成为剑桥学生生活中必不可少的一部分。

L: 说到它的起源，关于联合会的起源的确有很多传说。但是据说联合会是在三个较小的学院辩论社团的成员喝醉酒争吵过后成立起来的，那年是1815年。

V: 这三个社团的名字中都包含“联合会”这个词，这就是“剑桥联合会”的来源。

L: 联合会起初只是一个男生俱乐部，只招收家庭富裕、有社会背景的男士。随后以联合会为典范，牛津大学也成立了一个相似的社团。

V: 今天的情况和以往大不相同，会员制的多样化使得剑桥大学的所有学生都能成为联合会的一员。

L: 联合会辩论各种各样的话题，如犯罪、毒品、卖淫、种族、法律、堕胎、同性恋者权利和媒体等。

V: 在过去的几年中，联合会的辩论话题还涉及到寻求政治避难者、欧洲、伊拉克、色情作品和学费等。

L: 国际事务的辩论通常是最具争议性的。20世纪80年代早期，在南非大使参加辩论后，联合会大楼外爆发了大规模的暴动，窗户都被砖块砸破了。

V: 一场名为“我们认为巴勒斯坦人索取太多而付出太少”的辩论极具争议，以至于当时联合会的主席接到了死亡威胁，警察还要在联合会大楼外警戒。

L: 过去，联合会曾就20世纪一些重要事件进行过辩论。1938年，时任英国首相的张伯伦访问了联合会，同年联合会就征兵问题展开辩论。

V: 当时的报纸说这项动议以绝大多数人反对征兵的结果通过了，引起了很多争论和恐慌。

1 Speaking of its origin, the exact origin of the Society remains **steeped in legend**, ...

be steeped in history\tradition 意为“有丰富的历史\传统”。

➢ a town steeped in history
历史悠久的小城

2 The Union originally existed as a gentleman's club, the sole preserve of the rich and **well connected** and, using the Union as a model, a similar society was subsequently formed in Oxford.

well connected 意为“有优越社会关系的，有关系（后台硬）的”。

➢ a well-connected Edinburgh family
社会关系优越的爱丁堡家族

➢ He's well connected in political circles.
他在政界结识了不少有权有势的人物。

3 Topics like asylum seekers, Europe, Iraq, pornography and tuition fees have all **taken place** over the last few years.

take place 意为“发生，举行，进行”。

➢ When did the accident take place?
事故是什么时候发生的？

➢ When will the marriage take place?
婚礼什么时候举行？

4 Following the attendance of the Ambassador of South Africa at a debate in the early 1980s there was a **full-scale** riot outside the building with bricks being hurled through the windows.

full-scale 意为“最大限度的，彻底的，全面的”，仅用于名词前。

➢ a full-scale inquiry into the train crash
对列车撞毁事故的全面调查

➢ a full-scale campaign against the use of nuclear power plants
反对建立核工厂的大规模运动

Cambridge Union Society

The Cambridge Union Society, commonly referred to simply as the Cambridge Union, is the largest student society at the University of Cambridge and one of the oldest in the world. Additionally, the Cambridge Union served as a model for the **subsequent**[①] foundation of similar societies at several other prominent universities including the Oxford Union and the Yale Political Union.

The Union has always been famous for its controversial debates. Few other places in the world are able to bring together so many **high profile**[②] speakers of such diverging views and make them defend what they passionately believe in. Uniquely, the Union opens public figures up to your questions, for which they cannot be prepared. Debates are highly relevant to current issues and often mirror discussion in parliament and the media.

The Cambridge Union was founded on February 13th, 1815 as a union of three debating societies and quickly rose to **prominence**[③] in University life. Early officers have included the historian and **essayist**[④], Thomas Babington Macaulay and many subsequent Presidents and officers have gone on to become influential leaders in a wide variety of fields and professions. The Union has always served as a **pinnacle**[⑤] of free speech and open debate and was even temporarily shut down by the University in its early years for being too contentious! After nearly 200 years, the Cambridge Union is still best known for its debates which often receive national or international media attention. It also organizes lectures by visiting speakers, film evenings and other social events for its members. The top members of its debating team compete internationally against other top debating societies, and Cambridge regularly **fields**[⑥] one of the most successful teams at the World Universities Debating

---

① subsequent *adj.* 随后的
② high profile 知名度高的
③ prominence *n.* 声望，杰出
④ essayist *n.* 随笔作家
⑤ pinnacle *n.* 顶峰
⑥ field *v.* 派出

Championships.

The Cambridge Union is sometimes confused with the Cambridge University Students' Union, the representative body for undergraduate students set up much more recently in 1971.

The Cambridge Union is a private society and traditionally membership is only open to members of the University of Cambridge, although more recently membership has been made available to students at other educational institutions in Cambridge. The society is not open to the general public. However, members are often able to bring guests to certain functions and some events are made available to the public for free or through the purchase of a ticket.

唇枪舌剑

剑桥联合会，一般简称为剑桥联会，是剑桥大学最大的学生社团，也是世界上历史最悠久的学生社团之一。此外，剑桥联会成立之后，其他几个著名大学还以它为典范成立了类似的社团，这其中包括牛津联会和耶鲁政治联盟。

剑桥联合会一直以颇具争议性的辩论而闻名。世界上很少有其他地方能像联合会这样能聚集起这么多观点迥异、知名度高的演讲者，还能让他们为自己坚信的观点辩护。更独特的是，联合会还能让民众随意向公共人物提问题，他们不可能对这些问题提前准备。辩论和时事紧密相关，还经常反映出议会和媒体讨论的话题。

剑桥联合会成立于 1815 年 2 月 13 日，是三个辩论社团的联合，并很快在剑桥大学声名远扬。早期的联合会官员包括历史学家和随笔作家托马斯·巴宾顿·麦考雷，联合会随后的多任主席和官员都成为很多不同领域和行业的领导者，并颇具影响力。联合会一直以来都崇尚言论自由和公开辩论，还曾因为太容易引起争论，在创立初期被剑桥大学暂时关闭。在近 200 年之后，剑桥联合会仍然以其辩论闻名于世，并经常受到国内外媒体的关注。联合会还邀请来访的演讲者给会员做讲座，并为会员组织了电影之夜和其他社交活动。联合会辩论会的顶尖成员还参与国际竞争，和其他优秀的辩论社团一争高下。在世界大学生辩论锦标赛中，剑桥大学派出的辩论队通常都是世界上最成功的辩论队之一。

人们经常把剑桥联合会和剑桥学生会搞混。剑桥学生会是剑桥本科生的代表团体，成立于 1971 年，比剑桥联合会晚得多。

剑桥联合会是一个私人社团，虽然近年来剑桥市的其他教育机构的成员也可以申请成为会员，但是传统上只有剑桥大学的学生才能成为会员。联合会是不向公众开放的，但是联合会的会员可以经常邀请客人参加活动。还有一些活动向公众免费开放，或以向公众售票的形式开放。

10 The Eagle Pub
老鹰酒吧

焦点对话

Tom and Wendy are drinking beer at a pub.

T: Tom　　W: Wendy

T: I often go to pubs and I drink beer, chat with my friends and watch the show there. I quite enjoy going to pubs. Do you have any recommendation?

W: I think you should go to Cambridge, then. The small city is the house of about 200 pubs. And there are so many interesting pubs in the University of Cambridge.

T: I heard that the students in Cambridge like drinking and some of them even go to **binge drinking**[①].

W: That's because they are so stressful due to intensive courses and hard exams. Students like to go to drinking societies and pubs around the campus.

T: My friend said that she once went to the Eagle Pub and it's really nice.

W: Yeah. If you are looking for a pub that is historically **fascinating**[②], conveniently placed and large, then this is the one for you.

T: The Eagle Pub has a long and interesting history. First opened in 1667 during the era of the Great Fire of London and the Black Death, it was originally a **coaching inn**[③].

W: During the Second World War, it was particularly popular with the **airmen**[④] **stationed**[⑤] on the **airfields**[⑥] dotted around the city.

---

① binge drinking 酗酒，滥饮寻欢
② fascinating *adj.* 迷人的，吸引力大的
③ coaching inn 车站酒馆
④ airman *n.* 飞行员
⑤ station *v.* 驻扎
⑥ airfield *n.*（较小的无建筑的）飞机场

T: According to the newspaper, if you take a look at the **RAF**[①] bar out the back, you can still see **graffiti**[②] on the ceiling, made by the RAF and US **aircrews**[③] who scorched their names with candles and **cigarette lighters**[④].

W: And it stands as clear **proof**[⑤] of Cambridge as a place of innovation. It was in this very pub, on the 28 February 1953, that Cambridge scientists James Watson and Francis Crick first announced they had discovered "secret of life".

T: "Secret of life"? You mean DNA, **deoxyribonucleic acid**[⑥]?

W: Yes. When the University of Cambridge's **Cavendish Laboratory**[⑦] was still at its old site nearby Free School Lane, the pub was a popular lunch destination for staff working there.

T: Oh, I see, so it became the place where Francis Crick and James Watson often visited.

W: But just do not expect good beer or good food at the Eagle Pub.

T: Eagle Pub was prosecuted by Cambridge City Council for alleged poor food hygiene standards.

W: The charges, all of which related to May 2008, included **accusations**[⑧] that the pub did not provide soap for customers to wash their hands with in the bathrooms, and that the equipment used to prepare food was not sufficiently cleaned or **disinfected**[⑨].

T: As well as this the pub was accused of leaving windows open allowing flies to enter and failing to store raw meat in hygienic conditions.

---

① RAF 英国皇家空军
② graffiti *n.* 涂鸦
③ aircrew *n.* 机组人员
④ cigarette lighter 打火机
⑤ proof *n.* 证明，证据
⑥ deoxyribonucleic acid 脱氧核糖核酸
⑦ Cavendish Laboratory 卡文迪什实验室，著名实验室，也是剑桥大学物理系的代称。
⑧ accusation *n.* 指责，控告
⑨ disinfected *v.* 消毒

W: I'm so sorry to hear that, because Eagle Pub is a part of Cambridge's heritage, dating back to Tudor times when it served as a coaching inn in the 17th Century.

T: I'm not happy to hear that, too. It was popular among students and tourists alike.

W: A girl said online that she often **pops in**① the Eagle Pub as it's close to her work. But she can assure people that convenience is the only draw.

T: 我经常去酒吧，我在那儿喝酒、聊天、看演出。我很喜欢去酒吧，你有什么推荐的地方吗?

W: 那么我想你应该去剑桥，那个小城有 200 多家酒吧，并且剑桥大学里还有很多有意思的酒吧。

T: 我听说剑桥大学的学生们喜欢喝酒，一些学生甚至还酗酒。

W: 那是因为他们课程太多、考试太难、压力太大了。他们喜欢去饮酒社团和校园里的酒吧。

T: 我朋友说过她曾去过老鹰酒吧，感觉很好。

W: 是啊。如果你想寻找一个有历史魅力、交通便利且宽敞的酒吧，那么老鹰酒吧就是最佳选择。

T: 老鹰酒吧历史悠久，史上还发生过不少趣事。当它在伦敦大火和黑死病（鼠疫）肆虐时期的 1667 年开放时，它只是一个车站酒馆。

W: 二战期间，它颇受驻扎在剑桥附近飞机场的飞行员的欢迎。

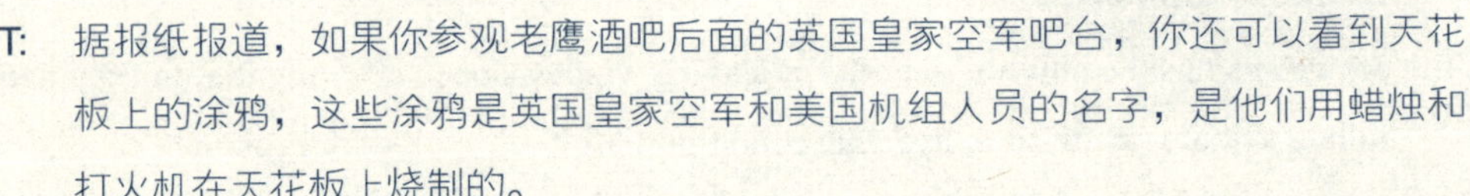

T: 据报纸报道，如果你参观老鹰酒吧后面的英国皇家空军吧台，你还可以看到天花板上的涂鸦，这些涂鸦是英国皇家空军和美国机组人员的名字，是他们用蜡烛和打火机在天花板上烧制的。

W: 而且老鹰酒吧还是剑桥大学作为创新基地的有力证明。1953 年 2 月 28 号，正是在这个酒吧，剑桥大学的科学家詹姆斯·沃森和弗朗西斯·克里克首次宣布他们发现了“生命的秘密”。

T: “生命的秘密？”你指的是 DNA（脱氧核糖核酸），是吗?

W: 是的。那时剑桥大学的卡文迪什实验室还位于自由学院路（靠近该酒吧）附近的

① pcp in 突然进来，出现

旧址，实验室的工作人员都喜欢去老鹰酒吧吃午餐。

T: 哦，我知道了，所以老鹰酒吧也就是弗朗西斯·克里克和詹姆斯·沃森经常光顾的地方。

W: 但是不要期待这个酒吧有爽口的啤酒和美味的食物。

T: 老鹰酒吧被剑桥市议会指控，市议会宣称其食物卫生标准低。

W: 指控是在 2008 年 5 月提出的，包括酒吧在洗手间里不提供香皂，顾客无法洗手，烹制食物的厨具没有清洗或消毒干净等等。

T: 酒吧还被指控不关窗户，从而蝇虫乱飞，并且在不卫生的情况下保存生肉。

W: 很遗憾听到这些，因为老鹰酒吧是剑桥大学的遗产，早在 17 世纪的都铎王朝时期，它就作为一个车站酒馆存在了。

T: 听到这些，我也开心不起来，因为它曾在学生和游客当中广受好评。

W: 一女孩在网上说，因为老鹰酒吧离她工作的地方近，所以她经常光顾，但是她能向大家保证，“便利”是这家酒吧吸引人的唯一地方。

1 During the Second World War, it was particularly popular with the airmen stationed on the airfields **dotted around** the city.

dot around 意为“散布，分布”。

➢ The company now has over 20 stores dotted around the country.
该公司现拥有 20 多家商店，遍布全国。

2 According to the newspaper, if you take a look in the RAF bar **out the back**, you can still see graffiti on the ceiling,...

out the back 意为“在房屋（建筑物）的后面”。

➢ We keep the bikes in a shed out the back.
我们把自行车放在屋后的车棚里。

3 Eagle Pub is **prosecuted** by Cambridge City Council for alleged poor food hygiene standards.

prosecute 意为“检举、告发某人，对某人提起公诉”。

➢ He was prosecuted for murder.
他因谋杀罪而被起诉。

➢ A court has power to prosecute for traffic offences.
法庭有权对违反交通的行为进行起诉。

4 I'm so sorry to hear that, because Eagle Pub is a part of Cambridge's heritage, **dating back** to Tudor times when it served as a coaching inn in the 17th Century.

date back 意为“追溯到……”。

➢ The history of hockey can date back to thousands ago.
曲棍球的历史可以追溯到数千年前。

The Eagle Pub

Originally opened in 1667 as the "Eagle and Child", The Eagle pub is one of Cambridge's most popular drinking establishments and one with an impressive historical legacy. It can be found on Benet Street, just to the South of the Senate House at the heart of Cambridge. It's one of the larger pubs in the city with access to a beautiful beer garden and serves a number of domestic beers and international wines.

The Eagle is famous for housing the so-called RAF bar, named as such because the pub was popular during the Second World War with local RAF and American Air personnel. A **permanent**[①] and moving reminder of those **momentous**[②] days has been left here in the form of some unusual yet historic graffiti. It became custom for the **pilots**[③] to burn their names, **squadron numbers**[④] and messages to loved ones into the

① permanent *adj.* 永久的
② momentous *adj.* 重大的，极重要的
③ pilot *n.* 飞行员
④ squadron number 部队番号

ceiling and walls of the pub using candles **whilst**[1] standing on the shoulders of their fellow airmen! It's impossible to imagine any **landlord**[2] today allowing this form of risky **vandalism**[3] but it demonstrates that at that time these men were seen very much as heroes. These **poignant**[4] **signatures**[5] can still be seen today and one remembers that many of the **scribes**[6] never returned home from their combat missions.

The pub is now owned by Corpus Christi College and is popular amongst its students and fellows. As well as the college, the world famous Cavendish Laboratory was also a past neighbor of the Eagle before it moved to its current location on JJ Thomson Avenue. As a result the pub was often frequented by the researchers of the lab. Two such scientists were Francis Crick and James Watson. It was at the Eagle at lunchtime on 28th February 1953, that Crick and Watson proudly announced they'd discovered the "secret of life" having **unraveled**[7] the mystery of DNA and its double helix structure. Quite a lunch it must have been for the patrons that afternoon! The event is commemorated on a **plaque**[8] next to the entrance and accounted in Watson's book, "The Double Helix".

A drink in the Eagle is a chance to **step into**[9] history.

老鹰酒吧

1667 年开放、原名为“老鹰和孩子”的老鹰酒吧是剑桥大学最受欢迎的酒吧之一，此外，它还拥有另人难忘的历史遗产。老鹰酒吧位于本尼特街，即在剑桥大学中心的议事大楼南侧，它有一个漂亮的花园，供顾客喝啤酒，还提供许多英国国产啤酒和世界各地的名酒，是剑桥市规模较大的酒吧之一。

老鹰酒吧以拥有英国皇家空军吧台而闻名。这样命名吧台的原因是因为在二战期间，驻扎在当地的英国皇家空军和美国空军都很喜欢这家酒吧。二战时，人们并肩作战，共抗敌军，那些岁月给人们留下了永恒而又感人的回忆，人们用涂鸦——一种不太寻常却极富历史意义的方式把回忆保存了下来。飞行员们骑在他们同伴的肩膀上，用蜡

---

① whilst conj. 当……的时候
② landlord *n.* 房东，店主
③ vandalism *n.* 恣意破坏公物行为
④ poignant *adj.* 令人心酸的
⑤ signature *n.* 签名
⑥ scribe *n.* 抄写员
⑦ unravel *v.* 拆开，解开
⑧ plaque *n.* 匾
⑨ step into 干预，涉及

烛把他们的名字、部队番号和信息烧制到酒吧的天花板和墙壁上，献给他们所爱的人已经成了一种风俗。很难想象今天有哪个店主能允许这种恣意破坏公物的冒险行为，但是这恰恰说明了在那个时代，飞行员是被视作英雄的。今天人们仍可看到那些令人心酸的“签名”，有人还记得，许多“签上”名字的飞行员在执行战斗任务后就再也没有回来。

老鹰酒吧现在隶属于剑桥大学圣体学院，很受学生和教职工欢迎。和圣体学院一样，世界知名的卡文迪什实验室在搬去现址——J.J. 汤姆生大道之前也是老鹰酒吧的邻居。所以在过去，老鹰酒吧里经常挤满了实验室的研究人员。其中包括这样两位科学家：弗朗西斯·克里克和詹姆斯·沃森。1953 年 2 月 28 号的午餐时间，克里克和沃森在老鹰酒吧自豪地宣布他们发现了“生命的秘密”，他们解开了 DNA 及其双螺旋结构的奥秘。那天中午的午餐对于酒吧里的顾客来说是多么美妙的一顿午餐啊！这件事被记录在酒吧入口旁的一块牌匾上，沃森的著作《双螺旋》中也有记载。

在老鹰酒吧浅酌一杯就有一次涉足历史的机会。

11 Great Court Run

庭院中的赛跑

James and Louise are visiting Trinity College, Cambridge.

J: James L: Louise

J: There are so many **time-honored**① buildings in Trinity College and I guess that's one of the reasons that they call Trinity College the most **aristocratic**② college in College.

L: And Trinity College is also famous for its **Great Court**③. It's the main court of Trinity College and reputed to be the largest enclosed court in Europe.

J: We are walking on the Great Court now. It feels really good.

L: Yeah. The court was completed by Thomas Nevile, **master**④ of the college, in the early years of the 17th century, when he rearranged the existing buildings to form a single court.

J: And there is a great competition in the The Great Court. Do you know?

L: Of course I know. It's **The Great Court Run**⑤. It's an attempt to run round the **perimeter**⑥ of Great Court (approximately 367 metres), in the 43-45 seconds during the clock striking twelve.

① time-honored *adj.* 历史悠久的
② aristocratic *adj.* 贵族气派的，高贵的
③ Great Court 巨庭
④ master *n.* 院长
⑤ The Great Court Run 巨庭赛跑
⑥ perimeter *n.* 周长

J: Students of Cambridge like to challenge themselves by taking part in it. They traditionally attempt to complete the circuit on the day of the **Matriculation Dinner**[①].

L: It's a rather difficult challenge: one needs to be a fine **sprinter**[②] to achieve it.

J: But it is by no means necessary to be of Olympic standard, despite assertions made in the press.

L: David Burghley, who in 1927 first beat the clock, running the course in 43.1 seconds, went on to win gold in the 400-metre hurdles at the 1928 Olympic Games.

J: Sebastian Coe, another gold medalist and chairman of the organizing committee for 2012 London Olympics, is generally accepted as the second person to have completed the race.

L: Yes. Sebastian Coe successfully completed the run when he beat Steve Cram in a **charity** [③]race in October 1988.

J: Coe's time on 29th October 1988 was reported to have been 45.52 seconds, but it was actually 46.0 seconds (confirmed by the video tape), while Cram's was 46.3 seconds.

L: The clock on that day took 44.4 seconds and the video film confirmed that Coe was some 12 metres short of his finish line when the **fateful**[④] final stroke occurred.

J: The television **commentators**[⑤] were more than a little **disingenuous**[⑥] in suggesting that the dying sounds of the bell could be included in the striking time, thereby allowing Coe's run to be claimed as successful.

L: One reason Olympic runners Cram and Coe found the challenge so tough is that they started at the middle of one side of the Court, thereby having four right-angle turns.

J: But in the days when students started at the corner, only three turns were needed.

L: Until the mid 1990s, the run was traditionally attempted by first year students, at midnight following their Matriculation Dinner.

J: Following a number of accidents of drunken undergraduates running on slippery cobbles, the college now organizes a more formal Great Court Run, at 12 noon. The challenge is only open to fresher, many of whom compete in fancy dress.

J: 三一学院有很多历史悠久的建筑，我猜这就是他们为什么认为三一学院是剑桥大

---

① Matriculation Dinner 入学晚宴
② sprinter *n.* 短跑运动员
③ charity *n.* 慈善
④ fateful *adj.* 重大的
⑤ commentator *n.* 评论员
⑥ disingenuous *adj.* 不真诚的

学最具贵族气质的学院的原因之一。

L: 三一学院还以它的巨大庭院出名。那是三一学院的主要庭院，据说是欧洲最大的封闭式庭院。

J: 我们现在就走在巨庭的道路上，感觉真好。

L: 是啊。这个庭院是在 17 世纪早期，在时任学院院长的托马斯·纳维尔的指导下建成的，他重新规划了已有的建筑，构建了一个单独的庭院。

J: 有一个重大的比赛在巨庭举行，你知道吗?

L: 我当然知道了，是巨庭赛跑，在学院大钟敲 12 下的 43 ~ 45 秒内（正午和午夜，大钟都要敲 12 下），沿着巨庭跑一圈（大概 367 米）。

J: 剑桥大学的学生都想参加这个比赛，挑战自我。他们通常在举行入学晚宴当天会尝试跑完一圈。

L: 这个挑战相当困难，只有优秀的短跑选手才能完成比赛。

J: 虽然媒体声称这是个艰难的挑战，但是选手并不需要具备参加奥运会的水平。

L: 大卫·伯利 1927 年用了 43.1 秒跑完全程，首次“击败了”大钟。随后他在 1928 年的奥运会中夺得了 400 米栏的冠军。

J: 另一位金牌得主，2012 年伦敦奥运会组委会主席塞巴斯蒂安·科被人们认为是完成该项比赛的第二个人。

L: 是的。在 1988 年 10 月的一个慈善赛跑中，塞巴斯蒂安·科击败了史蒂夫·克拉姆，成功跑完了全程。

J: 他在 1988 年 10 月 29 号跑完全程的时间据报道是 45.52 秒，但实际上是 46.0 秒（录像带证实），而克拉姆的成绩是 46.3 秒。

L: 那天的大钟敲完 12 下用了 44.4 秒。纪录片证实，当决定命运的最后一下敲响时，他离终点大概还有 12 米远呢。

J: 电视评论员很不真诚地点评到，大钟最后的声响延续的时间应该被算到敲钟时间内，所以他的赛跑挑战被认为是成功的。

L: 奥运会选手科和克拉姆之所以认为这个挑战很难的原因之一是因为他们分别在巨庭两侧道路的中心起跑，所以要经历 4 个直角转弯。

J: 但到了学生们可以在巨庭转角处起跑的时代时，他们只需经历 3 个直角转弯。

L: 直到 20 世纪 90 年代中期，这个跑步比赛传统上仍是由大一学生参加，校方在入学晚宴当天的午夜就举行比赛。

J: 但是有些本科生喝醉后，经常跑到光滑的鹅卵石上，在许多这样的事件发生后，现在三一学院决定在正午 12 点组织一个比较正式的巨庭赛跑。这项活动只允许大一新生参加，他们当中很多人穿着奇装异服来参加比赛。

难点解析

1 It's the main court of Trinity College and **reputed to be** the largest enclosed court in Europe.

reputed 是形容词，仅用于名词前，意思是"据说的，普遍认为的，号称的"，通常的用法是：be reputed to be。

➤ He is reputed to have a good memory.
传闻他记性很好。

➤ She is reputed to be extremely rich.
据说她极为富有。

2 But it is **by no means** necessary to be of Olympic standard, despite assertions made in the press.

by no means 意为"决不，并没有"。

➤ He will by no means surrender to intimidation.
他绝不会屈服于协迫。

➤ By no means can theory be separated from practice.
理论决不能脱离实践。

3 The television commentators were **more than a little** disingenuous in suggesting that the dying sounds of the bell could be included in the striking time,...

more than a little 意为"很，非常，极度地，简直"。

➤ Graham was more than a little frightened by what he had seen.
格雷厄姆被他所看到的事吓了一大跳。

4 the challenge is only open to **fresher**, many of whom compete in fancy dress.

fresher 意为"大一新生"，大一新生还可以说是 freshman，大二学生是 sophomore，大三学生是 junior，大四学生是 senior。

➢ a freshers' party
一年级新生聚会

Great Court Run

The course of the Great Court Run now is 341 meters long. The length of time between the start and the finish of the **chimes**① is about 43 seconds, but this varies according to the state of winding and **atmospheric**② conditions. It is customary for athletically-inclined members of Trinity to attempt the run every year at noon on the day of the Matriculation Dinner.

The Great Court Run forms a central scene in the film *Chariots of Fire* (David Puttnam, 1981) (although it was not in fact filmed at Trinity).

In October 1988 the race was **recreated**③ for charity by Britain's two foremost middle-distance runners at that time, Sebastian Coe and Steve Cram. The **decathlete**④ Daley Thompson was a **reserve**⑤. Coe won, getting round in 45.52 seconds. The runners started when the clock began to chime, and the final chime was **dying away**⑥ as Coe crossed the line.

On 20 October 2007 Sam Dobin, a student majoring in economics, completed the run within the sound of the final chime, with a time of 42.77 seconds. The course taken by the runners of that year was slightly different to that of 1988 in that competitors ran on the cobbles as well as the **flagstones**⑦.

It must be noted that the route taken by competitors around the court has changed over

① chime *n.* 钟声
② atmospheric *adj.* 大气的
③ recreate *v.* 再创造，再现
④ decathlete *n.* 十项全能运动员
⑤ reserve *n.* 后补队员，后备队员
⑥ die away（尤指声音、光、风等）逐渐消失，停止
⑦ flagstone *n.* 石板路

the years, thus making the accomplishment much more **attainable**[1] today. The current route — running on the path rather than the cobbles—cuts the distance down to 299m (the perimeter of the grass) as opposed to 341m (the perimeter of the cobbles). This is 12% shorter, reducing the pace required from Olympic to a level manageable by hundreds of good club athletes across the country. It also enables the four sharp corners to be "**rounded off**[2]" so that runners do not need to slow down **appreciably**[3] when taking the corners.

It is interesting to note that the two men who are reckoned to have achieved the Great Court Run prior to 2007, David Cecil and Sebastian Coe, both achieved the **multiple**[4] **distinctions**[5] of Olympic Champion, Member of both Houses of Parliament, and Chairman of London Olympics Organising Committee.

庭院中的赛跑

现在巨庭赛跑的赛程是341米，钟声从响起到结束大概用时43秒，但是这个时间会根据风力和大气条件的不同而变化。三一学院爱好竞技运动的学生会在每年举行入学晚宴的当天跑完全程，这已经成为了一项传统。

巨庭赛跑构成了电影《烈火战车》(1981年，戴维·普特内姆担任制片的著名电影）的一个中心场景（虽然并没有真正在三一学院拍摄)。

1988年10月，为了举行慈善募捐活动，人们重新组织了巨庭赛跑比赛，并邀请了英国两位最著名的中长跑选手塞巴斯蒂安·科和史蒂夫·克拉姆参加比赛，还邀请了十项全能选手戴利·汤普森做替补队员。结果是科赢了，跑完全程用了45.52秒。当大钟开始鸣响时，选手们就起跑，最后的钟声停止时，科冲过了终点线。

2007年10月20日，剑桥大学一位经济学专业的学生山姆·多宾在大钟最后的钟声消逝之前，跑完了全程，成绩是42.77秒。这名学生跑的路程和1988年的选手跑的

① attainable *adj.* 可获得的
② round off 变圆
③ appreciably *adv.* 明显地，可察觉地
④ multiple *adj.* 多重的
⑤ distinction *n.* 荣誉，殊荣

路程有些不同，在1988年的比赛中，选手们既要在鹅卵石上跑，又要在石板路上跑。

我们应该注意到，随着时光流逝，巨庭赛跑的路线已经发生了变化。所以，现在的选手们更容易“击败大钟”，跑完全程。现在是 在小道上跑，而不是在鹅卵石上跑，这样就把路程缩短到了299米(草地的周长),而不是原来的341米(鹅卵石道的长度)。路程缩短了12%，以前参加比赛的选手要达到奥运会水准，现在参赛难度下降，全英国很多的优秀俱乐部运动员都有能力参加。这样的路线也使得原先比赛中要经过的急转弯“变圆了一些”，所以参赛者在跑过转弯处时就不用紧急减速了。

有意思的是，公认的2007前跑完巨庭赛跑的两位运动员大卫·伯利和塞巴斯蒂安·科都获得过多项奥运会殊荣，他们都是议会议员，都担任过伦敦奥运会组委会主席（大卫·伯利是1948年伦敦奥运会组委会主席，塞巴斯蒂安·科是2012年伦敦奥运会组委会主席）。

12 May Ball 炫彩五月舞会

焦点对话

Catherine is looking for an **evening dress**① at a **department store**② and Tina is a saleswoman helping her.

C: Catherine T: Tina

C: I'm looking for a **sapphire**③ blue gown. Do you have any gown suits me?

T: Yes, please follow me.

C: I bought a ticket for Queens' May Ball this year, so I really want to find a gorgeous evening dress for the ball.

T: You mean the **May Ball**④ held by Queens College, Cambridge?

C: Exactly. A May Ball is a ball at the end of the academic year that happens at any one of the colleges of the University of Cambridge.

T: Oh, I heard of that. It's the formal affair, requiring evening dress, with ticket price of about 100 pounds.

C: The balls are held in the college gardens, lasting from around 9 p.m. until well after dawn, with some colleges offering rides in **balloons**⑤ when the ball ends, and even breakfast in Paris, or more traditionally, punting to River Cam.

T: It sounds interesting. So the May Balls are held in May?

C: Many Cambridge colleges originally held the balls in May, sometimes in the week **preceding**⑥ year-end exams. Today, they take place in May Week.

---

① evening dress 晚礼服
② department store 百货公司
③ sapphire *n.* 宝蓝色
④ May Ball 五月舞会
⑤ balloon *n.* 热气球
⑥ preceding *adj.*（时间或地点上）在先的，在前的

T: May Week?

C: May Week is the name used within Cambridge to refer to a period of time at the end of the **academic year**[①]. Originally May Week took place in the week during May before year-end exams began. Today, May Week takes place in June and lasts about ten days, after exams are over.

T: Oh, I see. And I know that the balls operate a strict **dress code**[②]. Magdalene is the only college that insists on white tie, which is recommended but not required at Trinity and **Peterhouse**[③], while all the others have a minimum of only black tie.

C: Well, it seems you know a lot about the May Ball.

T: Because some Cambridge students pick evening dress here, too.

C: Iget it. And talking about the balls, most balls are themed, though Magdalene's and Trinity's are notable for their lack of a theme.

T: But Trinity May Ball will offer a variety of **spectacles**[④] to entertain you all night long. And usually a **fireworks**[⑤] display would be performed at that night.

C: It's true. And it's difficult to buy a ticket of Trinity May Ball.

T: With tickets priced at over £100 and in short supply, there maybe students trying to gain **unauthorized**[⑥] access to the ball.

C: Some students climb high walls, others arrive dressed as **gorillas**[⑦] pretending to be part of the evening's entertainment, still others pose as journalists.

T: Do the colleges adopt any measures to deal with it?

C: Typically, college porters are joined by professional security staff and, at larger balls, police to identify and apprehend the crashers.

T: I read on a piece of news that Some colleges have painted walls with anti-burglar paint, which stains the crashers' clothes with luminous green paint, making it somewhat difficult to blend in.

---

① academic year 学年
② dress code 着装要求
③ Peterhouse 彼得学院
④ spectacle *n.* 奇观
⑤ fireworks *n.* 烟花
⑥ unauthorized *adj.* 未经许可的
⑦ gorilla *n.* 大猩猩

C: But, you know what? More courageous crashers can be seen swimming down the river Cam holding their clothes in a plastic bag above the water in an attempt to enter colleges from the banks.

C: 我在找一件宝蓝色的晚礼服，你们这儿有适合我穿的吗？

T: 有，请跟我来。

C: 我买了今年女王学院五月舞会的门票，所以很想找一件漂亮的晚礼服参加这个舞会。

T: 你指的是剑桥大学女王学院举办的五月舞会吗？

C: 就是那个舞会。五月舞会是指在剑桥大学各学院的学年末举行的舞会。

T: 哦，我听说过那个舞会。那可是个正式的舞会，要求穿晚礼服，持票入场，门票大概 100 英镑。

C: 这个舞会一般在各学院的花园举行，从晚上 9 点持续到第二天黎明后。一些学院在舞会结束时还让学生们乘坐热气球当作短途旅行，甚至还可以去巴黎吃早餐，或者还有更传统的活动——在剑河撑船。

T: 听起来很有意思。那么五月舞会是在五月举行吗？

C: 剑桥大学的很多学院最初是在五月份举行舞会的，有时在学年末考试的前一周举行。现在各学院在“五月周”举行舞会。

T: 五月周？

C: “五月周”这个名字是在剑桥大学内部使用的，指的是学年末（考试结束后的）一段时期。最初“五月周”是指在五月份学年末考试开始前的那一周。现在“五月周”指的是 6 月份考试结束后的十来天里。

T: 哦，我知道了。我知道五月舞会有严格的着装要求。麦格达伦学院是唯一一个要求穿燕尾服、系白领结的学院。三一学院和彼得学院虽然要求没那么严，但是也建议这样穿。其他的学院则要求至少要穿小礼服。

C: 哇，看起来你对五月舞会还挺了解的。

T: 那是因为有些剑桥学生也到这儿来挑晚礼服。

C: 哦，原来是这样。说到五月舞会，虽然麦格达伦学院和三一学院的舞会以缺少主题而闻名，但是绝大多数学院的舞会都是有主题的。

T: 但是三一学院的舞会在整个晚上都会举行很多新奇的娱乐活动。在举行舞会的那天晚上，学院通常都有烟花表演。

C: 嗯，是这样的。所以三一学院五月舞会的票很难买到。

T: 这些舞会门票的价格都在 100 英磅以上，又供不应求，所以可能会有学生试图混进舞会吧。

C: 有些学生翻高墙，还有的学生扮作大猩猩到舞会现场，假装要来舞会表演节目，甚至还有学生扮成记者。

T: 各学院有没有采取什么措施来应对?

C: 一般来说，专业安保人员会加入到学院的保安队伍中，在规模较大的舞会上，警察还在现场巡逻，逮捕擅闯舞会的人。

T: 我看过一则新闻，说的是一些学院在墙上涂上“防盗油漆”，谁擅自闯入，谁的衣服就会沾上夜光绿漆，这样一来，没买票的人就很难混进来了。

C: 但是，你知道吗? 更有甚者竟然游过剑河，把衣服装在塑料袋里，高举过水面，试图从岸边进入学院。

难点解析

1 Magdalene is the only college that insists on **white tie**, which is recommended but not required at Trinity and Peterhouse, while all the others have a minimum of only **black tie**.

white tie 指的是非常正式的晚礼服，男士要系白领结、穿燕尾服，white-tie 是形容词形式；black tie 指的是较正式的晚礼服，没有 white tie 那么正式，black-tie 是形容词形式。

- It is going to be a very formal party, white tie and tails for men, full-length gowns for women.
  这将是非常正式的宴会，男士要打领带，穿燕尾服，女士要穿拖地长裙。

- It was a black-tie function.
  它是一次半正式集会。

2 Typically, college porters are joined by professional security staff and, at larger balls, police to identify and apprehend the **crashers**.

crasher 意为“不速之客，擅自闯入者”，或者可以说是 gate-crasher。

- To be a great party crasher, you really have to have balls of steel.
  要想成为令人讨厌的不速之客，得要有钢铁般的意志。

3 I read on a piece of news that Some colleges have painted walls with **anti-burglar** paint, which stains the crashers' clothes with luminous green paint, making it somewhat difficult to blend in.

anti-burglar 意为“防盗的，”anti- 这个前缀用得很多，意为“反对……”，如 anti-

American，反美国的；"防（止）……" antiseptic，防腐的、抗菌的。

➢ With the development of society and economy, people demand better food, so we should utilize natural food antiseptic adequately.
随着社会、经济的发展，人们对食品的要求越来越高，更应充分利用天然食品防腐剂。

4 More courageous crashers can be seen swimming down the river Cam holding their clothes in a plastic bag above the water **in an attempt to** enter colleges from the banks.

in an attempt to 意为"试图……，力图……"。

➢ That decision rattled many economists, who feared that Mr Obama would backtrack on his free trade promises in an attempt to pacify the politically important US unions.
上述决定令许多经济学家感到不安，他们担心，奥巴马会为了安抚政治上重要的美国工会，而放弃自由贸易的承诺。

May Ball

May balls held by colleges in the University of Cambridge are famous around the world. St. John's May ball is named "the seventh best party in the world" by *Time* Magazine. Trinity Boat Club May ball (named after the boat club, but run by Trinity College) is always held on the first Monday of May Week. Though it has no theme, its tickets are also among the most highly sought. Magdalene's and Peterhouse's white tie balls also prove highly popular. Other desirable May balls are held annually by Clare, who has some of the most beautiful gardens, and **Jesus**[①], whose ball is popular amongst first year students. Robinson hosts the first ball of May Week, and is also one of the least expensive black tie balls. Christ's is known for securing **high-profile**[②] acts. Trinity, Clare and St. John's are **situated**[③] directly on the River Cam, along the Backs. As a result, when several balls are held on the same

① Jesus 基督学院
② high-profile *adj.* 引人注目的，高调的
③ situate *v.* 位于

evening, the river is lit up in different colours from the lights and the fireworks, creating a memorable **backdrop**[①] to the evening's festivities.

Most balls have fundamental similarities: all will offer guests a variety of food, entertainment, and a **bevy**[②] of alcoholic drinks. The quality and diversity of all of these vary markedly between different balls. While all claim to offer luxury, some have distinctive **hallmarks**[③]: Peterhouse is famed for its Ferris wheel, Magdalene for its dining. Trinity for its near-unlimited champagne and St. John's for having the most spectacular fireworks.

Several colleges host a **variation**[④] on these balls, a June Event. These are cheaper, tend to be focused on live music, and frequently have less formal dress codes. Some colleges alternate June events and May balls from year to year.

In order to spread the fun throughout the year, a number of colleges have broken with tradition to hold balls at different times, normally either in the winter at the end of **Michaelmas term**[⑤], i.e. the beginning of December, or in spring at the end of **Lent term**[⑥]. Selwyn is the only college to hold a yearly winter ball, known as the Snowball; in 2008 Selwyn also held a May Ball to celebrate its 125th Birthday. Fitzwilliam holds a winter ball every two years, the most recent one being December 2008. Of the spring balls, that of Girton is held every other year, whereas Churchill continues to produce an annual ball.

炫彩五月舞会

剑桥大学各学院举办的五月舞会闻名世界。圣约翰学院的五月舞会就被《时代》杂志评为“全球排名第七的派对。”三一学院划船俱乐部五月舞会（以剑桥大学划船俱乐部命名，但由三一学院举办）总是在五月周的第一个星期一举行。虽然这个舞会没有主题，但是它的门票也跻身于学生们最想买的舞会门票之列。麦格达伦学院和彼得学院要求穿晚礼服的舞会也很受欢迎。其他一些五月舞会也不错，包括克莱尔学院和耶稣学院的年度舞会，克莱尔学院有一些全校最漂亮的花园，耶稣学院的舞会则很受大一新生的欢迎。罗宾森学院的舞会是五月周第一个舞会，它也是要求穿小礼服的舞会中门票最便宜的一个。基督学院舞会上的活动总是很引人注目。三一学院、克莱尔学院和圣约翰学院的舞会就沿着后园景观，在剑河岸边举行。所以，当几个舞会都在同一天晚上举行时，整个剑河都被舞会灯光和烟花的不同的色彩照亮了，为那天晚上的活动创造了难忘的背景。

---

① backdrop *n.* 背景
② bevy *n.* 一群，一批
③ hallmark *n.* 特点，标志
④ variation *n.* 变动，变种
⑤ Michaelmas term 圣米迦勒学期，每学年第一个学期
⑥ Lent term 春季学期

大部分舞会都基本相同，都会给来宾提供很多食物、娱乐活动、酒水饮料，但是其质量和品种在不同的舞会差别很大。虽然所有的学院都宣称他们会提供奢华的享受，有些学院却与众不同。彼得学院以摩天轮出名，麦格达伦学院的晚宴很精致，三一学院几乎无限量地提供香槟，圣约翰学院的烟花表演最为壮观。

有几个学院举办了“六月节（舞会）”，是以上各学院五月舞会的改编版。这些舞会门票较便宜，注重现场音乐表演，一般不要求正式着装。一些学院的五月舞会和六月节舞会是隔年交替举办的。

为了使全年都有舞会这种娱乐活动，许多学院打破传统，在一年中的不同时间举办舞会。通常不是在圣米迦勒学期末的冬天，比如11月初，就是在春季学期末的春天举行舞会。塞尔文学院是唯一每年都举办冬季舞会的学院，该舞会被称作雪球舞会。2008年塞尔文学院也举办了一个五月舞会，庆祝学院成立125周年。菲茨威廉学院每两年举办一次冬季舞会，最近的一次是2008年11月。格顿学院每隔一年举办一次春季舞会，丘吉尔学院则保持着每年都举办春季舞会的传统。

Unit 4 Literature & Art
浪漫芳草园

13 John Milton
失明诗人弥尔顿

Mike and Lucy are reading *Paradise Lost* together.

M: Mike　　L: Lucy

M: John Milton is a genius. His **masterpieces**① *Paradise Lost*, *Paradise Regained* and *Samson Agonistes* are pearls of world literature.

L: I cannot agree with you more. The works of today's poets are not half as brilliant as those of Milton. And he excels in languages studying, too. He can speak and write in Greek, Latin, and Italian.

M: Milton is a **life-long**② student. His schooling started at home before he went to read the works of Homer and Virgil in Greek and Latin at St Paul's School in London.

L: And he entered Christ's College, Cambridge in 1625 with the intent to become a minister.

M: But Milton did not adjust to university life. He was called, half in **scorn**③, "The Lady of Christ's".

---

① masterpiece *n.* 杰作，代表作
② life-long *adj.* 终身的
③ scorn *n.* 鄙视，轻蔑

L: While Milton was a hardworking student, he was also **argumentative**[①]. Only a year later, in 1626, he got suspended after a dispute with his tutor.

M: During his **temporary**[②] return to London, Milton attended plays, and began his first **forays**[③] into poetry.

L: At his return to Cambridge, Milton was assigned a new tutor. But life at Cambridge was still not easy on Milton; he felt he was disliked by many of his fellow students and he was dissatisfied with the curriculum.

M: But he did learn a lot in Cambridge. It was at Cambridge that he **composed**[④] "On the Morning of Christ's Nativity".

L: You're quite right. Upon graduation in 1632 with a Master of Arts degree, he retired to the family homes, for years of private study and literary composition.

M: That's true. Milton had given up his plan to become a priest. He adopted no profession but spent six years at leisure in his father's home, writing literary works.

L: At the same time Milton decided to further his studies in languages including **Hebrew**[⑤]. And he travelled many countries in the late 1630s where he immersed himself in their history and culture.

M: He met many **prominent**[⑥] learned men during the travelling including Galileo Galilei.

L: Yes, he also had a long and meaningful conversation with Galileo Galilei. Their conversation was recorded in his celebrated plea for a free speech and free discussion, AREOPAGITICA (*On Liberty*).

M: And I remember that there are references to Galileo's **telescope**[⑦] in *Paradise Lost*.

L: The intense work of translating and writing created much **strain**[⑧] on his eyes and by 1652 he was entirely blind and relied on the assistance of other people.

M: But it seems that Milton was not unduly **grieved**[⑨] by his loss of sight. Instead, blindness helped him to stimulate his verbal richness.

L: He sacrificed his sight, and then he remembered his first desire, that of being a poet.

---

① argumentative *adj.* 好辩的，好争论的
② temporary *adj.* 暂时的
③ foray *n.* 尝试
④ compose *v.* 创作
⑤ Hebrew *n.* 希伯来语
⑥ prominent *adj.* 杰出的，卓越的
⑦ telescope *n.* 望远镜
⑧ strain *n.* 压力
⑨ grieved *adj.* 伤心的

During the **plague**[1] years he left London and lived in a **cottage**[2] in the village of Chalfont St Giles, Buckinghamshire.

M: It was here that Milton prepared for publication *Paradise Lost* and *Paradise Regained*.

M: 约翰·弥尔顿真是个天才。他的杰作《失乐园》、《复乐园》和《力士参孙》是世界文学的明珠。

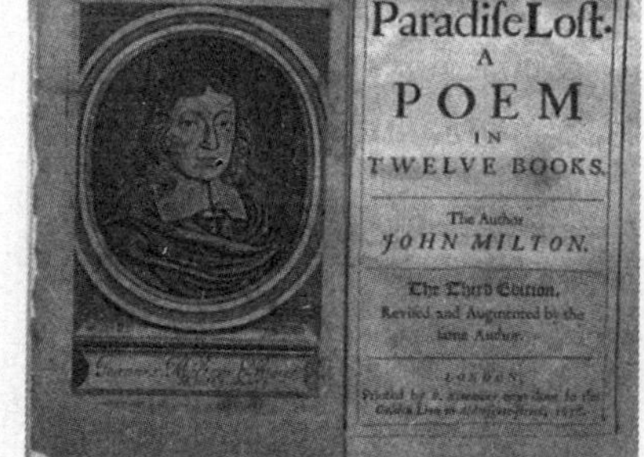

L: 我非常同意你的观点。现在很多诗人的作品远不如弥尔顿的精彩。弥尔顿还精通多种语言。他通晓希腊语、拉丁语和意大利语。

M: 弥尔顿终身都在学习。在他到伦敦圣保罗学校学习希腊语的荷马著作和拉丁语的维吉尔著作之前，他在家里就开始学习了。

L: 1625 年，他抱着要当牧师的念头考入了剑桥大学基督学院。

M: 但是弥尔顿并不适应大学生活。同学们半带蔑视地称他为“基督学院的女士。”

L: 虽然弥尔顿是一个刻苦学习的学生，他却喜欢和老师争论。入学后仅一年，也就是 1926 年，由于与导师产生了矛盾，他被迫辍学。

M: 在弥尔顿暂返伦敦的这段时间里，他参加了戏剧演出，并开始尝试写诗。

L: 回到剑桥后，校方为弥尔顿重选了一个新导师。但弥尔顿仍感到在剑桥大学生活不易。他觉得许多同学都不喜欢他，对课程设置也不满意。

M: 但是弥尔顿的确在剑桥学到了很多东西。《基督诞生的早晨》这首诗正是他在剑桥创作的。

L: 你说得很对。1632 年毕业拿到文学学士学位后，弥尔顿退隐家中，花费数年时间自学和创作文学。

M: 的确如此。弥尔顿放弃了成为牧师的计划。他没有找任何工作，6 年来的闲暇时光都待在父亲的房子里，进行文学创作。

L: 同时弥尔顿决定加强语言学习，包括希伯来语的学习。17 世纪 30 年代晚期，他去了很多国家旅游，并沉浸于所到国家的历史和文化之中。

M: 在旅行中，他遇到了包括伽利略·伽利雷在内的很多杰出的博学之人。

L: 是的。他还和伽利略·伽利雷有过一次长时间富有意义的谈话。他们的对话被记录在弥尔顿著名的呼吁自由演讲和讨论的《论自由》一书中。

M: 我还记得弥尔顿在《失乐园》中也谈到了伽利略的望远镜。

---

① plague *n.* 瘟疫

② cottage *n.* 小屋，村舍

L: 翻译和写作的高强度工作使他的眼睛不堪重负，到了 1652 年，他已经完全失明了，要依赖别人的帮助才能工作。

M: 但是弥尔顿对于自己的失明似乎并不怎么伤心。相反，失明有助于刺激他语言的表达。

L: 弥尔顿虽然失明了，但是他想起了他最初的梦想，那就是成为一名诗人。在伦敦大瘟疫期间，他离开伦敦，住在了白金汉郡查尔芬特·圣贾尔斯村子的一个小屋里。

M: 正是在这里，弥尔顿创作书了《失乐园》和《复乐园》，并准备出版。

难点解析

1 The works of today's poets are **not half as** brilliant as those of Milton.

not half as 意为“远远不，几乎不”，经常用 not half as good\interesting (as) 意为“远不如……好\有趣”等。

➢ The movie wasn't half as entertaining as the book.
这部电影远不如原书好看。

2 And he **excels in** languages studying, too.

excel in 意为“擅长、优于……”，也可以说 excel at。

➢ I never excelled in sport.
我从不擅长体育。

3 And he travelled many countries in the late 1630s where he **immersed himself in** their history and culture.

immerse yourself in 意为“使自己专心于\沉浸于……”。

➢ Jane was determined to immerse herself in the African way of life.
简决定潜心研究非洲人的生活方式。

4 **It was here that** Milton prepared for publication *Paradise Lost* and *Paradise Regained*.

it is… that 是强调句句型，用法是：It is/was + 强调部分 + that (who) + 其他成分

注意：强调句即便强调时间、地点也不能用 when 或 where, 而只能用“that”，当然如果强调人时，用 that/who 都可以。

强调时间：It was yesterday evening that my father did the experiment in the lab. (注意没

有用 when)

强调地点：It was in the lab that my father did the experiment yesterday evening. (注意没有用 where)

强调人：It was I that lost the book on the playground yesterday.

John Milton

One of the greatest poets of the English language, John Milton, is best-known for his **epic poem**① *Paradise Lost*. Milton's powerful prose and poetry had an immense influence especially on the 18th-century verse. Besides poems, Milton published **pamphlets**② defending civil and religious rights.

John Milton was born into a rich family in London. Milton's first teachers were his father, from whom he inherited love for art and music, and the writer Thomas Young, a graduate of St Andrews University.

Milton traveled in France and Italy in the late 1630s, meeting in Paris the **jurist**③ and **theologian**④ Hugo Grotius and the **astronomer**⑤ Galileo Galilei in Florence. Milton returned to London in 1639, and set up a school with his nephews. He had planned to write an epic based on the **Arthurian**⑥ legends, but then gave up his literary pursuits, partly due to the Civil War, which divided the country as Oliver Cromwell fought against the king, Charles I.

England was in a great state of **flux**⑦ during his lifetime. Milton sided with the Puritans and Oliver Cromwell, rejected popular political and religious beliefs, adopted an **anti-roy-**

---

① epic poem 史诗
② pamphlet *n.* 小册子
③ jurist *n.* 法理学家
④ theologian *n.* 神学家
⑤ astronomer *n.* 天文学家
⑥ Arthurian *adj.* 亚瑟王的
⑦ flux *n.* 不稳定的状态

alist[①] stance against King Charles I, and joined the pamphlet wars, writing many pamphlets on the Church of England. Milton also wrote pamphlets on various political issues like free speech and the **censorship**[②] exerted by Parliament as in *Areopagitica.*

Milton was appointed Cromwell's Latin secretary of foreign affairs and wrote many articles in defense of the republicanism. Milton's poor eyesight, which was born with, was increasingly worsened over time and the intensive work led to his blindness.

After the Restoration of Charles II in 1660, Milton was arrested as a noted defender of the republicanism, but was soon released. Milton escaped from more punishment, but he became a poor man because he was forced to pay a massive **fine**[③]. The manuscript of *Paradise Lost* he sold for £5 to Samuel Simmons, and was promised another £5 if the first edition of 1,300 copies sold out.

Milton created a powerful and sympathetic portrait of Satan in *Paradise Lost*. His character bears similarities with Shakespeare's hero-villains Iago and Macbeth. Milton's view influenced deeply such Romantic poets as William Blake and Percy Bysshe Shelley, who regarded Satan as the real hero—a **rebel**[④] against the **tyranny**[⑤] of Heaven.

失明诗人弥尔顿

弥尔顿是用英语写作的最著名的诗人之一，他创作的史诗《失乐园》享誉世界。弥尔顿气势磅礴的散文和诗歌对18世纪的韵文写作影响深远。除了诗歌，弥尔顿还发表了维护民权和宗教权利的小册子。

约翰·弥尔顿出生于伦敦的一个富裕家庭。弥尔顿的启蒙老师是他的父亲和毕业于圣安德鲁大学的作家托马斯·杨。弥尔顿继承了父亲对艺术和音乐的热爱。

17世纪30年代晚期，弥尔顿到法国和意大利旅游，并在巴黎和佛罗伦萨分别遇到法理学家、神学家胡果·格劳秀斯和天文学家伽利略·伽利雷。1639年，弥尔顿回到英国，和他的侄子们共同创办了一个学校。他原本打算根据亚瑟王的传奇写一部史诗，但后来由于英国内战和其他一些原因，他放弃了这个计划。在英国内战中，奥利弗·克伦威尔起兵反对国王查理一世，国家被分裂了。

在弥尔顿的有生之年，英格兰一直局势动荡。弥尔顿站在清教徒和克伦威尔一边，反对主流政治和宗教信仰，采取反保皇主义者立场，反对国王查理一世，还奋笔疾书，写了很多关于英国国教的小册子。弥尔顿还写了其他小册子，讨论众多政治议题，如

① anti-royalist *n.* 反保皇主义者
② censorship *n.* 审查（制度）
③ fine *n.* 罚金
④ rebel *n.* 反抗者，叛逆者
⑤ tyranny *n.* 暴政

他在《论出版自由》中谈到了言论自由和议会实施的审查制度。

弥尔顿被任命为克伦威尔的外交事务拉丁语秘书，并写了很多维护共和制的文章。弥尔顿天生就视力不佳，随着时间的推移，他的视力日益下降，高强度的工作最终导致了他的失明。

作为知名的共和制拥护者，弥尔顿在查理二世1660年复辟后被捕，但很快就被释放。虽然弥尔顿逃脱了更多的惩罚，但他却因被迫付一大笔罚金而变得穷困潦倒。弥尔顿以5英镑的价格把《失乐园》的手稿卖给了塞缪尔·西蒙斯。西蒙斯承诺，如果第一版的1300本书售完，他还可以再拿到5英镑。

弥尔顿在《失乐园》中创造了一个强有力而又令人同情的撒旦形象。他创造的角色和莎士比亚创造的亦正亦邪的埃古和麦克白有相似之处。浪漫主义诗人如威廉·布莱克和珀西·比希·雪莱深受弥尔顿的影响。他们把撒旦视作真正的英雄——一个与天国暴政抗争的反抗者。

14 Byron — the Play Boy
花花公子拜伦

Lucy is reading *Childe Harold's Pilgrimage* while Matt is walking towards her.

L: Lucy　　M: Matt

M: Lucy, what are you reading?

L: *Childe Harold's Pilgrimage,* the talented poem of Lord Byron.

M: You mean Lord George Gordon Byron, the **playboy**①?

L: Yes, it is him. He did have a lot of **love-affairs**② during his short life. But he is a poet of overflowing brilliance in the first place.

M: Indeed. Byron is a household name. His works, *Childe Harold's Pilgrimage* and *Don Juan* are well-known.

L: Besides this, there are many **romances**③ about him that are well-known even when he was in **Harrow**④.

M: His **complicated** relationship with women may have been influenced by his childhood experience. At home Byron's **alcoholic**⑤ governess made sexual advances when he was nine.

L: And according to some sources, Byron was also **seduced**⑥ by the lord who rented his mansion before he inherited it.

M: At Cambridge, he even aroused **alarm**⑦ with **bisexual**⑧ love affairs.

---

① playboy *n.* 花花公子
② love-affair *n.* 风流韵事
③ romance *n.* 爱情故事，浪漫史
④ Harrow 哈罗公学，英国最顶级的公学之一
⑤ alcoholic *adj.* 嗜酒成性的
⑥ seduce *v.* 诱奸
⑦ alarm *n.* 恐慌
⑧ bisexual *adj.* 双性的

L: When he was in Cambridge, he wasn't a hardworking student, but he read many books on history, literature and philosophy. And he spent his leisure time on drinking, **hunting**[1], shooting and swimming.

M: Byron's first two cantos of *Childe Harold's Pilgrimage* became blockbusters when they were published.

L: He became an adored character of London society. He spoke in the **House of Lords**[2] effectively on liberal themes, and had a hectic relationship with Lady Caroline Lamb.

M: But Byron married Anne Isabella Milbanke in 1815, and their daughter Ada was born in the same year. The marriage was unhappy, and they obtained legal separation next year.

L: When the **rumors**[3] of his **incest**[4] with his **half-sister**[5], Augusta and accumulating debts started to rise, Byron left England in 1816, never to return.

M: "The only virtue they honor in England is **hypocrisy**[6]," he once wrote a friend.

L: Byron settled in Geneva with **Percy Bysshe Shelley**[7], Mary Shelley and Claire Clairmont, who became his mistress. There he wrote the two cantos of *Childe Harold* and *The Prisoner of Chillon*.

M: At the end of the summer Byron decided to continue his travels, spending two years in Italy. While staying in Venice Byron proudly claimed he had different woman on 200 **consecutive**[8] evenings.

L: During the years in Italy, Byron wrote *The Lament of Tasso* and started *Don Juan*, his **satiric**[9] masterpiece.

M: After a long creative period, Byron had come to feel that action was more important

---

① hunting *n.* 打猎
② House of Lords 上议院
③ rumor *n.* 谣言
④ incest *n.* 乱伦
⑤ half-sister *n.* 同父异母或同母异父的姐妹
⑥ hypocrisy *n.* 虚伪，伪善
⑦ Percy Bysshe Shelley 珀西·比希·雪莱，英国文学史上最有才华的抒情诗人之一。
⑧ consecutive *adj.* 连续的
⑨ satiric *adj.* 含讽刺意味的

than poetry. He armed a **brig**[①], the Hercules, and sailed to Greece to aid the Greeks, who had risen against their Ottoman overlords.

L: However, before he saw any serious military action, Byron **contracted**[②] a fever from which he died in Missolonghi on 19 April 1824.

M: Byron's body was returned to England but refused by the deans of both Westminster and St Paul's. Finally Byron's coffin was placed in the family vault at Hucknall Torkard, near Newstead **Abbey**[③] in Nottinghamshire.

M: 露西，你在读什么?

L: 拜伦勋爵的天才诗作《恰尔德·哈罗德游记》。

M: 你指的是花花公子乔治·戈登·拜伦勋爵?

L: 是的，就是他。在其短暂的一生中，他的确有很多风流韵事，但他毕竟是一个才华横溢的诗人。

M: 的确是这样。拜伦是个家喻户晓的名字。他的作品《恰尔德·哈罗德游记》和《唐璜》很有名。

L: 拜伦的私生活也很引人注目，当他还在哈罗公学念书时，他的爱情故事就广为人知。

M: 他和女性的复杂关系可能是受童年经历的影响，当拜伦只有 9 岁时，嗜酒成性的女家庭教师就对他进行了性侵犯。

L: 一些资料表明，他还受到过一个贵族的引诱，后者在拜伦继承房产前曾租住在他家。

M: 在剑桥时，拜伦甚至还因双性恋风流韵事引起了公众的恐慌。

L: 在剑桥念书时，拜伦并不是一个刻苦学习的学生，但他读了很多历史、文学和哲学等方面的书。而他的闲暇时间则用在喝酒、打猎、射击和游泳上。

M: 拜伦的《恰尔德·哈罗德游记》的头两章出版后，曾轰动一时。

L: 拜伦成为伦敦社会的宠儿。他在上议院就“自由”这一主题高效地阐述了自己的观点，还和卡罗琳·兰姆夫人有过一段炽热的爱情。

M: 但是拜伦在 1815 年和安妮·伊莎贝拉·米尔班克结婚。同年，他们的女儿艾达出生。不过这段婚姻并不幸福，在第二年，他们就分居了。

---

① brig *n.* 双桅船

② contract *v.* 染上（恶习、疾病等）

③ Abbey *n.* 修道院

L: 当关于他和同父异母的姐姐奥古斯塔乱伦以及债务不断攀升的谣言开始广泛传播后，拜伦于 1816 年离开了英格兰，就再也没有回来了。

M: 拜伦有一次写信给朋友，说道："在英格兰，人们唯一推崇的美德就是虚伪。"

L: 拜伦和珀西·比希·雪莱、玛丽·雪莱以及其情妇克莱尔·克莱蒙特一起定居在日内瓦。在那里他创作了《恰尔德·哈罗德游记》的另外两个章节和《锡隆的囚徒》。

M: 夏末，拜伦决定继续他的旅行，花两年时间去游历意大利。待在威尼斯时，拜伦骄傲地宣布连续 200 个晚上都有不同的女人和他共度良宵。

L: 在游历意大利的年月里，拜伦撰写了《塔克的哀歌》，并开始创作讽刺诗代表作《唐璜》。

M: 经过长时间的创作后，拜伦发觉行动比诗歌更重要。于是他驾着英国大船"赫拉克勒斯号"前往希腊，协助希腊人反抗土耳其领主。

L: 然而，在拜伦目睹任何正规的军事活动之前，他就发了高烧，并因此于 1824 年 4 月 19 日在梅索朗吉昂辞世。

M: 拜伦的遗体被运回英格兰，但威斯敏斯特教堂和圣保罗教堂的主教都拒绝把他的遗体安葬入内。最终拜伦的棺木被安葬在诺丁汉郡纽斯台德修道院附近赫克诺尔的家族墓穴内。

1 But he is a poet of overflowing brilliance **in the first place**.

in the first place 意为"首先，第一位的是"。

➢ In the first place, we should solve this problem.
首先，我们应该解决这个问题。

➢ Well, in the first place, I can't afford it, and in the second place I'm not really interested.
首先我没钱去，其次我也不怎么感兴趣。

2 Byron **is a household name**.

be a household name\word 意为"家喻户晓，十分出名"。

➢ *Coca Cola* is a household name around the world.
可口可乐是全世界家喻户晓的品牌。

3 At home Byron's **alcoholic**[1] governess **made** sexual **advances** when he was nine.

make advances 意为“对异性挑逗、侵犯”。

➢ She accused her boss of making advances to her.
  她指控老板对她图谋不轨。

4 Byron's first two cantos of *Childe Harold's Pilgrimage* became **blockbusters** when they were published.

blockbuster 意为“轰动一时的电影、书籍”。

➢ the latest blockbusters from Hollywood
  好莱坞最新大片

Byron, the Play Boy

More than any other poet Lord Byron has been identified with his own heroes — with Childe Harold, the romantic traveler; with Manfred, the **outcast**[2] from society; with Don Juan, the **cynical**[3] lover. Although Byron did use his own life as the material for much of his poetry, it is by no means purely **autobiographical**[4]. It is, however, in his long poems that Byron's genius most truly resides rather than in the **lyrics**[5] which usually represent him in **selections**[6].

Byron was born into an aristocratic[7] family of doubtful reputation. His father died of drink and **debauchery**[8] when Byron was 3, and when he was 10 his great-uncle — the 'wicked' Lord Byron also died. So Byron inherited the title.

He was born with a **malformed**[9] foot—a disability which tortured him with self-consciousness in his youth. He went to Harrow and to Trinity College, Cambridge, where,

① alcoholic *adj.* 嗜酒成性的
② outcast *n.* 被社会遗弃的人
③ cynical *adj.* 愤世嫉俗的
④ autobiographical *adj.* 自传的
⑤ lyric *n.* 抒情诗
⑥ selection *n.* 选集
⑦ aristocratic *adj.* 贵族的
⑧ debauchery *n.* 道德败坏，生活腐化
⑨ malformed *adj.* 畸形的

amongst other **eccentricities**[①], he kept a bear. While an undergraduate he published his first book of poems *Hours of Idleness*. The criticism it got stung Byron not to despair but to revenge, and he replied with a **satire**[②] in the manner of Pope called *English Bards and Scotch Reviewers*. After Cambridge, Byron went on **the grand tour**[③] of Europe, traditional for men of his education. For nearly 2 years he wandered about Greece and the Aegean Islands. This was the shaping time of his imagination.

On 20 February 1812, the first two **cantos**[④] of *Childe Harold's Pilgrimage* were published. They took the town by storm. Byron became famous overnight. And in the next 4 years he wrote a series of romantic poems; the best among them being *The Corsair* and *The Bride of Abydos*. It is said that 14, 000 copies of *The Corsair* were sold in a day.

Byron had always been **susceptible**[⑤] to women and attractive to them. Now that he was successful they threw themselves at his head. For 3 years he lived in the **limelight**[⑥], and then, quite unaccountably, married Ann Milbanke, a **frigid**[⑦] and correct woman, entirely unsuited to him, but with a lot of money. She bore him a daughter and left him within a year.

In 1823 he left Italy for Greece, but the next year, worn out with the **ardours**[⑧] of the campaign, he caught rheumatic fever and died at Missolonghi, mourned as a national hero by the Greeks.

花花公子拜伦

人们认为拜伦勋爵比其他任何诗人更像自己创造的英雄人物，富于浪漫色彩的旅游者恰尔德·哈罗德、被社会摈弃的曼弗雷德、愤世嫉俗的情人唐·璜。虽然拜伦用自己的生活经历作为素材写了很多诗篇，但这些诗篇决不纯粹是自传性质的。最能体现拜伦天赋的还是他的那些长诗，而不是通常在选集里作为他的代表作的抒情诗。

拜伦出生于一个名声不太好的贵族家庭。他3岁时，父亲就死于酗酒和放荡的生活。

---

① eccentricity *n.* 古怪行为
② satire *n.* 讽刺诗
③ the grand tour 英国大学生毕业前的大陆旅行（上流社会子弟作为毕业的最后一部分）
④ canto *n.* 篇章
⑤ susceptible *adj.* 易受影响的，易动感情的
⑥ limelight *n.* 众人关注的中心
⑦ frigid *adj.* 冷漠的
⑧ ardour *n.* 热情，激情

10岁时，他的叔祖，“邪恶的”拜伦勋爵也去世了。因此拜伦继承了爵位。

拜伦出生时，他的一只脚就带有残疾，敏感的拜伦因此在年少时代备受折磨。拜伦就读于哈罗公学和剑桥大学三一学院。在剑桥念书时，他行为古怪，还养了一只熊。但是在大学期间，拜伦就出版了第一本诗集《闲散的时光》。人们对这本诗集的批评深深刺痛了拜伦的心，但他没有绝望，而是想报复，他以蒲柏的风格写了一篇名为《英格兰诗人和苏格兰评论家》的讽刺诗反驳那些批评。离开剑桥大学以后，拜伦启程前往欧洲开始长途旅行，这是受过像他这种教育的人的惯常做法，在将近两年的时间里，他游历了希腊和爱琴海群岛。这是拜伦想象力形成的时期。

1812年2月20日《恰尔德·哈罗德游记》第一、二章出版了，全城为之轰动，拜伦也一夜成名。在接下来的4年里，他写了一系列浪漫诗篇，其中最好的有《海盗》和《阿比多斯的新娘》。据说，《海盗》一天就销售了14000册。

拜伦喜好女色，而女子也钟情于他。由于他已飞黄腾达，女人们更愿意投怀送抱。3年里他出够了风头，然后，莫名其妙地和安妮·米尔班克结了婚。她是一个冷漠的、严肃的妇女，对拜伦来说根本不合适，只是家境殷实罢了。她为拜伦生下了一个女儿，不到一年就离开了他。

1823年，拜伦离开意大利前往希腊，但是第二年，由于热心独立运动而劳累过度，染上了风湿病，最终在梅索朗吉昂辞世，成为希腊人所缅怀的一位民族英雄。

15 William Wordsworth
湖畔诗人华兹华斯

John and Vera are reading ***The Solitary Reaper***[1] *together.*

J: John　　V: Vera

J: *William Wordsworth's poem is so beautiful that I can scarcely take my eye off it.*

V: His poem is full of emotion, just like *The Solitary Reaper.* When many poets at his time still wrote about ancient heroes in **grandiloquent**[2] style, Wordsworth focused on the nature, children, the poor, common people.

J: Exactly, and he used ordinary words to express his personal feelings. His definition of poetry is "the **spontaneous**[3] **overflow**[4] of powerful feelings".

V: A man's interest is influenced by the **surroundings**[5]. The magnificent landscape of Wordsworth's hometown deeply affected him and gave him a love of nature.

J: As a writer Wordsworth made his debut in 1787, when he published a **sonnet**[6] in *The European Magazine*. In that same year he entered St. John's College, Cambridge, from where he took his B.A. in 1791.

V: When he was in Cambridge, he went on a **walking tour**[7]

---

① *The Solitary Reaper*《孤独的割麦女》，华兹华斯的名作。
② grandiloquent *adj.* 夸张的
③ spontaneous *adj.* 自发的
④ overflow *n.* 流露
⑤ surroundings *n.* 环境
⑥ sonnet *n.* 十四行诗
⑦ walking tour 徒步旅行，远足

through revolutionary France and Switzerland during a summer vacation in 1790.

J: Revolutionary fervor in France made a powerful impact on the young Wordsworth. His French experience was a powerful factor in turning his inbred sympathy to plain common people.

V: When Wordsworth's political ideas and poetic talent were beginning to **take shape**, he fell passionately in love with a French girl.

J: Yes. It happened on his second journey in France. Wordsworth had an affair with Annette Vallon by whom he had an **illegitimate**[①] daughter Anne Caroline.

V: The affair was basis of one of his poems, but otherwise Wordsworth did his best to hide the affair from **posterity**[②].

J: After his journeys, Wordsworth spent several aimless and unhappy years until he met **Coleridge**[③] in 1795.

V: And Wordsworth's financial situation became better in 1795 when he received a legacy and was able to settle at Racedown, Dorset, with his sister Dorothy.

J: Encouraged by Coleridge and stimulated by the close contact with nature, Wordsworth composed his masterwork, *Lyrical Ballads* with Coleridge.

V: *Lyrical Ballads* is an important work in the English Romantic Movement. But the volume had neither the name of Wordsworth nor Coleridge as the author. The second edition, published in 1800, had only Wordsworth listed as the author.

J: The winter 1798-99 Wordsworth spent with his sister and Coleridge in Germany. And due to the **homesickness**[④], he and his sister moved back to England, settled in Dove Cottage, Grasmere, in the Lake District.

V: This time he was accompanied by fellow poet Robert Southey nearby. And Wordsworth, Coleridge and Southey came to be known as the "Lake Poets".

J: Wordsworth's **path-breaking**[⑤] works were produced between 1797 and 1808. Through this period, many of his poems revolved around themes of death, endurance, separation and grief.

---

① illegitimate *adj.* 非婚生的，私生的

② posterity *n.* 子孙后裔

③ Coleridge 柯勒律治，英国浪漫主义诗人、评论家。

④ homesickness *n.* 思家

⑤ path-breaking *adj.* 开创性的

V: Wordsworth's Grasmere period ended in 1813 when he moved to Rydal Mount, Ambleside, where he spent the rest of his life.

J: 威廉·华兹华斯的诗真是太美了，以至于我难以把目光从他的诗上移开。

V: 华兹华斯的诗歌充满了情感，就像这首《孤独的割麦女》。当他那个年代的很多诗人还在用浮夸的风格描写古代英雄时，华兹华斯却关注自然、孩子、穷人和普通人。

J: 的确是这样。华兹华斯还用平实的语言表达个人情感。他对诗歌的定义是“强烈情感的自然流露。”

V: 一个人的兴趣是受到环境的影响的。故乡壮丽的风景深深地打动了华兹华斯，他对自然充满了爱。

J: 当华兹华斯 1787 年在《欧洲杂志》发表了一首十四行诗时，他的作家生涯就开启了。同年他进入剑桥大学圣约翰学院学习，并在 1791 年获得学士学位。

V: 华兹华斯还在剑桥念书时，就在 1790 年的暑假到爆发大革命的法国和瑞士徒步旅行。

J: 年轻的华兹华斯深受法国革命热潮的影响。华兹华斯生性善良，他在法国的经历使得他对贫苦大众更加同情。

V: 当华兹华斯开始展露政治抱负和诗人才能时，他疯狂地爱上了一位法国姑娘。

J: 是的，这发生在他的第二次法国之行。华兹华斯和阿内特·瓦隆关系暧昧，并育有一个私生女安妮·卡洛琳。

V: 这段感情是他的一首诗歌的灵感来源，但除此之外，华兹华斯极力向他的后人隐瞒这一段感情。

J: 这段旅程结束后，华兹华斯度过了几年浑浑噩噩、郁郁寡欢的时光，直到他在 1795 年遇到柯勒律治。

V: 同样是在 1795 年，华兹华斯继承了一笔遗产，经济状况得到了好转。他和妹妹多萝西可以定居在多塞特郡的雷斯唐农庄。

J: 和大自然的亲密接触激发了华兹华斯的灵感，在柯勒律治的鼓励下，华兹华斯和他合写了著名的《抒情歌谣集》。

V:《抒情歌谣集》是英国浪漫主义运动中的一部重要作品。但是这卷诗集并没有署上华兹华斯和柯勒律治的名字。1800 年出版的第二版也只把华兹华斯列为作者。

J: 1798 ~ 1799 年的冬天，华兹华斯和他的妹妹以及柯勒律治是在德国度过的。由于思乡心切，他和妹妹回到了英格兰，并定居在格拉斯米尔湖区的鸽舍。

V: 这一次陪伴他的是住在附近的诗人罗伯特·骚塞。华兹华斯、柯勒律治和骚塞被并称为“湖畔诗人”。

J: 华兹华斯具有开创性的作品写于 1797 ~ 1808 年。在这段时期内，他的很多诗作都是围绕着死亡、忍耐、分离和悲痛等主题展开的。

V: 1813 年，华兹华斯把家搬到安布尔赛德的赖德尔山，并在此度过余生，结束了他在格拉斯米尔湖区的定居生活。

1 As a writer Wordsworth made his **debut** in 1787, when he published a sonnet in *The European Magazine*.

debut 意为“（演员或运动员等的）首次公开露面，首次登台”。

➤ a young actress making her debut on Broadway
在百老汇首次登台演出的女演员

2 His French experience was a powerful factor in **turning** his inbred sympathy **to** plain common people.

turn to 意为“（把注意力等）转向……”；turn your attention\thoughts\efforts etc. to sth 意为“开始注意到\想到\致力于某事”。

➤ Tough studying Chinese, he turned his attention to English literature.
虽然他学习中文，他把注意力转向英语文学。

3 When Wordsworth's political ideas and poetic talent were beginning to **take shape**, he fell passionately in love with a French girl.

take shape 意为“形成，使成形”。

An idea was beginning to take shape in his mind.

一个主意在他脑子里成形。

4 The affair was basis of one of his poems, **but otherwise** Wordsworth did his best to hide the affair from posterity.

but otherwise 意为“然而在别的方面却……”。

➢ The rent is a bit high, but otherwise the house is satisfactory.
这所房子租金贵了点，但在其他方面倒是令人满意的。

William Wordsworth

Wordsworth was one of the most influential of England's Romantic poets.

William Wordsworth was born on 7 April 1770 at Cockermouth in Cumbria. His father was a lawyer. Both Wordsworth's parents died before he was 15, and he and his four **siblings**[①] were left in the care of different relatives. As a young man, Wordsworth developed a love of nature, a theme reflected in many of his poems.

While studying at Cambridge University, Wordsworth spent a summer holiday on a walking tour in Switzerland and France. He became an **enthusiast**[②] for the ideals of the French Revolution.

In 1795, Wordsworth received a legacy from a relative and he and his sister Dorothy went to live in Dorset. Two years later they moved again, this time to Somerset, to live near the poet Samuel Taylor Coleridge, who was an **admirer**[③] of Wordsworth's work. They collaborated on *Lyrical Ballads*, published in 1798. This collection of poems, mostly by Wordsworth but with Coleridge contributing *The Rime of the Ancient Mariner*, is generally taken to mark the beginning of the Romantic Movement in English poetry. The poems

---

① sibling *n.* 兄弟，姐妹
② enthusiast *n.* 热衷者
③ admirer *n.* 崇拜者，爱慕者

were greeted with **hostility**[1] by most **critics**[2] at that time.

In 1799, after a visit to Germany with Coleridge, Wordsworth and Dorothy settled at Dove Cottage in Grasmere in the Lake District. Coleridge lived nearby with his family. Wordsworth's most famous poem *I Wandered Lonely as a Cloud* was written at Dove Cottage in 1804.

In 1802, Wordsworth married a childhood friend, Mary Hutchinson. The next few years were personally difficult for Wordsworth. Two of his children died, his brother was **drowned**[3] at sea and Dorothy suffered a mental breakdown. His political views underwent a **transformation**[4] around the turn of the century, and he became increasingly conservative, **disillusioned**[5] by events in France **culminating in** [6]Napoleon Bonaparte taking power.

In 1813, Wordsworth moved from Grasmere to nearby Ambelside. He continued to write poetry, but it was never as great as his early works. In 1843, wordsworth became poet **Laureate**[7]. Wordsworth died on 23 April 1850 and was buried in Grasmere churchyard. His great **autobiographical**[8] poem, *The Prelude*, which he had worked on since 1798, was published after his death.

湖畔诗人华兹华斯

华兹华斯是最有影响力的英格兰浪漫主义诗人之一。

威廉·华兹华斯在1770年4月7日出生于昆布兰郡科克茅斯。他的父亲是一名律师。他15岁之前父母就双亡了，他和四兄弟姐妹由不同的亲戚抚养成人。年轻的华兹华斯对自然产生了一种爱，这是他许多诗歌中所反映的主题。

还在剑桥大学读书时，华兹华斯就用一个暑假徒步到瑞士和法国旅行。他成为了法国大革命的狂热支持者。

1795年，华兹华斯从他一个亲戚那里继承了一笔遗产，随后他和妹妹多萝西搬去多塞特郡居住。两年之后他们又搬家，这次是搬到萨默塞特郡，诗人塞缪尔·泰勒·柯勒律治就住在附近。柯勒律治非常欣赏华兹华斯的作品。他们俩合作完成了《抒情歌

---

① hostility *n.* 敌意
② critic *n.* 评论家
③ drown *v.*（使）淹没，溺死
④ transformation *n.* 转变
⑤ disillusion *v.* 使理想破灭，不再抱幻想
⑥ culminate in 达到顶峰
⑦ poet laureate 桂冠诗人，英国颁给优秀诗人的称号。
⑧ autobiographical *adj.* 自传体的

谣集》，并在 1798 年出版。这本诗集里的诗绝大部分是由华兹华斯所作，而柯勒律治只写了《古舟子咏》。这本诗集被普遍认为是英国诗歌浪漫主义运动的开端。但当时大部分评论家对这些诗歌持否定态度。

1799 年，在和柯勒律治游历了德国之后，华兹华斯和多萝西定居在格拉斯米尔湖区的鸽舍。柯勒律治则住在他家附近。华兹华斯最有名的诗《我好似一朵流云独自漫游》就是在 1804 年作于鸽舍的。

1802 年，华兹华斯和儿时的玩伴玛丽·郝金生结婚。但华兹斯在接下来的几年里备受煎熬，他的两个孩子不幸夭折，他的兄弟溺水而亡，妹妹多萝西精神崩溃。大约在世纪之交，华兹华斯的政治观念发生了转变，他变得越来越保守。法国发生的事情使他的政治幻想破灭，尤其是拿破仑·波拿巴的掌权使他失望透顶。

1813 年，华兹华斯从格拉斯米尔搬到了附近的安布尔赛德。他继续写诗，但所取得的成就不如他早期的创作。1843 年华兹华斯荣获“桂冠诗人”称号。华兹华斯于 1850 年 4 月 23 日辞世，葬于格拉斯米尔墓。他伟大的自传体诗《序言》写于 1798 年，他去世后才得以发表。

16 *Winnie the Pooh* and Milne
《小熊维尼》与米尔恩

Betty is picking toys at a shop and Carl is a saleswoman of this shop.

B: Betty C: Carl

B: Excuse me, do you have any **teddy bear**① here? I want to buy the teddy bear **Winnie-the-Pooh**② as a birthday gift for my friend.

C: Of course. Please follow me.

B: Winnie-the-Pooh is my friend's favorite toy, so I'd like to get her one.

C: Pooh Bear is so cute that people love it. Ever since its birth in 1920s, it brings endless **mirth**③ to children.

B: Wow, it has a long history. Winnie-the-Pooh is created by Alan Alexander Milne, right?

C: Yes. At the age of 42, Milne published *When We Were Very Young*, a collection of poetry for children, included a poem about the bear. And then he published *Winnie the Pooh* in 1926 and *The House at Pooh Corner* in 1928.

B: I heard that Milne is most famous for his two *Pooh* books about a boy named Christopher Robin after his son, and various characters inspired by his son's **stuffed animals**④, most notably the bear named Winnie-the-Pooh.

C: Well, you know a lot of Winnie-the-Pooh, too. Christopher Robin Milne's stuffed bear was originally named "Edward".

B: It was renamed "Winnie-the-Pooh" after a Canadian black bear named Winnie, which was used as a military **mascot**⑤ in World War I, and left to London Zoo during the war.

---

① teddy bear 玩具熊
② Winnie-the-Pooh 小熊维尼
③ mirth *n.* 欢乐
④ stuffed animal 毛绒玩具
⑤ mascot *n.* 吉祥物

C: All three books were **illustrated**[1] by E. H. Shepard, using his own son's teddy as the model.

B: Later Pooh became an industry, producing toys, comics, and such films as *Winnie-the-Pooh and the Honey Tree* from Disney.

C: Speaking of Milne, he is not only good at writing, but also good at math.

B: He is a gifted **mathematician**[2] and he won a scholarship to Westminster School when he was only eleven.

C: He studied mathematics at Trinity College, Cambridge, and edited the undergraduate magazine *Granta*. After receiving his B.A. in 1903, he started his career as a **freelance writer**[3].

B: During World War I he served in the Royal Warwickshire Regiment as a **signals officer**[4]. The horrors he witnessed in the war left him a lifelong **nostalgia**[5] for the idyllic childhood.

C: "A children's book' must be written, not for children, but for the author himself," he once said.

B: When the **disillusioned**[6] post-war writers depicted the "**lost generation**[7]" of the 1920s, Milne returned in his Pooh books into the safety of his early years.

C: In the 1930s and 40s Milne was active in religious and **pacifist**[8] polemics. At the age of fifty-six he published his **autobiography**[9] *It's Too Late Now*, which focused mostly on his childhood years.

B: After the success of Milne's books, his son Christopher Milne has later confessed that he had problems coping with the legendary literary figure created about him.

---

① illustrate *v.* 给……画插图
② mathematician *n.* 数学家
③ freelance writer　自由撰稿人
④ signals officer 信号官
⑤ nostalgia *n.* 怀旧
⑥ disillusioned *adj.* 幻想破灭的
⑦ lost generation 迷惘的一代
⑧ pacifist *n.* 和平主义者，反战主义者
⑨ autobiography *n.* 自传

C: Christopher Milne has also said that his mother, Daphne, invented stories about toy animals and provided most of the material for his father's books.

B: 打扰一下，你们这儿有玩具熊卖吗？我想要买维尼玩具熊作为生日礼物送给我朋友。

C: 当然有，请跟我来。

B: 维尼熊是我朋友最喜欢的玩具，我想给她买一个。

C: 维尼熊是那么的可爱，所有人都喜欢它。自从它在 20 世纪 20 年代诞生以来，就给孩子们带来了无尽的欢乐。

B: 哇，它有这么长的历史啊。维尼熊是艾伦·亚历山大·米尔恩创作的，对吗？

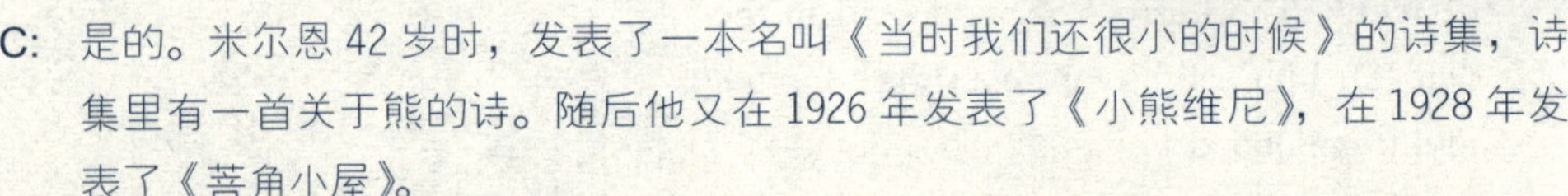

C: 是的。米尔恩 42 岁时，发表了一本名叫《当时我们还很小的时候》的诗集，诗集里有一首关于熊的诗。随后他又在 1926 年发表了《小熊维尼》，在 1928 年发表了《菩角小屋》。

B: 我听说米尔恩是以两本维尼熊故事书而闻名于世的。那两本书讲述的是一个叫克里斯多夫·罗宾的小男孩的故事。书中的小男孩是以米尔恩儿子的名字命名的。书中的其他角色也是受他儿子的毛绒玩具启发而创造出来的，其中最著名的就是维尼熊。

C: 关于维尼熊，你知道的也很多。克里斯多夫·罗宾·米尔恩的毛绒玩具熊原来的名字叫“爱德华”。

B: 它是以一只澳大利亚黑熊维尼的名字重命名的。那只澳大利亚黑熊是一战时的军队吉祥物，住在伦敦动物园里。

C: 米尔恩的三本书的插图都是由 E.H. 谢培德画的，谢培德以他儿子的玩具熊作为模特画了插图。

B: 随后维尼熊发展成了一个产业，生产玩具、连环画和《小熊维尼和蜂蜜树》这样的迪斯尼电影。

C: 说到米尔恩，他不仅擅长写作，还擅长数学。

B: 他是个天才的数学家，在 11 岁时就获得威斯敏斯特学校的奖学金。

C: 米尔恩在剑桥大学三一学院学习数学，并编辑了一本本科生杂志《格兰特》。1903 年他拿到学士学位后，开始了自由撰稿人的职业生涯。

B: 一战期间，米尔恩作为一名信号官在皇家沃里克郡军团工作。他在战争中所目睹的恐惧使他余生都迷恋于快乐的童年生活。

C: 米尔恩曾经说过：“儿童读物有创作的必要，这不是为了满足儿童的需要，而是为了让作者找回童年的感觉。"

B: 当战后幻想破灭的作家在描写 20 世纪 20 年代的"迷惘的一代"时，米尔恩却把注意力转向他的"小熊维尼"系列书，重温快乐的童年生活。

C: 20 世纪 30 年代至 40 年代，米尔恩活跃于宗教和反战辩论运动中。56 岁时，他出版自传《现在已经太迟了》，着重描述他的童年生活。

B: 在米尔恩的书大受欢迎后，他的儿子克里斯多夫·米尔恩后来承认他在处理根据他本人创作的传奇文学形象时感到疑惑。

C: 克里斯多夫·米尔恩还说，毛绒玩具的故事是他母亲达芙妮创作的，他父亲著作里的大部分材料也是他母亲提供的。

1 ...and various characters inspired by his son's stuffed animals, most **notably** the bear named Winnie-the-Pooh.

notably 意为"特别地，显著地"，经常和 most 连用，表示强调。

- Even so, they have made remarkable progress, notably with drugs such as inhaled steroids.
  既使如此，他们已经有了非凡的进步，明显体现在可吸入的类固醇药物上。
- Most notably, the kids are readily identified as not being part of the adoptive family when they're adopted by Caucasians.
  最重要的是，当他们被白种人收养时，这些孩子不容易融入收养家庭。

2 It was **renamed** "Winnie-the-Pooh" after a Canadian black bear named Winnie, which was used as a military mascot in World War I, and left to London Zoo during the war.

rename 意为"给……重新命名"，一般用作被动态。

- Can I rename my account?
  我可以更改账户名吗？

3 I heard that Milne is most famous for his two *Pooh* books about a boy named Christopher Robin after his son, and various characters **inspired by** his son's stuffed animals,...

inspire by 意为"受……鼓舞，鼓励，启发"。

➢ We were greatly inspired by reading the joint communique.
联合公报使我们大受鼓舞。

➢ The story was inspired by a chance meeting with an old Russian duke.
这个故事的创作灵感来自于和一位俄国老公爵的不期而遇。

4 The horrors he **witnessed** in the war left him a lifelong nostalgia for the idyllic fantasies of childhood.

witness 作动词用，意为“目击，亲眼看见（尤指罪行或事故发生）”

➢ Police are appealing to any driver who may have witnessed the accident.
警方正呼吁曾目睹这起事故的司机协助。

Winnie the Pooh and Milne

Alan Alexander Milne was born on the 18th of January 1882 in Hampstead, London. He studied at Westminster School and Trinity College, Cambridge, where he graduated with a degree in mathematics in 1903. Milne's first literary efforts were published in the humorous magazine Punch, where, in 1906 Milne started to work as Assistant Editor. In 1913 Milne married Daphne, the **God-daughter**① of Punch editor.

With the **outbreak**② of the First World War, Milne joined the army as a signaling officer in February 1915, despite being a pacifist. He was sent to France but he left the front lines later suffering from fever. After his **recovery**③ he was placed in charge of a signaling company at Fort Southwick until his **discharge**④ from the army in February 1919. After leaving the army, Milne **resigned**⑤ his post at Punch and concentrated on writing plays. In 1923 his first children's poem *Vespers* was published in *Vanity Fair*. The poem featured his son Christopher.

In 1924, after the success of *Vespers* Milne published a book of children's poems entitled *When We Were Very Young*, with drawings by Punch **illustrator**⑥, Ernest Shepard. This

① God-daughter *n.* 教女
② outbreak *n.* 爆发
③ recovery *n.* 康复
④ discharge *n.* 准许离开（尤指病人出院、服役的人退伍等）
⑤ resign *v.* 辞职
⑥ illustrator *n.* 插图画家

book included a poem about a Teddy Bear. This was Pooh's first unofficial appearance in Milne's writing. *When We Were Very Young was* proved to be an instant success and sold over 50,000 copies within eight weeks.

It was not until 1925 that Pooh officially came into being. Milne's contribution for the Christmas Eve issue was a **bedtime story**① that he had made up for his son about adventures he had with his Teddy Bear who was later known as Winnie the Pooh.

This bedtime story formed the first chapter of Milne's next book entitled *Winnie-the-Pooh*. This book was followed by *The House at Pooh Corner* in 1928. In an attempt to **shield**② his son from the publicity generated by the success of the Pooh stories, Milne announced that *The House at Pooh Corner* would be his last Christopher Robin book.

He also never read the stories and poems to his son Christopher, preferring rather to amuse him with the works of P.G. Wodehouse, one of Milne's favourite authors. Although Milne went on to write plays and novels, these Pooh stories remain his best known works.

《小熊维尼》与米尔恩

1882 年 1 月 18 日，艾伦·亚历山大·米尔恩出生于伦敦汉普斯特德。他就读于威斯敏斯特学校和剑桥大学三一学院，1903 年，他从剑桥大学数学专业毕业，并获得学士学位。米尔恩的第一部文学作品发表在幽默杂志《笨拙》上，而从 1906 年开始，米尔恩就作为一名助理编辑开始工作。1913 年，米尔恩和《笨拙》杂志一位编辑的教女达芙妮结婚。

尽管米尔恩是反战主义者，随着第一次世界大战的爆发，他还是在 1915 年 2 月参军了，并成为一名信号官。他被派到法国，但不久就因高烧不退被迫离开前线。米尔恩康复以后，开始负责管理索思威克要塞的一家信号公司，直到 1919 年 2 月退伍。退伍后，米尔恩辞去了他在《笨拙》杂志社的工作，

① bedtime story 睡前故事
② shield *v.* 保护，庇护

专心致力于话剧写作。1923 年他的第一首儿童诗《晚祷》发表在著名杂志《名利场》上，这首诗以他的儿子克里斯多夫为原型。

继《晚祷》的成功发表后，1924 年，米尔恩又发表了一本儿童诗集《当我们还很小的时候》，诗集里配有《笨拙》插图画家欧内斯特·谢泼德画的插图。这本诗集里收藏了一首关于玩具熊的诗。这是维尼熊在米尔恩写作生涯中的首次非正式现身。《当我们还很小的时候》一经出版便大受欢迎，8 周内卖出了 5 万本。

直到 1925 年，玩具熊维尼才正式进入人们的视野。米尔恩为圣诞前夕发行物所做的贡献就是创作了一个睡前故事，这个故事是为他儿子准备的，讲的是他儿子和玩具熊的冒险故事，这只玩具熊后来被称为“小熊维尼”。

这个睡前故事构成了米尔恩的下一本书《小熊维尼》的第一章。在 1928 年，米尔恩又发表了《菩角小屋》。“小熊维尼”系列故事书的成功使得公众开始密切关注他的儿子，为了保护儿子，米尔恩宣布《菩角小屋》将是以他儿子克里斯多夫·罗宾为原型的最后一本书。

米尔恩再也没有给克里斯多夫读故事书和诗歌，而是选择用他最喜欢的作家 P.G. 沃德豪斯的作品供儿子阅读。虽然米尔恩继续创作话剧和小说，“小熊维尼”系列仍是他最出名的作品。

Unit 5 Science & Technology

行行出状元

17 The Genius in the Wheelchair

轮椅上的天才霍金

Edison met Jenny outside the library.

E: Edison J: Jenny

E: Have you heard the news that American President Obama presented Presidential Medal of Freedom① to Prof Hawking at the White House?

J: Yes, of course, it's such big news. President Obama addressed: "His popular books have advanced the cause of science itself. From his **wheelchair**②, he's led us on a journey to the farthest reaches of the **cosmos**③**.** " Prof Hawking is one of the greatest scientists in the world and he deserved it!

E: I can't agree with you more. As a scientist in wheelchair, he makes a huge progress in the field of physics despite the difficulties in speaking and writing.

J: After he was diagnosed with a rare, disease and be told to have just a few years to live, he chose to live with new purpose.

---

① Presidential Medal of Freedom 总统自由勋章，是由美国总统向在科学、文化、体育和社会活动等领域作出杰出贡献的平民颁发的一种勋章，是美国对普通人的最高奖励。

② wheelchair *n.* 轮椅

③ cosmos *n.* 宇宙

E: At the very beginning, Hawing was in low spirits until he saw an unpleasant sight.

J: What exactly this unpleasant sight was?

E: While Hawking had been in hospital, he had seen a boy die of **leukemia**[①], in the bed opposite him. And suddenly Hawking realized that there were people who were worse off than him. Whenever he felt sorry for himself, he remembered that boy.

J: Well, to some extent, that boy saved Hawking's life.

E: Speaking of Hawking's research, he always keeps critical thinking. He is brave to challenge famous theories like black hole theory[②], **big bang theory**[③] and **string theory**[④].

J: Without the doubts of authorities[⑤], he cannot explore more in physics and be closer to the truth.

E: As a physicist, Hawking wants to see the outer space.

J: He underwent a **zero-gravity**[⑥] flight in 2007 and planned to go into space in 2009. Hawking announced this plan at his 65th birthday in 2007.

E: Prof Hawking's next step towards the cosmos then depended on the Virgin Galactic space tourism plans of Sir Richard Branson, whose Spaceship Two carried six passengers into space in 2008.

J: Usually a flight costs about £100,000, but Sir Richard will sponsor Prof Hawking's flight. But Hawking didn't go to space in 2009.

E: By the way, have you read Hawking's **masterpiece**[⑦] *A Brief History of Time: From the Big Bang to Black Holes*?

J: Of course. I bought this book as soon as it came into the market.

E: It became a best-seller of long standing and established his reputation as an accessible genius. And he wrote other popular articles and appeared in movies and television.

J: He remains extremely busy, his work hardly slows by Lou Gehrig's disease for which he uses a wheelchair and speaks through a computer and voice **synthesizer**[⑧].

---

① leukemia *n.* 白血病
② black hole theory 黑洞理论
③ big bang theory 大爆炸理论
④ string theory 弦理论
⑤ authority *n.* 权威
⑥ zero-gravity 零重力
⑦ masterpiece *n.* 代表作，杰作
⑧ synthesizer *n.* 合成器

E: But I found *A Brief History of Time* was difficult to read.

J: It is said that there are just a few people in the world could truly understand this book.

E: We are just ordinary people, but not physicists. What I'm trying to say is Hawking and his books have attracted people's attention to the world of physics.

E: 你知道美国总统奥巴马在白宫给霍金教授颁发总统自由勋章的消息吗?

J: 我当然知道了，这可是一条重大消息。奥巴马总统在颁奖辞中说道："他（霍金）的畅销书推动了科学事业的发展。他在轮椅上引领我们踏上一条通往宇宙最深处的道路。"霍金教授是最杰出的科学家之一，这个奖项他当之无愧!

E: 我很赞同你的说法。作为一个坐在轮椅上的科学家，尽管霍金在说话与写作上有障碍，但他在物理学领域作出了巨大的贡献。

J: 当霍金被诊断患有一种罕见的疾病并被告知只有几年时间活在世上后，他选择了为新的目标和意义而活。

E: 一开始霍金意志消沉，直到他亲眼目睹了悲惨的一幕。

J: 这悲惨的一幕到底是什么?

E: 当霍金还在医院的时候，他看到一个男孩死于白血病，那男孩的床就在他对面，突然间霍金意识到自己并不是世界上最悲惨的人。每当他为自己感到难过的时候，他就会记起那个男孩。

J: 从某种程度上来说，那个男孩救了霍金的命。

E: 说到霍金的研究，他总是保持批判性思维。他勇敢地去挑战诸如黑洞理论、大爆炸理论和弦理论之类的著名学说。

J: 没有对权威的质疑，他就不能探索发现物理学的更多奥秘，也不会离真理越来越近。

E: 作为一个物理学家，霍金想去太空看看。

J: 他在 2007 年进行了一次零重力飞行，并计划 2009 年进入太空。在 2007 年霍金 65 岁生日的时候，他宣布了这一计划。

E: 霍金教授的下一步走向宇宙的计划取决于里查德·布兰森爵士的"维珍银河"太空旅行计划。2008 年，里查德·布兰森爵士的"太空飞船 2 号"把 6 名乘客送入了太空。

J: 一般来说，一次太空飞行要花费 10 万英镑，但里查德·布兰森爵士将会赞助霍金教授的太空飞行。然而由于种种原因，霍金并没有在 2009 年进入太空。

E: 对了，你看过霍金的代表作《时间简史：从大爆炸到黑洞》吗？

J: 我当然看过啦，这本书一上市我就买了。

E: 很长一段时间以来，这本书都很畅销。这本书奠定了霍金作为一个平易近人的天才的地位。他还写了很多大受欢迎的文章，还出现在电影和电视上。

J: 霍金仍然很忙，但是他的工作并没有因卢伽雷氏症而延缓：他以轮椅代步，通过电脑和声音合成器说话。

E: 不过我觉得《时间简史》很难读懂。

J: 据说世上只有很少的人能真正读懂这本书。

E: 我们只是普通人，不是物理学家。我觉得霍金和他的书让人们把目光投向了物理世界，去探索这个有趣的领域。

1 At the very beginning, Hawing was **in low spirits** until he saw an unpleasant sight.

in a low sprit 意为“意志消沉，情绪低落”。

➢ Don’t play with her; she is in low spirits.
别跟她开玩笑，她情绪不好。

2 Well, **to some extent**, that boy saved Hawking’s life.

to some extent 意为“在某种程度上”。

➢ The central services of that broadcasting company *to some extent* feed off the regional stations.
那家广播公司的中心业务在某种程度上是依靠地方台供应材料的。

➢ National economic growth accelerated to some extent.
国民经济增长速度有所加快。

3 I bought this book as soon as it **came into the market**.

come into the market 意为“上市，开始销售”。

➢ This kind of car will come into the market soon.
这款车即将投放市场。

➢ When did this soup come into the market?
这种香皂什么时候上市?

4 It became a best-seller of long standing and established his reputation as an **accessible** genius.

accessible 意为“容易取得的、容易获得的;可接近的、平易近人的、可与之打交道的”。

➢ A manager should be accessible to his staff.
一个管理人员应该让职员感到平易近人。

The Genius in the Wheelchair

Stephen Hawking was born on 8 January 1942, the 300th anniversary of Galileo's death. He has come to be thought of the greatest mind in physics since Albert Einstein.

Hawking grew up outside London in an intellectual family. His father was a physician and specialist in tropical diseases; his mother was active in the Liberal Party. He was an **awkward**① schoolboy, but knew from early on that he wanted to study science. In 1959 he won a scholarship to Oxford University, where his intellectual capabilities became more noticeable. In 1962 he went to Cambridge University to pursue a PhD in **cosmology**②. There he became **intrigued**③ with **black holes**④ and "**space-time singularities**⑤".

However, Hawking's life was threatened by a terrible disease. He had never been very well coordinated physically as a child, and in his third year at Oxford, he noticed that he seemed to be getting clumsier. Shortly after his 21st birthday, he

① awkward *adj.* 怪异的
② cosmology *n.* 宇宙学
③ intrigue *v.* 激起……的好奇心
④ black holes 黑洞
⑤ space-time singularities 时空起点

went into hospital for tests. It was a great shock to Hawking to discover that he had Lou Gehrig's disease (a disease that affects muscle control). The realization that he had an incurable **disease**① was likely to kill him in the first few years.

The doctors suggested Hawking to go back to Cambridge and carry on with the research he had just started in general **relativity**② and cosmology. Shortly after he came out of hospital, he dreamt that he was going to be executed. He suddenly realized that there were a lot of **worthwhile**③ things he could do if he were **reprieved**④. Hawking then began to make progress with his research. And he got engaged to a girl called Jane Wilde, whom he had met just about the time his condition was **diagnosed**⑤. That engagement changed Hawkins's life. It gave him something to live for. Jane cared for Hawking until 1991 when the couple separated, reportedly due to the pressures of fame and his increasing disability. Hawking then married his nurse, Elaine Mason in 1995. But they divorced in October 2006.

Stephen Hawking has worked on the basic laws which govern the universe. He received the Albert Einstein Award, the most **prestigious**⑥ in **theoretical physics**⑦ in 1978. And in 1979, he was appointed Lucasian Professor of Mathematics at Cambridge, the same post held by Sir Isaac Newton 300 years earlier.

轮椅上的天才霍金

斯蒂芬·霍金出生于1942年1月8日，这一天正好是伽利略逝世300周年纪念日。人们认为他是自爱因斯坦以来最伟大的物理学家。

霍金出生于伦敦郊区的一个知识分子家庭，他的父亲是名擅长医治热带病的内科医生，母亲是名活跃的英国自由党分子。上学时，霍金就表现得有些怪异，和其他孩子不同。但很早人们就知道他有志于科学研究。1959年霍金获得了牛津大学的奖学金，在那里他的研究能力得到了很大提高。1962年霍金前往剑桥大学攻读宇宙学博士学位。在剑桥大学，他对黑洞理论和时空奇点理论产生了兴趣。

但是霍金的生命却因一种严重的疾病而受到威胁。当霍金还小时，他的身体动作就不太协调。在牛津大学的第三年，他就注意到自己看起来更笨拙了。在他21岁生

① incurable disease 不治之症
② general relativity 广义相对论
③ worthwhile *adj.* 值得的，有价值的
④ reprieve *v.* 暂缓，缓期执行
⑤ diagnose *v.* 诊断
⑥ prestigious *adj.* 受尊敬的，有声望的
⑦ theoretical physics 理论物理学

日过后不久，他去医院做了检查。他发现自己患有卢伽雷氏症（一种影响肌肉控制的疾病），这对霍金来说是一个巨大的打击。在最初的几年里，发现自己患有不治之症这件事差点“杀”了霍金。

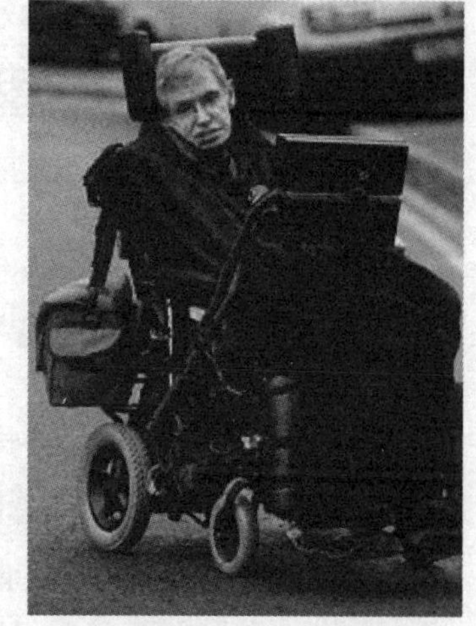

医生建议霍金回到剑桥大学继续他在广义相对论和宇宙学方面的研究。在他出院后不久，他就梦到自己要被处死。他突然意识到如果“处死”能够被暂缓，还有很多有价值的事情等着他去做。从那时起，霍金的研究开始取得进展。他还和简·王尔德订了婚，霍金在病情刚诊断出来时就遇到了这个女孩。订婚改变了霍金的生活，给了他活下去的动力。简一直照顾霍金直到 1991 年夫妇俩离婚，据报道婚姻破裂是受霍金的名声和残疾加剧所累。1995 年，霍金和他的护士伊莱恩·梅森结婚，但两人于 2006 年 10 月离婚。

斯蒂芬·霍金一直致力于掌控宇宙的基本定理的研究。1978 年，霍金获得了物理学理论研究领域的最高奖爱因斯坦奖。1979 年，他受聘于剑桥大学任卢卡斯数学教授。300 年前，这个职位是由艾萨克·牛顿爵士担任的。

18 The Secret of Life in the Pub

克里克和沃森

焦点对话

Thomas and Kate are discussing questions.

T: Thomas K: Kate

T: Do you know why we look different? And why the colour of our hair is different? Someone is blond, but the others are brown, still others are black.

K: That's because we have different DNA. DNA is a **molecule**[①] which carries genetic information. Each one of us has unique DNA, so we have different facial features.

T: Wow, DNA is so magical! **No wonder**[②] the discovery of the structure of DNA was one of the most significant scientific discoveries of the 20th century.

K: well, it is a big thing. And the scientists, mainly James Watson and Francis Crick who discovered the **double helix**[③] of DNA played very important roles in the history of molecular biology.

T: In a best-selling book, *The Double Helix*, Watson claimed that Crick announced the discovery by walking into the nearby Eagle Pub and blurting out that "we had found the secret of life."

K: Both Watson and Crick were so excited to discover this secret, because they were so desperate to find the truth.

---

① molecule *n.* 分子

② no wonder 怪不得

③ double helix 双螺旋结构

T: When Watson came to Cambridge, Crick was a 35-year-old post-graduate student and Watson was only 23, but he already had a Ph.D.

K: Though Crick was 12 years older than Watson, they got along quite well. These two men shared similar interests: they liked to talk in a loud voice, no matter if they were walking along the river bank or drinking in the Eagle Pub.

T: More importantly, they were interested in the **fundamental**[①] problem of how genetic information might be stored in molecular form. They talked endlessly about DNA and the idea that it might be possible to guess a molecular model of its structure.

K: Both of them were deeply influenced by a book *What is Life?* which was written by Erwin Schrödinger, the father of **Quantum mechanics**[②]. The author proposed the concept of a complex molecule with the genetic code for **living organisms**[③]. After reading this book, they determined to discover what exactly this complex molecule is.

T: In the early 1950s, Watson and Crick were only two of many scientists working on figuring out the structure of DNA. California chemist Linus Pauling suggested an incorrect model at the beginning of 1953, **prompting**[④] Watson and Crick to try and beat Pauling at his own game.

K: At that time Maurice Wilkins and Rosalind Franklin, both working at King's College, London, were using **X-ray diffraction**[⑤] to study DNA.

T: Crick and Watson used their findings in their own research.

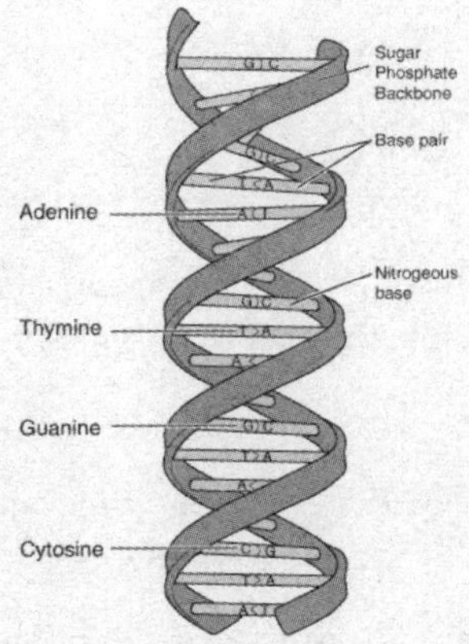

K: On the morning of February 28, 1953, they determined that the structure of DNA was a double-helix polymer, or a **spiral**[⑥] of two DNA strands, each containing a long chain of **monomer nucleotides**[⑦], wound around each other.

T: Watson, Crick and Wilkins shared the Nobel Prize in Medicine in 1962 "for their discoveries concerning the molecular structure of **nucleic acids**[⑧] and its

① fundamental *adj.* 基本的，基础的
② quantum mechanics 量子物理学
③ organisms *n.* 有机体
④ prompt *v.* 促使
⑤ X-ray diffraction X- 光衍射
⑥ spiral *n.* 螺旋
⑦ monomer nucleotide 单体核苷酸
⑧ nucleic acid 核酸

significance for information transfer in living material”.

K: Franklin had died in 1958 and, despite her key experimental work, the prize could not be received **posthumously**①. Crick and Watson both received numerous other awards and prizes for their work.

T: 你知道为什么我们长得不一样吗？为什么我们头发的颜色不同？有些人是金发，有些人是棕发，还有一些人是黑发。

K: 那是因为我们有不同的 DNA。DNA 是一种携带遗传信息的分子。我们每一个人的 DNA 都是独特的，所以我们有不同的面部特征。

T: 哇，DNA 这么神奇啊！怪不得 DNA 结构的发现是 20 世纪最重大的科学发现之一。

K: 是啊，这的确是一件大事。而发现 DNA 双螺旋结构的科学家主要是詹姆斯·沃森和弗朗西斯·克里克，他们在分子生物学的历史上扮演了非常重要的角色。

T: 在一本叫《双螺旋》的畅销书中，沃森声称是克里克走进附近的“老鹰酒吧”（剑桥大学内,老卡文迪什实验室附近的一家酒吧）宣布这一发现的。克里克脱口而出：“我们已经发现了生命的秘密。”

K: 发现这个奥秘后，沃森和克里克都很兴奋，因为他们一直致力于发现真理。

T: 当沃森来到剑桥时，克里克是一名已经 35 岁的硕士研究生，沃森虽然只有 23 岁，但已经有了一个博士学位。

T: 虽然克里克年长沃森 12 岁，他们俩却相处得很愉快。这两人有着相似的兴趣，不管是沿着河边散步还是在老鹰酒吧喝酒，他们都喜欢大声说话。

T: 更为重要的是，他们都对遗传信息是如何以分子形式储存的问题感兴趣。 他们不停地谈论 DNA，以及 DNA 有可能出现的分子形式。

K: 他们都深受《生命是什么》这本书的影响。这本书是量子物理学之父埃尔温·薛定谔写的，薛定谔在书里大胆地设想了生物有机体的一种带遗传密码的复杂分子形式。读了这本书之后，沃森和克里克决心要找出这种复杂的分子到底是什么。

T: 在 20 世纪 50 年代早期，许多科学家都致力于研究发现 DNA 结构，沃森和克里克只是其中的两个。加利福尼亚化学家莱纳斯·鲍林在 1953 年年初提出了一个错误的模型，误导了很多科学家，这促使沃森和克里克尝试在鲍林擅长的建构分子模型方面打败他。

K: 那时，一同在伦敦国王学院工作的莫里斯·威尔金斯和罗莎琳德·富兰克林正用 X 光衍射研究 DNA。

① posthumously *adv.* 在死后

T: 他们两人的发现被用于克里克和沃森的研究中。

K: 1953 年 2 月 28 日，克里克和沃森认定 DNA 的结构是一个双螺旋聚合物，或者说是一个包含DNA双链的螺旋，每条链包含着一长串单体核苷酸，缠绕在另一条链上。

T: 沃森、克里克和威尔金斯“因他们关于核酸分子结构的发现以及这一发现对于生物遗传信息传送的重大意义”一起分享了 1962 年的诺贝尔医学奖。

K: 尽管富兰克林的实验工作取得了巨大成就，但她于 1958 年过世，而诺贝尔奖只能颁发给在世的人。克里克和沃森两人还获得了其他无数的奖励和奖项。

1 Watson claimed that Crick announced the discovery by walking into the nearby Eagle Pub which and **blurting out** that "we had found the secret of life."

blurt out 意为“脱口而出，不假思索地说出”。

➢ He was apt to blurt out the whole truth, in cases where other people would have kept silence.
他常常直言不讳地说出全部真情，而其他人在这种情况下则往往会保持沉默。

2 Both Watson and Crick were so excited to find out this secret, because they were so **desperate** to looking for the truth.

desperate 意为“令人绝望的，不顾一切的，拼命的，孤注一掷的，迫切需要的”。

➢ Ben was desperate to get a job.
本急切地想找一份工作。

➢ By then I was desperate for a holiday.
到那时，我已经特别渴望休假了。

3 In the early 1950s, Watson and Crick were only two of many scientists working on **figuring out** the structure of DNA.

figure out 意为“计算出，解决，断定，领会到”。

➢ Can you figure the total cost out?
你能把全部成本算出来吗？

➢ I just can't figure him out.
我简直摸不透他。

4 California chemist Linus Pauling suggested an incorrect model at the beginning of 1953, prompting Watson and Crick to try and **beat** Pauling **at his own game**.

beat someone at his own game 意为“在某人拿手的方面胜过某人”。

➢ John wanted to take us in, but we beat him at his own game.
约翰想骗我们，但这位骗人老手反而受了我们的欺骗。

主题延伸

The Secret of Life in the Pub

The names of James Watson and Francis Crick are bound together forever because the scientific discovery they made was truly a **joint enterprise**①. Watson and Crick were the first to describe the structure of **deoxyribonucleic acid**②, or DNA, the molecule that carries our genes and determines everything from the color of our eyes to the shape of our fingernails. Even though Watson and Crick's collaboration lasted only a few years, their achievement was huge enough to tie their names together forever in the history of science and to establish a firm **footing**③ for what was then a radical new branch of science: **molecular biology**④. In doing so, they paved the way for the early detection of genetic diseases such as sickle-cell anemia, and for new **scientific leaps**⑤ such as **animal cloning**⑥.

Francis Harry Compton Crick was born on 8 June 1916 near Northampton. He studied physics at **University College of London**⑦, and during World War Two he worked for the Admiralty Research Laboratory, from which emerged a group of many notable scientists. He

① joint enterprise 共同事业
② deoxyribonucleic acid 脱氧核糖核酸
③ footing *n.* 立足点，地位
④ molecular biology 分子生物学
⑤ scientific leap 科学飞跃
⑥ animal cloning 动物克隆
⑦ University College of London 伦敦大学学院

changed from physics to biology and in 1947 began to work at Cambridge University. By 1949, he was working at the Medical Research Council unit at the Cavendish Laboratory in Cambridge. In 1951, an American student, James Watson, arrived at the unit and the two began to work together.

James Dewey Watson was born on 6 April 1928 in Chicago and studied at the universities of Chicago, Indiana and Copenhagen. He then moved to Cambridge University. Watson and Crick worked together on studying the structure of DNA (deoxyribonucleic acid), the molecule that contains the **hereditary**① information for cells.

In April 1953, they published the news of their discovery, a molecular structure of DNA based on the double helix. Their model served to explain how DNA **replicates**② and how hereditary information is coded on it. This set the stage for the rapid advances of molecular biology.

Francis Crick continued to work in genetics and then moved into brain research, becoming a professor at the Salk Institute for Biological Studies in California. He died on 28 July 2004.

From 1988 to 1992, James Watson directed the **Human Genome Project**③ at the American National Institutes of Health. He was **instrumental**④ in obtaining funding for the project and in encouraging cooperation between governments and leading scientists.

克里克和沃森

詹姆斯·沃森和弗朗西斯·克里克这两个名字永远联系在了一起，因为他们取得的重大科学发现是两人共同的事业。沃森和克里克是第一次向世人描述脱氧核糖核酸或DNA 结构的两位科学家。DNA 这种分子携带着人类的基因并决定着从眼珠的颜色到手指甲形状的人身上的一切部位。尽管沃森和克里克的合作仅持续几年，两人取得的成就之大足以令他们名垂科学史。他们还为分子生物学的发展打下了坚实的基础，而那时的分子生物学只是门新兴学科。两人的发现为诸如镰状细胞性贫血等遗传疾病的早期诊断和诸如动物克隆等的新科学飞跃铺平了道路。

① hereditary *adj.* 遗传的

② Replicate *v.* 复制

③ Human Genome Project 人类基因组计划，是 1990 年正式启动的。美、英、法、德、日和中国科学家共同参与，按计划在 2005 年，要把人体内约 10 万个基因的密码全部解开，同时绘制出人类基因的谱图。

④ instrumental *adj.* 有帮助的，乐器的

1916 年 6 月 8 日，弗朗西斯·哈里·康普顿·克里克出生于北安普敦附近。他在伦敦大学学院学习物理。二战期间，克里克为英国海军研究实验室工作，那里涌现出了很多知名的科学家。后来他从物理系转到生物系并于 1947 年开始在剑桥大学工作。1949 年，克里克开始在剑桥大学卡文迪什实验室的医学研究中心工作。1951 年，一位美国学生詹姆斯·沃森来到了中心，于是两人开始一起工作。

詹姆斯·杜威·沃森 1928 年 4 月 6 日出生于芝加哥并先后在芝加哥大学、印第安纳大学和哥本哈根大学学习。后来他去了剑桥大学。沃森和克里克一同致力于 DNA 结构的研究，DNA（脱氧核糖核酸）是一种携带细胞遗传信息分子。

1953 年 4 月，克里克和沃森宣布了他们的发现：DNA 的双螺旋结构。他们提供的 DNA 分子结构模型解释了 DNA 是怎样复制遗传信息，而遗传信息又是如何在 DNA 上编码的。这一发现为分子生物学的快速发展创造了条件。

弗朗西斯·克里克继续自己在遗传学方面的研究，而后转到脑研究，成为美国加州萨克生物研究学院的教授。他于 2004 年 7 月 28 日辞世。

从 1988 年到 1992 年，詹姆斯·沃森指导了美国国家卫生研究院的人类基因组计划。他在为该项目获得资金及鼓励政府和顶尖科学家合作等方面起了重要作用。

19 The Cavendish Laboratory
卡文迪什实验室的风水

焦点对话

Mark and Jane are looking for books about Nobel Prize Winners in a book store.

M: Mark　　J: Jane

M: It's October now, and Nobel Prize Winners are usually announced in this month. I wonder who will be the winners of this year's Nobel Prize in Physics.

J: Well, maybe the winners will be scientists who work in Cavendish Laboratory. There are 29 Nobel Prize winners in the history of Cavendish after all.

M: Twenty-nine winners! That's the brilliant achievement.

J: The Cavendish Laboratory is the Department of Physics of the University of Cambridge. The Department is itself part of the School of Physical Sciences.

M: It was built in 1873 as a teaching laboratory. It was **initially**① on Free School Lane, in the centre of Cambridge. After **perennial**② space problems, it moved West Cambridge, in the early 1970s.

J: The need for the practical training of scientists and engineers was emphasized by the success of the **Great Exhibition of 1851**③ and the requirements of an industrial society.

M: William Cavendish, the Seventh Duke of **Devonshire**④, provided £6,300 to meet the costs of building a physics laboratory, on condition that Cambridge provided the funding

---

① initially *adv.* 最开始，最初

② perennial *adj.* 持续多年的

③ Great Exhibition of 1851 指 1851 年英国伦敦万国工业产品博览会，它的开幕标志了第一届世界博览会的诞生。

④ Devonshire 德文郡

for a **Professorship**[1] of **Experimental Physics**[2].

J: Cavendish has been in the center of Physics for a long time. It has an extraordinary history of discovery and innovation in Physics since its opening in 1874, so it is not surprising that there are so many Nobel Prize Winners who come from Cavendish.

M: I also heard that Cavendish has a long history and it plays an important role in the development of Cambridge. Oh! I remember that Watson and Crick, the discoverers of the DNA structure also worked in Cavendish.

J: Yes. Crick had already worked in the Cavendish Laboratory when Watson came from the U.S.A. and together they discovered the DNA double helix. The Cavendish Laboratory has had important influence on **biology**[3], mainly through the application of X-ray **crystallography**[4] to the study of structures of **biological molecules**[5].

M: It seems that Cavendish is influential not only in Physics, but also in many other areas.

J: Do you know whom the Cavendish Laboratory is named after?

M: Of course, it is named after William Cavendish, because he gives money to endow the laboratory in memory of his **learned**[6] relative.

J: His learned relative? Who he is?

M: He is Henry Cavendish, a famous physicist. He is famous for the discovery of **hydrogen**[7] and Cavendish experiment.

J: Oh, I have read an article about the Cavendish experiment. This is the first experiment

---

① professorship *n.* 教授职位
② Experimental Physics 实验物理学
③ biology *n.* 生物学
④ crystallography *n.* 晶体学
⑤ biological molecule 生物分子
⑥ learned *adj.* 博学的
⑦ hydrogen *n.* 氢

to measure the **force of gravity**① in the laboratory, and the first to **yield**② **accurate**③ values for the **gravitational constant**④ and the **mass**⑤ of the Earth.

M: What is the current situation of Cavendish?

J: Currently there are 65 teaching staff, **approximately**⑥ 150 **postdoctoral**⑦ fellows, and about 250 graduate students. There are 700 people at large, including **administrative**⑧ and technical support staff. Total research grant income was over £14m in 2004, and has roughly doubled in the last decade.

M: 现在是十月，诺贝尔奖获得者通常会在这个月公布。我在想今年的诺贝尔物理学奖会颁给谁呢?

J: 可能得奖者会是在卡文迪什实验室工作的科学家吧。毕竟在卡文迪什实验室的历史上，总共有 29 位科学家获得诺贝尔奖。

M: 29 位获奖者，这个成就真是辉煌啊！

J: 卡文迪什实验室是剑桥大学的物理系。而这个物理系本身就是（剑桥大学）物理科学学院的一部分。

M: 这个实验室始建于 1873 年，当时是作为教学实验室使用的。它最初位于剑桥大学中心一个叫“自由学派巷”的小巷子。被持续多年的空间问题困扰着，后来卡文迪什实验室于 20 世纪 70 年代早期搬到了剑桥西区。

J: 1851 年伦敦万国博览会的成功举办，凸显了通过实践培养人才的重要性。而工业社会要发展也需要通过实践培养更多的科学家和工程师。

M: 在剑桥大学保证为实验物理教授提供一定资助后，德文郡七世公爵威廉·卡文迪什出资 6300 英镑为剑桥建了一间物理实验室。

J: 很长一段时间以来，卡文迪什实验室一直是物理学的中心。自 1874 年建成以来，

① force of gravity 重力
② yield *v.* 产生
③ accurate *adj.* 精确的
④ gravitational constant 重力常数
⑤ mass *n.* 质量
⑥ approximately *adv.* 大概，近乎
⑦ postdoctoral *adj.* 博士后的
⑧ administrative *adj.* 行政的，管理的

它就在物理学的探索和创新上创造了辉煌的历史。所以卡文迪什实验室出现过那么多诺贝尔奖获得者并不令人感到惊讶。

M: 我也听说卡文迪什实验室有很悠久的历史，它在剑桥大学的发展历程中起到了重要的作用。啊！我想起来了，DNA 结构的发现者沃森和克里克就曾在卡文迪什实验室工作过。

J: 是的。当沃森从美国来到卡文迪什实验室时克里克已经在那工作了，他们两人一起发现了 DNA 的双螺旋结构。卡文迪什实验室对生物学有重要影响，因为它将 X 射线结晶学应用到了生物分子结构的研究当中。

M: 看起来卡文迪什实验室不仅在物理学领域，而且在其他很多领域都颇具影响力。

J: 你知道卡文迪什实验室是以谁的名字命名的吗?

M: 我当然知道，它是以威廉·卡文迪什的名字命名的，因为威廉·卡文迪什捐了一大笔钱给这个实验室，以纪念他博学的亲戚。

J: 他博学的亲戚？是谁?

M: 他就是亨利·卡文迪什，著名的物理学家。他以发现氢和做出卡文迪什实验而出名。

J: 我在一篇文章上看到过卡文迪什实验。这是首次能在实验室中测试出重力的实验。这次实验也首次得出重力常数和地球质量的精确数值。

M: 卡文迪什实验室现在的情况怎么样?

J: 现在该实验室有 65 名教员，近 150 名博士后研究生，约 250 名研究生。包括行政人员和教辅人员在内，该实验室总共有 700 人。2004 年，实验室总的研究赞助经费超过 1400 万英镑，赞助经费在上一个 10 年中增长了一倍左右。

难点解析

1 William Cavendish, the Seventh Duke of Devonshire, provided £6,300 to meet the costs of building a physics laboratory, **on condition that** Cambridge provided the funding for a Professorship of Experimental Physics.

on condition that 意为“在……条件下，如果”。

➤ I'll come on condition that John is invited too.
如果约翰也受到邀请，我就来。

2 Do you know that the Cavendish Laboratory is **named after** whom?

name sb\sth after 意为“以……的名字给某人、某物命名”。

➢ Bill is named after his father.
比尔以其父亲的名字命名。

➢ The college is named for George Washington.
这所学院以乔治·华盛顿的名字命名。

3 Of course, it is named after William Cavendish, because he gives money to endow the laboratory **in memory of** his learned relative.

in memory of 意为“为了纪念（已经故去的某人）”，也可以说 to the memory of。

➢ She set up a charitable fund in memory of his father.
她设立了一项慈善基金以纪念他的父亲。

➢ A monument was dedicated to the memory of the national hero.
人们建立了一座纪念碑以纪念这位民族英雄。

4 There are 700 people **at large**, including administrative and technical support staff.

at large 意为“一般来说，普遍来说，（囚犯）在逃”。

➢ It is disturbing to think that a dangerous wild animal is still at large in the quiet countryside.
一想到这头危险的野生动物还游荡在宁静的乡村里，真是让人担心。

The Cavendish Laboratory

Since its foundation, the Laboratory has had great fortune in appointing Cavendish professors who, between them, have changed completely our understanding of the physical world.

In 1871, James Clerk Maxwell was elected as the first professor at the Cavendish, but the laboratory itself was not finally completed until 1874. **Whilst**① he was at the Cavendish he did not add greatly to his original contributions. However, he established a laboratory where students were taught that properly conducted experiments constituted the only true ba-

① whilst 当……时，可是，虽然

sis of physics, and he began the research **school**[①] whose standards or experiments and **theoretical**[②] work played a vital role in the birth of modern physics.

Maxwell's successor, Lord Rayleigh, was appointed in 1879, and continued work on electrical standards **initiated**[③] by Maxwell as well as carrying out research into a very wide range of subjects from **telescopes**[④] to sound waves. By the time Rayleigh had left, the Cavendish was well established as a leading research laboratory.

Under its new head, J. J. Thomson, it grew into an outstanding institution in which many of the world's greatest physicists were either to be trained or in which they were able to conduct their researches. Thomson himself, though no great experimenter, was able, with **primitive**[⑤] and simple equipment, to unravel many of the secrets of the atom. He discovered the electron, and this discovery was the first step in the development of modern atomic theory.

One of the scientists who was attracted by the reputation of the Cavendish was the young New Zealander, Ernest Rutherford. He succeeded Thomson as professor of physics in 1918. Many of his famous experiments which helped explain the nature of **radioactivity**[⑥] and the structure of the atom were conducted with **apparatus**[⑦] of astonishing simplicity, in keeping with the traditions of the laboratory.

The list of Nobel Prize winners who passed through the Cavendish in the time of Thomson and Rutherford is imposing, the 50 years of their combined **tenures**[⑧] marking a period in which the laboratory played a central role in the development of nuclear science.

The next phase of development is the reconstruction of the Laboratory to meet the challenges of the 21st century. The major redevelopment program continues the tradition of innovation and **originality**[⑨] that has been at the heart of the Laboratory's program since its foundation.

---

① school *n.* 学派
② theoretical *adj.* 理论上的
③ initiate *v.* 开始，创始
④ telescope *n.* 望远镜
⑤ primitive *adj.* 原始的，简陋的
⑥ radioactivity *n.* 放射能
⑦ apparatus *n.* 装置，设备
⑧ tenure *n.* 任期
⑨ originality *n.* 独创性，原创性

卡文迪什实验室的风水

自成立以来，卡文迪什实验室在指派卡文迪什教授（指的是上文的实验物理学教授，即实验室或物理系主任，译者注）方面取得了极大的收获。杰出的卡文迪什教授们彻底改变了我们对物理世界的看法。

1871年，詹姆斯·克拉克·麦克斯韦当选第一任卡文迪什教授，但是卡文迪什实验室直到1874年才完全建好。虽然身处设备一流的卡文迪什实验室，麦克斯韦并没有为自己的研究锦上添花。但是，他“创立”了一个实验室，在那里学生们被告知，准确执行的实验才是组建物理学基础的唯一方法。麦克斯韦还创立了一个研究学派，该学派的操作规范或实验、理论工作在现代物理学诞生中起到了至关重要的作用。

麦克斯韦的继任者——瑞利勋爵于1879年上任。他继续致力于研究麦克斯韦提出的电学标准，同时还把研究范围扩大，从望远镜到声波，包罗万象。当瑞利卸任时，卡文迪什实验室已经是研究工作实验室的领头羊了。

在新领导J. J. 汤姆生的领导下，卡文迪什实验室已经发展成了一个杰出的机构，世界上顶尖的物理学家要么在这里接受培训，要么在这里进行研究。虽然汤姆生本身不是一个杰出的实验员，他却能用简陋的的设备发现原子能的许多秘密。汤姆生还发现了电子，这一发现是现代原子理论发展的第一步。

很多科学家被卡文迪什实验室的声望所吸引，年轻的新西兰学者欧内斯特·卢瑟福就是其中之一。1918年，他成为继汤姆生之后的实验物理学教授。他的许多有助于解释放射能本质和原子结构的著名实验都是用极为简单的设备完成的，和卡文迪什实验室的传统保持了一致。

在汤姆生和卢瑟福领导时期，获得诺贝尔奖的卡文迪什实验室的科学家名单数量惊人。汤姆生和卢瑟福在任的50年里，卡文迪什实验室始终在世界核科学的发展中占据核心地位。

卡文迪什实验室的下一个发展时期则是重组、改造以适应21世纪挑战的时期。主要的改造项目延续了创新和原创的传统，自成立以来，这一直是卡文迪什实验室项目的核心本质。

20 Origin of Species and Darwin
物种起源与达尔文

William and Alice are watching a documentary film about Darwin.

W: William　　A: Alice

W: Do you believe that human beings are created by God?

A: I'm an **antitheist**[①], so I can't say yes to that. It is now generally believed that men have evolved from the **ape-men**[②].

W: I'm not a Christian either. I tend to agree with what Darwin wrote in his book *Origin of Species*.

A: Darwin was really a genius. His **natural selection theory**[③] was a very **radical**[④] thought at that time.

W: At the 19th century, almost everyone believed in religion and Darwin's theory was a real thunderbolt to them. And there were people who try to deny Darwin's theory.

A: It had been supposed that Darwin **renounced**[⑤] evolution on his **deathbed**[⑥]. Shortly after his death, **temperance**[⑦] campaigner and **evangelist**[⑧] Lady Elizabeth Hope claimed she visited Darwin on his deathbed, and witnessed the renunciation. Her story was printed in a Boston newspaper and subsequently spread.

---

① antitheist *n.* 无神论者
② ape-man *n.* 猿人
③ natural selection theory 自然选择学说
④ radical *adj.* 激进的
⑤ renounce *v.* 放弃，否认
⑥ deathbed *n.* 临终前
⑦ temperance *n.* 禁欲
⑧ evangelist *n.* 福音传道者

W: But Lady Hope's story was **refuted**① by Darwin's daughter Henrietta. Henrietta stated, "I was present at his deathbed. He never **recanted**② any of his scientific views, either then or earlier."

A: Darwin truly believed in his theory. Though he avoided arguing the **evolution**③, natural selection and the **origins of species**④ with people, he never gave up his thought.

W: By the way, Darwin entered the Christ's College, Cambridge when he was a youth. How would he become a naturalist and antitheist?

A: It was his father's idea to go to Cambridge. He was not interested in medicine and he neglected to study when he was in the University of Edinburgh Medical School. This annoyed his father, who **shrewdly**⑤ sent him to Christ's College, Cambridge, for a Bachelor of Arts degree as the first step towards becoming an **Anglican parson**⑥.

W: Darwin wasn't interested in religion either. But his studies at the University of Cambridge encouraged his passion for natural science.

A: That's true. And he met two influential scholars who helped him a lot in his research on species in Cambridge.

W: But Darwin's research was not a plain sailing. When he was going to join Beagle to conduct a **scientific expedition**⑦ around the world, his father objected to this two-year planned **voyage**⑧. His father regarded it as a waste of time, but was at last persuaded by his brother-in-law, Josiah Wedgwood, to agree to his son's participation.

A: This scientific expedition laid the first stone for Darwin's future study. Without the specimens he collected during the expedition, he couldn't have come up with the theory of natural selection and evolution.

W: Darwin's work had a tremendous impact on religious thought. Many people strongly opposed the idea of evolution because it conflicted with their religious convictions.

A: Darwin avoided talking about the **theological**⑨ and sociological aspects of his work, but other writers used his theories to support their own ideas.

---

① refute *v.* 驳斥
② recant *v.* 放弃主张，撤销
③ evolution *n.* 进化
④ origins of species 物种起源
⑤ shrewdly *adv.* 精明地，机灵地
⑥ Anglican parson 英国国教教区牧师
⑦ scientific expedition 科学探险
⑧ voyage *n.* 航行
⑨ theological *a.* 神学的

W: 你相信人类是由上帝创造的吗?

A: 我是个无神论者，所以不赞同这个说法。今天大家普遍相信人是由猿人进化而来的。

W: 我也不是一个基督徒，所以我比较认同达尔文在《物种起源》中的说法。

A: 达尔文真是一个天才。他的自然选择学说在当时是一个很激进的学说。

W: 在19世纪，几乎每一个人都有宗教信仰，达尔文的理论对他们来说真是一个晴天霹雳。所以有人试图否定达尔文的学说。

A: 据说达尔文在临终前宣布放弃进化论学说。他死后不久，禁欲活动者和福音传道者伊丽莎白·霍普女士宣称她在达尔文临终前拜访了他，并亲眼目睹了上述那一幕。她的故事被刊登在波士顿的一家报纸上，随后传播开来。

W: 但是达尔文的女儿亨利埃塔反驳了霍普女士的说法。亨利埃塔声明:“父亲临终前我在场，他从来没有放弃过他的科学见解，以前没有，临死前也没有。”

A: 达尔文对自己的理论深信不疑。虽然他避免和别人争论进化论、自然选择和物种起源等学说，但他从来没有放弃过自己的观点。

W: 对了，达尔文年轻时曾在剑桥大学基督学院念书。他怎么会成为一个博物学者和无神论者呢?

A: 去剑桥是他父亲的主意。当达尔文在爱丁堡大学医学院念书时他对医学并不感兴趣，荒废了学业，这使他父亲感到苦恼。但他父亲灵机一动，把达尔文送到了剑桥大学基督学院，想让他获得一个文学学士学位，成为英国国教教区牧师。

W: 达尔文对宗教也不感兴趣。但是，在剑桥大学的学习激发了他对自然科学的热情。

A: 的确是这样。而且他在剑桥遇到了两位颇具影响力的学者，他们对达尔文的物种研究帮助很大。

W: 但是达尔文的研究并不是一帆风顺的。当他准备加入贝格尔号进行环游世界的科学探险时，他的父亲反对这个预期两年的航行。他的父亲认为这是浪费时间，但最后他父亲还是被达尔文的舅舅乔舒亚·威基伍德说服了，最后同意他参加科学探险。

A: 这次科学探险为达尔文后来的研究打下了基础。没有这次科学探险收集的标本，他就不会提出自然选择和进化论学说。

W: 达尔文的学说极大地影响了人们的宗教观念。许多人强烈反对进化论，因为这和他们的宗教信仰相冲突。

A: 达尔文避免谈论他工作中有关神学和社会学的方面。但是其他学者会运用达尔文的学说来支撑自己的观点。

1 At the 19th century, almost everyone believed in religion and Darwin's theory was a real **thunderbolt** to them.

thunderbolt 意为"雷电，晴天霹雳，（突然且具毁灭性的猛烈行动的）人或物"。

➢ The unexpected defeat came as a thunderbolt.
这意外的失败犹如晴天霹雳。

2 Shortly after his death, temperance campaigner and evangelist Lady Elizabeth Hope claimed she visited Darwin on his **deathbed**, and witnessed the renunciation.

deathbed，名词，意为"临终前"，通常的用法是 on your / his / her deathbed。

➢ Mrs. Reed's husband, a brother of Jane's mother, instructs his wife on his deathbed to care as tenderly for Jane as for her own three children.
里德太太的丈夫是简·爱母亲的兄弟，临终前他嘱咐妻子亲切关照简，要像对待她自己的三个孩子一样。

➢ The deathbed struggles of the enemies can only hasten their own doom.
敌人的垂死挣扎只能加速他们的灭亡。

3 But Darwin's research was not a **plain sailing**.

plain sailing 意为"一帆风顺"。

➢ Life is difficult navigation and it will not be plain sailing.
人生是艰难的航行，绝不会一帆风顺。

➢ After we solved that problem the rest was a plain sailing.
当我们解决了这个问题，剩余的就顺利了。

4 This scientific expedition **laid the first stone** for Darwin's future study.

lay the first stone 意为"打下基础"。

> What he has learned from school lays the first stone for his future career.
他在学校所学的知识为他将来的职业奠定了基础。

> This article lay the first stone for the design of the personal computer.
本文为设计个人电脑打下了基础。

Origin of Species and Darwin

Charles Darwin was the British naturalist who became famous for his theories of evolution and natural selection. Like several scientists before him, Darwin believed all the life on earth evolved over millions of years from a few common ancestors.

Born in Shrewsbury, Shropshire, England, on February 12, 1809, Darwin was the fifth child of a wealthy family. After graduating from the elite school at Shrewsbury in 1825, young Darwin went to the University of Edinburgh Medical School to study medicine. In 1827 he **dropped out**① of medical school and entered the Christ's College, Cambridge, in preparation for becoming a **clergyman**② of the Church of England. There he met two stellar figures: Adam Sedgwick, a **geologist**③, and John Stevens Henslow, a naturalist. Henslow not only helped build Darwin's self-confidence but also taught him to be a **meticulous**④ and **painstaking**⑤ observer of natural phenomena and collector of specimens. After graduating from Cambridge in 1831, the 22-year-old Darwin was taken aboard the English survey ship Beagle, largely on Henslow's recommendation, as an unpaid naturalist on a scientific expedition around the world.

In South America Darwin found fossils of extinct animals that were similar to modern

---

① dropped out 辍学
② clergyman *n.* 牧师
③ geologist *n.* 地质学家
④ meticulous *a.* 一丝不苟的
⑤ painstaking *a.* 勤勉的，不辞劳苦的

species. On the Galapagos Islands in the Pacific Ocean he noticed many **variations**[①] among plants and animals of the same general type as those in South America. The expedition visited places around the world, and Darwin studied plants and animals everywhere he went, collecting **specimens**[②] for further study.

Upon his return to London in 1836, Darwin conducted thorough research of his notes and specimens. Out of this study grew several theories: one, evolution did occur; two, evolutionary change was gradual, requiring thousands to millions of years; three, the primary mechanism for evolution was a process called natural selection; and four, the millions of species alive today arose from a single original life form through a process called "**speciation**[③]."

Darwin's theory of evolutionary selection holds that **variation**[④] within species occurs **randomly**[⑤] and that the survival or **extinction**[⑥] of each organism is determined by that organism's ability to adapt to its environment. He set these theories forth in his book called *The Origin of Species* (1859). After publication of *Origin of Species*, Darwin continued to write on **botany**[⑦], **geology**[⑧], and **zoology**[⑨] until his death in 1882.

物种起源与达尔文

查尔斯·达尔文是英国博物学者，因提出进化论和自然选择学说而闻名于世。和科学界前辈一样，达尔文相信地球上的所有生命都是由少数共同的祖先历经数百万年进化而来的。

达尔文于1809年2月12日出生在英格兰希施罗普郡什鲁斯伯里的一个富裕家庭，在家中排行第五。1825年毕业于什鲁斯伯里的一个精英学校后，年轻的达尔文考入爱丁堡大学医学院学习医学。1827年他从医学院辍学并进入剑桥大学基督学院学习，准备成为英国国教牧师。在剑桥达尔文遇见了两位一流的人物：地质学者亚当·塞奇威克和博物学者约翰·斯蒂文·亨斯楼。亨斯楼不仅帮助达尔文建立自信，还教导他要一丝不苟、不辞辛劳地观察自然现象和收集标本。1831年从剑桥大学毕业后，在亨斯楼的大力推荐下，22岁的达尔文作为一名不收报酬的博物学者开始了他环游世界的科学探

① variation *n.* 变种
② specimen *n.* 标本
③ speciation *n.* 物种形成
④ variation *n.* 物种
⑤ randomly *adv.* 随机地
⑥ extinction *n.* 灭绝
⑦ botany *n.* 植物学
⑧ geology *n.* 地质学
⑨ zoology *n.* 动物学

险。

达尔文在南美洲发现了和现代物种相似的灭绝动物的化石。在太平洋的加拉帕哥斯群岛，他注意到，和南美洲的情况一样，同一个大类的动植物的很多变种都是相似的。达尔文随探险队拜访了世界上的许多地方，每到一处，他就开始研究当地的动植物，收集标本以备更深一步的研究。

1836 年回到伦敦后，达尔文对他的笔记和标本就行了深入的研究。他的研究衍生出一些学说：第一，进化的确发生了；第二，进化对于物种的改变是渐进的，需要上千甚至上百万年的时间；第三，产生进化的最主要机制是一种被称为自然选择的进程；第四，当今世上的数百万物种是由一个单一的初级生命形式通过“物种形成”衍生出来的。

达尔文的进化选择学说认为物种的变异是随机发生的，每一个生物体的存活或灭绝是由那个生物体适应环境的能力决定的。1859 年，他在自己的著作《物种起源》中提出了这些学说。《物种起源》出版后，达尔文继续在植物学、地质学和动物学等方面著书立作，一直到 1882 年辞世。

Unit 6 Celebrities & Alumni 桃李满天下

21 Oliver Cromwell 颇具争议的克伦威尔

焦点对话

Adam and Beth are going to take a history class.

A: Adam　　B: Beth

A: Yesterday was the 350th **anniversary**① of Oliver Cromwell's death and this anniversary was "celebrated" by the publication of a new book.

B: I have read that book. That book suggests that the Lord Protector's reputation should be reassessed in the light of two **massacres**② he conducted in Ireland.

A: Oliver Cromwell is a controversial figure in the English history. The **overwhelming**③ majority of the 150 **biographies**④ of Cromwell published over the past century had been favorable. And Cromwell came third in a BBC poll to find the greatest Briton of the second **millennium**⑤. But in Ireland they have long taken a different view.

B: Yes, it is. According to an Irish historian, the **slaughters**⑥ at Drogheda and Wexford which were led by Cromwell in 1649 ranked among the greatest **atrocities**⑦ in Anglo-Irish history. Though Cromwell is England's great **parliamentarian**⑧, he should be

① anniversary *n.* 周年纪念
② massacre *n.* 大屠杀
③ overwhelming *adj.* 巨大的，压倒一切的
④ biography *n.* 自传
⑤ millennium *n.* 千年
⑥ slaughter *n.* 屠杀
⑦ atrocity *n.* 暴行
⑧ parliamentarian *n.* 国会议员

guilty of war crimes, **religious persecution**① and ethnic cleansing.

A: The first major town Cromwell and his army encountered when they landed in Ireland was Drogheda. He **summoned**② the royalist commander and asked him to surrender. When he refused, Cromwell's model army **seized**③ the town and put the entire **garrison**④ of 2,500 officers and men to the sword.

B: It was so cruel. And this act sent shock waves of fear through the rest of Ireland. Other towns **surrendered**⑤ as soon as Cromwell's army approached.

A: But in the eyes of many Britons, he is a hero in the battle between good and evil. And he is a man who restores **morale**⑥ in an age dominated by **expediency**⑦ and compromise, who presses a new political equality and a religious toleration.

B: I can't deny his popularity in England. He has more roads named after him than any other Englishman and woman except Queen Victoria. He is a dominant figure in the memory of British and Irish history, and probably the one with most disagreement.

A: This topic is so serious. Shall we switch to another topic?

B: Sure. Have you ever heard of the ghost of Cromwell? Rumor has it that Cromwell has returned as a ghost to his lifetime **haunts**⑧.

A: Yes. And I often think that, in order for someone to return as a ghost, his life must have been unfulfilled in some way, perhaps ending tragically, **prematurely**⑨, or violently.

B: There have been so many reported sightings of ghosts and odd happenings at Oliver Cromwell's House.

A: Oliver Cromwell's home in Ely has now been turned into a museum documenting Cromwell's life and the history of the Civil War period.

---

① religious persecution 宗教迫害
② summon *v.* 召唤，传召
③ seize *v.* 占领
④ garrison *n.* 守备部队
⑤ surrender *v.* 投降
⑥ morale *n.* 士气，斗志
⑦ expediency *n.* 权宜之计
⑧ haunt *n.* 常去的地方
⑨ prematurely *adv.* 过早地

B: A woman, who once stayed at the house with her husband, described seeing the figure of a powerful man who **gripped**① her arm firmly before disappearing. She believed it was the ghost of Cromwell.

A: Well, it seems we don't need to go to **Madame Tussauds**② to see famous dead British people.

B: Ha-ha, I'd rather choose to go to Madame Tussauds.

A: 昨天是克伦威尔逝世350周年纪念日，有人出版了一本新书，以"庆祝"这个纪念日。

B: 我看过那本书。那本书认为护国公克伦威尔的声誉应该要重新评价，因为他在爱尔兰进行了两次大屠杀。

A: 在英国历史上克伦威尔是一个有争议的人物。上世纪以来出版的150本克伦威尔的传记中的绝大多数都是对克伦威尔赞誉有加的。在BBC的一个"寻找2000年以来最杰出的英国人"的投票中，克伦威尔排名第三。但是爱尔兰人早就对他心怀不满。

B: 是的，他的确有争议性。一名爱尔兰历史学家认为，1649年由克伦威尔领导的德洛格达和韦克斯福德大屠杀在英国——爱尔兰历史上是最残酷的暴行之一。虽然克伦威尔是英格兰杰出的国会议员，他也应该为战争罪、宗教迫害和种族清洗感到内疚。

A: 当克伦威尔和他的军队登陆爱尔兰时，德洛格达是他们进入的第一个主要城镇。克伦威尔传召德洛格达的保皇党指挥官并让他投降。当指挥官拒绝投降时，克伦威尔的模范军就占领了整个城镇并杀死守备部队共计2500名军官和平民。

B: 这真是残酷。这一举动在爱尔兰的其他地方引起了恐惧的震动。克伦威尔的军队一接近某个城镇，那个城镇就投降。

A: 但在很多英国人眼里，克伦威尔是正义和邪恶之战中涌现出来的英雄。在一个充斥着权宜之计和妥协的时代，他重振了士气。他推动并执行了一种新的政治平等和宗教宽容。

B: 我不否认克伦威尔在英格兰很受欢迎。除了维多利亚女王外，以克伦威尔名字命

① grip *v.* 紧握，抓紧

② Madame Tussauds 杜莎夫人蜡像馆，是全世界水平最高的蜡像馆之一，有众多世界名人的蜡像。

名的道路比任何一个英国人都要多。在英国和爱尔兰历史的回忆中，他是一个主宰人物，可能也是争议最多的一个。

A: 这个话题太严肃了，我们换其他话题好吗？

B: 好啊。你听说过克伦威尔的幽灵吗？据传闻，克伦威尔化作鬼魂回到了他生前住的地方。

A: 我也听过这个传闻。而且我经常想，某人要化作鬼魂归来，他的生活必须是在某种意义上没有得到满足，可能是悲剧性、过早地死去或是死于非命。

B: 据报道，有很多人看见克伦威尔的房子里有鬼魂和奇怪的事情发生。

A: 克伦威尔在伊利的家现在已经变成一个博物馆，记录克伦威尔的生活和英国内战时期的历史。

B: 一个曾经和丈夫一起在克伦威尔房子里呆过的女人，说她看见了一个强壮的男人，那个男人在消失之前牢牢地抓住她的肩膀。她相信那就是克伦威尔的幽灵。

A: 那看来我们不必去杜莎夫人蜡像馆看故去的英国名人了。

B: 哈哈，我还是宁愿去杜莎夫人蜡像馆。

1 That book suggests that the Lord Protector's reputation should be reassessed **in the light of** two massacres he conducted in Ireland.

in the light of 意为"鉴于，由于"。

➤ He reviews his policy in the light of recent developments.
他根据最近的事态发展重新考虑自己的方针。

➤ He reviewed the proposals in the light of past experience.
他照老经验来评论那些建议。

2 When he refused, Cromwell's model army seized the town and **put** the entire garrison of 2,500 officers and men **to the sword**.

put… to the sword 意为"杀死，屠杀"。

➤ All the prisoners were put to the sword.
所有的囚犯都被处死了。

3 Other towns surrendered **as soon as** Cromwell's army approached.

as soon as 意为"一……，就……"; as soon as possible 意为"尽快，尽可能快"。

➢ We need to send the letter off as soon as possible.
我们要尽可能快地把这封信寄出去。

➢ I came as soon as I heard the news.
我一听到消息马上就来了。

4 Rumor has it that Cromwell has returned as ghosts to his lifetime haunts.

rumor has it 意为"据谣传，传闻"。

➢ Rumor has it that the Cabinet will be reshuffled in February next year.
传闻内阁将于明年二月改组。

➢ Rumor has it that the factory was burned down.
谣传那家工厂被大火烧毁了。

Oliver Cromwell

Oliver Cromwell was born on 25 April 1599 in Huntingdon, Cambridgeshire into a family of **minor genre**① and studied at Cambridge University. He became member of parliament for Huntingdon in the parliament of 1628-1629. In the 1630s Cromwell experienced a religious crisis and became convinced that he would be guided to **carry out**② God's purpose. He began to make his name as a radical **Puritan**③.

Civil war④ broke out between Charles I and parliament in 1642. Although Cromwell lacked military experience, he created and led a superb force of **cavalry**⑤, the 'Ironsides', and rose from the rank of **captain**⑥ to that of **lieutenant-general**⑦ in three years. He convinced parliament to establish a professional army, the New Model Army, which won the **decisive**⑧ victory over the king's forces at Naseby (1645). The king's **alliance**⑨ with the Scots

① gentry *n.* 贵族
② carry out 执行，实现
③ Puritan *n.* 清教徒
④ Civil war 英国内战，是 1642 年至 1651 年在英国议会派与保皇派之间发生的一系列武装冲突及政治斗争。
⑤ cavalry *n.* 骑兵
⑥ captain *n.* 上尉
⑦ lieutenant-general *n.* 中将
⑧ decisive *adj.* 决定性的
⑨ alliance *n.* 结盟

and his subsequent defeat in the Second Civil War convinced Cromwell that the king must be brought to justice. He was a prime mover in the trial and execution of Charles I in 1649 and subsequently sought to win conservative support for the new republic by suppressing radial elements in the army. Cromwell became army commander and lord lieutenant of Ireland, where he **crushed**① resistance with the massacres at Drogheda and Wexford (1649).

Cromwell then defeated the supporters of the king's son Charles II at Dunbar and Worcester, effectively ending the civil war. In 1653, frustrated with lack of progress, he dissolved the **rump**② of the Long Parliament and, after the failure of his Puritan convention made himself lord protector. At home, Cromwell reorganised the national church, established Puritanism **readmitted**③ Jews into Britain and supported over a certain degree of religious tolerance. Abroad, he ended the war with Portugal and Holland and allied with France against Spain, defeating the Spanish at the Battle of the Dunes.

In 1658 he was struck by a sudden bout of malarial fever, followed directly by illness of a urinary **complaint**④. He died on 3 September, 1658. When the **Royalists**⑤ returned to power in 1661, Oliver Cromwell's body was **exhumed**⑥ from Westminster Abbey, and was hung in chains and beheaded. **Symbolically**⑦, this took place on 30 January; the same date that Charles I had been executed.

颇具争议的克伦威尔

奥利弗·克伦威尔 1599 年 4 月 25 日出生于英国剑桥郡亨廷顿的一个小贵族家庭，求学于剑桥大学。他在 1628—1629 年议会中成为亨廷顿议会的议员。17 世纪 30 年代，克伦威尔经历了一次宗教危机，而后他开始相信他将受到指引，执行上帝的意愿。克伦威尔开始以激进的清教徒身份而闻名。

1642 年，国王查理一世和议会的矛盾激化，英国内战爆发。虽然克伦威尔缺乏军

① crush *v.* 镇压
② rump *n.* 余党，余众
③ readmit *v.* 重新接纳
④ complaint *n.* 并发症
⑤ Royalist *n.* 保皇党人
⑥ exhume *v.* 挖出，发掘出
⑦ symbolically *adv.* 象征性地

事经验，但他创建并带领了一支优秀的骑兵部队“勇敢之人”，仅用了3年，就从上尉升至中将。他说服议会组建一支专业军队—新模范军。1645年，新模范军在纳西比与国王军队的交锋中取得决定性胜利。国王和苏格兰的结盟以及国王随后在二次内战中的败北让克伦威尔坚信国王必须要归案受审。克伦威尔推动了1649年对查理一世的审判和处决。随后，为了新共和国，他镇压军中的激进力量，以寻求保守势力的支持。1649年，克伦威尔成为军队总司令和爱尔兰总督。他在德洛格达和韦克斯福德实施大屠杀，镇压爱尔兰的抵抗。

克伦威尔随后在登巴和沃塞斯特击败了国王的儿子查理二世，高效地结束了内战。1653年，长期议院的清教徒大会推举克伦威尔为护国公遭到失败，而后他苦于没有进展解散了长期议院。对内，克伦威尔重组了英国教会，建立了清教，重新接纳犹太人到英国来，并支持一定程度上的宗教宽容。对外，他结束了英国和葡萄牙、荷兰的战争，并和法国结盟对抗西班牙，最终在沙丘战役中击败了西班牙。

1658年，克伦威尔被一次突发的疟疾高烧袭倒，紧随高烧而来的是泌尿系统的并发症。他于1658年9月3日辞世。当1661年保皇党成员重新掌权后，奥利弗·克伦威尔的尸体被人从威斯敏斯特教堂掘出，人们还用铁链吊起他的尸体，并进行“斩首”。具有象征性意味的是，这发生在1月30日，和查理一世被处死是同一天。

22 Sherlock Holmes, Where is he
寻找福尔摩斯

焦点对话

Nete is reading a novel in a coffee shop while Steven is walking towards her.

N: Nete　　S: Steven

S: Hi, Nete, what are you reading?

N: *A Study in Scarlet*. Have you heard of it?

S: Oh, yes. The **hero**① of this novel is Sherlock Holmes. And I'm a huge fan of Holmes.

N: Holmes is renowned for his **astute**② observation and **deductive reasoning**③. And he uses **forensic**④ skills to solve difficult cases.

S: Every novel that featured in Holmes is so **thrilling**⑤ that you could hardly bear to put it down.

N: I can't agree with you more. As soon as I buy a novel about Holmes, I'll read it at a stretch.

S: Of the Sherlock Holmes novels, *The Hound of the Baskervilles* is probably the best known. It has been made into a film over twenty times with adaptations in languages as diverse as Indian, German, Russian and Italian.

N: That one is my favorite, too. And I'm interested not only in Holmes but also Watson.

S: In the novel, Holmes shared the majority of his professional years with his good friend

① hero *n.* 主人公
② astute *adj.* 敏锐的，精明的
③ deductive reasoning 演绎推理
④ forensic *adj.* 法医的
⑤ thrilling *adj.* 精彩刺激的

Watson. Watson lived with Holmes for some time before he got married in 1887, and again after his wife's death.

N: Watson has two roles in Holmes' life. First, he gives practical assistance in the conduct of Holmes' cases; second, he is Holmes' **chronicler**①.

S: Yes, most of the Holmes stories are frame **narratives**②, written from Watson's point of view as summaries of the detective's most interesting cases.

N: Where did Holmes and Watson live?

S: They lived in London at 221B Baker Street. This real house has been **converted into**③ a museum and is the first museum in the world to be dedicated to a **fictional**④ character.

N: This museum maybe added to the impression that Sherlock Holmes really existed.

S: Yes, exactly. According to a recent survey, 58% of British people thought that Sherlock Holmes really existed!

N: And given details in two of the adventures, fans thought that Holmes must have been at the University of Cambridge.

S: Perhaps Holmes studied biology and **anatomy**⑤ at **Sidney Sussex College**⑥, Cambridge, because that offered the greatest number of advantages to Holmes.

N: The fact is Holmes is the creation of Sir Arthur Conan Doyle. But Doyle had a love-hate relationship with his most popular creation. He killed Holmes off in a story called "The Final Problem" but the public **outcry**⑦ led him to bring the character back. The fact is Conan Doyle wanted to be respected for his other writing as well.

S: By the way, have you watched the movie *Sherlock Holmes* **starring**⑧ Robert Downey Jr and Jude Law.

N: Well, I'm going to watch it this weekend. I have watched the **trailer**⑨ of *Sherlock Holmes* and it seems quite nice.

S: In the Guinness book of World Records Sherlock Holmes is listed as the most portrayed movie character with over 70 actors playing the part in over 200 films.

---

① chronicler *n.* 年代记录者
② narrative *n.* 叙事
③ convert into 转变成……
④ fictional *adj.* 虚构的
⑤ anatomy *n.* 解剖学
⑥ Sidney Sussex College 悉尼·苏塞克斯学院
⑦ outcry *n.* 公开反对
⑧ star *v.* 主演
⑨ trailer *n.* 预告片

S: 嗨，内特，你在读什么呢?

N:《血字的研究》，你听过这本小说吗?

S: 当然了。这本小说的主人公是福尔摩斯。我是福尔摩斯的大粉丝。

N: 福尔摩斯因他敏锐的观察力和演绎推理能力而享誉于世。他还运用法医技巧来解决疑案。

S: 每一本关于福尔摩斯的小说都精彩得让人爱不释手。

N: 你说的太对了。每买一本福尔摩斯的小说，我都会一口气把它读完。

S: 在福尔摩斯的小说系列中，《巴斯克维尔的猎犬》可能是最有名的。它至少 20 次被改编为电影，以印度语、德语、俄语和意大利语等多种语言呈现。

N:《巴斯克维尔的猎犬》也是我最喜欢的小说。我不仅对福尔摩斯着迷，而且对华生也很感兴趣。

S: 在小说里，福尔摩斯职业生涯的大部分时光是和他的好朋友华生一起度过的。华生在 1887 年结婚之前，和福尔摩斯住了一段时间，他妻子去世后，又和福尔摩斯住在一起了。

N: 华生在福尔摩斯的生活中扮演着两个角色。首先，在福尔摩斯破案的过程中，华生给与了他很多帮助。其次，他还是福尔摩斯破案的记录者。

S: 是啊，绝大多数福尔摩斯故事都遵循着相同的叙事模式，都是借华生之口讲述福尔摩斯精彩的断案故事。

N: 福尔摩斯和华生住在哪里?

S: 他们住在伦敦贝克街 221B 号。这个真实存在的房子已经被改造成一个博物馆。这是世界上第一个为虚构角色而建立的博物馆。

N: 有了这个博物馆，人们更坚信有夏洛克·福尔摩斯这个人存在了。

S: 的确是这样。不久前的一个调查显示，58% 的英国人认为真的有福尔摩斯这个人!

N: 从关于福尔莫斯的小说中两次探险的细节来看，粉丝们认为福尔摩斯肯定在剑桥大学念过书。

S: 福尔摩斯可能在剑桥大学的悉尼·苏塞克斯学院学过生物学和解剖学，因为这会给福尔摩斯带来很大帮助。

N: 事实上福尔摩斯是阿瑟·柯南·道尔爵士虚构出来的角色。但是道尔爵士对这个最受欢迎的角色爱恨交加。在《最后一案》里，他把福尔摩斯“消灭”掉了，但是公众的义愤迫使他让福尔摩斯“死而复生”。事实上柯南·道尔希望他能够因其他的作品而受到尊重。

S: 对了，你看过由小罗伯特·唐尼和裘德·洛主演的电影《大侦探福尔摩斯》吗?

N: 我打算周末去看。我已经看了这部电影的预告片了，看起来还不错。

S: 在吉尼斯世界纪录中，夏洛克·福尔摩斯这个电影角色的扮演者是史上最多的，曾有 70 多个演员分别在 200 多部电影中扮演过福尔摩斯。

1 As soon as I buy a novel about Holmes, I'll read it **at a stretch**.

at a stretch 意为“一口气地，连续不断地”。

➢ She worked for six hours at a stretch.
她连续工作了 6 个小时。

➢ You are so great to tell those numbers at a stretch.
你一口气就能把那些数字说出来，真了不起。

2 It has been **made into** a film over twenty times with adaptations in languages as diverse as Indian, German, Russian and Italian.

make into 意为“把……做成，把……转化成，使成为”。

➢ The basement has been made into a workshop.
地下室已改成工作间了。

➢ I think it impossible that hydrogen can ever be make into a metal.
我认为氢气能被制成一种金属是不可能的。

3 This real house has been converted into a museum and is the first museum in the world to be **dedicated to** a fictional character.

dedicate to 意为“献(身)于……，把(时间、精力等)用于……，(写)……以献给某人”。

➢ The soldier dedicated himself to the service of the people.
这名战士献身于为人民服务。

➢ So, find what thrills you and dedicate your time to going for it.
所以，找到令你兴奋的事情，然后全身心地投入进去。

4 But Doyle had a **love-hate relationship** with his most popular creation.

love-hate relationship 意为“爱恨交加的关系”。

➢ Switzerland, in its love-hate relationship with the rich, has for years been fining wealthy drivers more than non-wealthy drivers.
瑞士是一个让富人既爱又恨的国家。在瑞士，由于罚金多少与财富多寡挂钩，富人驾车违规所受的罚金多年来一直高于普通人群。

Sherlock Holmes, Where Is He

Sherlock Holmes is a fictional character of the late nineteenth and early twentieth century who first appeared in **publication**① in 1887. He was the creation of Scottish author and **physician**② Sir Arthur Conan Doyle.

Sir Arthur Conan Doyle was born in **Edinburgh**③, Scotland. He studied to be a doctor at the University of Edinburgh and set up a small **practice**④ at Southsea in **Hampshire**⑤ during his 20s. While the practice proved largely unsuccessful, the lack of patients provided him with the opportunity to create possibly the most popular character ever introduced in the history of **fiction**⑥, Sherlock Holmes.

While at University, Conan Doyle had been greatly influenced by Dr. Joseph Bell, one of his professors. Bell was an expert in the use of deductive reasoning to diagnose disease. Conan Doyle was so impressed that he used these same principles when creating his famous **detective**⑦.

Sherlock Holmes was introduced in *A Study in Scarlet*, followed by *A Sign of Four* in 1890, but didn't really **take hold of**⑧ the public's imagination until *Strand* magazine, newly founded in 1890, published a series of short stories called *The Adventures of Sherlock Hol-*

---

① publication *n.* 出版物
② physician *n.* 内科医生
③ Edinburgh 爱丁堡
④ practice *n.* 诊所
⑤ Hampshire 汉普郡
⑥ fiction *n.* 小说
⑦ detective *n.* 侦探
⑧ take hold of 控制住，吸引

mes. From that point on the public couldn't get enough of Holmes and his always reliable confidant, John Watson.

Residing[1] in London at 221B Baker Street, with his **keen**[2] sense of observation, lean face, **hooked nose**[3], and his ever-present pipe, Holmes's character and personality set him apart from all others. This personality is what caught the reader's imagination.

From 1891 to 1893, Strand published stories featuring Holmes and Watson, all **avidly**[4] followed by the public. When in *The Final Problem*, Holmes and his longtime enemy, Professor Moriarty, are killed off, the public outcry was so great, Conan Doyle was forced to bring him back to life. He continued the **exploits**[5] of Holmes and Watson nine years later in *The Hound of the Baskervilles*.

Sherlock Holmes is without doubt one of the most beloved figures in the history of mystery fiction. In all, Holmes and Watson were featured in four novels and 56 short stories.

Despite the success of his most famous character, **throughout**[6] his adult life Conan Doyle sought to escape the Sherlock Holmes phenomenon and concentrate on writing about his other interests.

寻找福尔摩斯

夏洛克·福尔摩斯是19世纪晚期至20世纪早期的一个虚构角色，他第一次出现在公众视野是在1887年。福尔摩斯是由苏格兰作家、内科医生阿瑟·柯南·道尔爵士创作出来的。

阿瑟·柯南·道尔爵士出生于苏格兰爱丁堡。为了能成为医生，他到爱丁堡大学学习医学。20岁时，道尔在英国的汉普郡南海城开了一个小诊所。这个诊所开得不太成功，来看病的人很少，这使得他有机会创作出小说史上最受欢迎的角色——夏洛克·福尔摩斯。

大学期间，柯南·道尔受他的老师，约瑟夫·贝尔医生影响很大。贝尔是运用推理诊断疾病的专家，他给柯南·道尔留下了深刻印象。在创作侦探福尔摩斯这个著名角色时，柯南·道尔运用了同样的推

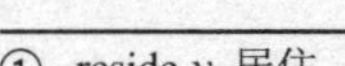

① reside *v.* 居住
② keen *adj.* 敏锐的
③ hooked nose 鹰钩鼻
④ avidly *adv.* 热心地
⑤ exploit *n.* 功绩，事迹
⑥ throughout *prep.* 自始至终，在……期间

理方法。

夏洛克·福尔摩斯是在《血字的研究》中出场的，在1890年的《四签名》中再次出现。但是直到创刊于1890年的《海滨杂志》刊登了一系列名为“福尔摩斯历险记”的短篇小说后，福尔摩斯才成为公众关注的焦点。从那时起，公众总是对福尔摩斯和他忠诚的密友约翰·华生的故事欲罢不能。

福尔摩斯居住在伦敦贝克街221B号，他观察敏锐、脸颊消瘦、鼻似鹰钩，经常叼着烟斗，不俗的长相和鲜明的个性让他在人群中卓尔不凡，正是这种人格魅力引发了读者的无限遐想。

从1891年到1893年，《海滨杂志》发表了一系列关于福尔摩斯和华生的小说，受到公众的热烈追捧。在《最后一案》中，福尔摩斯和他的死敌莫里亚蒂教授被“杀死”了，引起了民众很大的激愤，柯南·道尔不得不让福尔摩斯起死回生。在9年后的《巴斯克维尔的猎犬》中，他继续讲述着福尔摩斯和华生的故事。

在悬疑小说历史上，福尔摩斯无疑是最受人喜爱的一个角色。福尔摩斯和华生总共在4个长篇小说和56个短故事中出现过。

虽然柯南·道尔成功塑造了福尔摩斯这个著名角色，但在生活中，柯南·道尔总是试图逃避夏洛克·福尔摩斯现象并专注于其他方面的写作。

23 Samuel Pepys's Diaries
塞缪尔·佩皮斯的日记

焦点对话

Tina is writing a diary while Jim is walking towards her.

J: Jim　　T: Tina

J: What are you writing, Tina?

T: I'm writing a dairy.

J: Oh, keeping a dairy is a good habit, but I'm not used to it.

T: Influenced by Samuel Pepys, I started to keep a dairy last year.

J: Samuel Pepys? The guy who recorded great events, such as the **Great Plague of London**[1], the **Second Anglo–Dutch War**[2] and the **Great Fire of London**[3] in his diary?

T: Yes, it's him. *The Diary of Samuel Pepys* is the **collected works**[4] of his diaries. But *The Diary of Samuel Pepys* was collected by someone else, unlike other diarists of his time; Pepys had no **aspirations**[5] for publication.

J: And this freed him up to paint a frank portrait of life in London at the time of the Restoration.

T: Yes, you're right. Throughout the work, which spans from 1660 to 1669, Pepys offered his firsthand sources

---

① Great Plague of London 伦敦大瘟疫，在这次大瘟疫期间，伦敦死亡的人口超过了万人。

② Second Anglo–Dutch War 第二次英荷战争，英国与荷兰为争夺殖民地市场和海上霸权所进行的战争。

③ Great Fire of London 伦敦大火，伦敦历史上最严重的一次火灾，烧掉了许多建筑物，包括圣保罗大教堂。

④ collected works 文集，文选

⑤ aspiration *n.* 强烈的愿望，抱负

on the major events during the Restoration, including his own role in helping to bring Charles II back from **exile**[①] to become king.

J: His diaries recorded his aid in both the Great Plague of 1665 and the Great Fire of 1666, too.

T: The coverage gives *The Diary of Samuel Pepys* a historic distinction as well as a literary one.

J: In some degree, Pepys's diary is not so much a record of events as a re-creation of them. Pepys's achievement rests on his close observation and total recall of detail. It is the small **touches**[②] that achieve the effect.

T: And what contribute to his success is the freshness and **flexibility**[③] of the language. Pepys writes quickly in **shorthand**[④] and for himself alone. The words, often pile on top of each other without much respect for formal grammar, exactly reflect the impressions of the moment.

J: Instead of writing a **considered**[⑤] narrative, Pepys shows us hundreds of scenes from life — civil servants in committee, Members of parliament in debate, concerts of music, friends on a river outing.

T: The diary's contents are characterized also by its geographical setting. It is a London diary, with only occasional **glimpses**[⑥] of the countryside.

J: As luck would have it, Pepys wrote in the decade when London suffered two of its great disasters—the Plague of 1665 and the Great Fire of the following year.

T: He wrote the dairy in a **cryptic**[⑦] code, which was his own **variation**[⑧] on an existing form of shorthand.

J: Fearing that he was going blind from writing, Pepys stopped recording entries in his diary in 1669 and had his entire diary bound for his personal library, which he left to Magdalene College, Cambridge University—his **alma mater**[⑨].

T: It wasn't rediscovered until 1819, more than one hundred fifty years later, at which point the Master of the College had a student decipher Pepys's codes.

---

① exile *n.* 流亡
② touch *n.*（细节上的）润色，修饰，点缀
③ flexibility *n.* 弹性，灵活性
④ shorthand *n.* 速记（法）
⑤ considered *adj.* 深思熟虑的
⑥ glimpse *n.* 一瞥，一看
⑦ cryptic *adj.* 隐秘的
⑧ variation *n.* 变形，变种
⑨ alma mater 母校

J: 你在写什么，汤姆?

T: 我在写日记。

J: 噢，记日记是一个好习惯，但我就没有这个习惯。

T: 受塞缪尔·佩皮斯的影响，我从去年开始写日记。

J: 塞缪尔·佩皮斯? 就是那个在日记中记录了很多大事件，如伦敦大瘟疫、第二次英荷战争和伦敦大火的人吗?

T: 是的，就是他。《塞缪尔·佩皮斯日记》是他的日记集。和那时的日记作者不同的是，《塞缪尔·佩皮斯日记》是由其他人收集整理的，佩皮斯本人并不打算出版。

J: 这使得佩皮斯有精力来描绘一幅真实的王政复辟时期的伦敦生活画卷。

T: 是的，你说得很对。在 1660 年到 1669 年的日记中，佩皮斯提供了王政复辟时期重大事件的第一手资料，包括他是如何帮助流亡中的查理二世重登国王宝座的。

J: 佩皮斯的日记还记录了他在 1665 年大瘟疫和 1666 年大火中提供的援助。

T: 这些记载让《塞缪尔·佩皮斯日记》既有历史意义又有文学价值。

J: 从某种程度上来说，佩皮斯的日记与其说是事件的记录，不如说是事件的再创造。佩皮斯的成就有赖于细致的观察和完整的细节回忆。只是细节上的小小润色就会取得不俗的效果。

T: 清新灵活的语言是他成功的另一个原因。佩皮斯用速记法写日记，写得很快，而且这种速记法只有他自己才能识别。佩皮斯的文字不注重形式语法，经常是单词的首字母堆积在一起，准确地反映了他对于某个时刻的印象。

J: 佩皮斯并不打算写一篇经过深思熟虑的记叙文，他向我们展示的是生活中数以百计的场景——委员会中工作的公务员、辩论中的议员、音乐会和在河岸边郊游的朋友等。

T: 他的日记还以地理环境为特征。这是一本伦敦日记，只是偶尔涉及到乡村。

J: 碰巧的是，在佩皮斯写日记的那 10 年里，伦敦遭受了两次大灾难——1665 年大瘟疫和 1666 年大火。

T: 佩皮斯是用密码写日记的，是他对一种现有速记法的变形。

J: 由于害怕写作会致盲，佩皮斯于 1669 年停止了记日记，并将所有日记都收藏在他的私人图书馆里。佩皮斯后来把私人图书馆捐赠给他的母校——剑桥大学麦格达伦学院。

T: 直到150多年后的1819年，麦格达伦学院的院长让一个学生破解了佩皮斯的密码后，佩皮斯的日记才得以重新被发现。

1 And this **freed him up** to paint a frank, uncensored portrait of life in London at the time of the Restoration.

free up 意为“腾出，使……可用”。在本句中，free him up 意为“使他腾出空来”。在使用中，也可直接说 free。

➢ This would free recourses that are badly needed.
这就会腾出急需的资源。

2 In some degree, Pepys's diary is **not so much** a record of events **as** a re-creation of them.

not so much...as 意为“与其说是……不如说是……”。

➢ In many cases nursing is not so much a job as a way of life.
在许多情况下，护理与其说是一件工作倒不如说是一种生活方式。

➢ Success lies not so much as in luck as in hard work.
与其说成功在于运气不如说在于辛勤努力。

3 Pepys's achievement **rests on** his close observation and total recall of detail.

rest on 意为“依靠，有赖于”。

➢ We rest our hope on you alone.
我们把希寄托在你一个人身上。

➢ Success in management ultimately rests on good judgment.
管理的成功最终依靠正确的判断。

4 **As luck would have it**, Pepys wrote in the decade when London suffered two of its great disasters—the Plague of 1665 and the Great Fire of the following year.

as luck would have it 意为“碰巧，真走运或不走运”。

➢ As luck would have it, he recovered his lost watch.
幸运的是，他找回了丢失的表。

➢ As luck would have it, I was out when he called.
真不凑巧，他来访时我正好外出。

Samuel Pepys's Diaries

Samuel Pepys is famous for his diaries, which cover the years 1659 ~ 1669, and he also enjoyed a successful career as a naval administrator and **Member of Parliament**①.

Samuel Pepys was born on 23 February 1633 near Fleet Street in London, the son of a tailor. He was educated at St Paul's School in London and Cambridge University. After graduating, Pepys was employed as secretary to Edward Montagu, a distant relative who was a **councillor of state** during the Cromwellian **protectorate**② and later served Charles II. In 1655, Pepys married 15-year-old Elizabeth, daughter of a **Huguenot**③. In 1658, he underwent a dangerous operation for the removal of a **bladder stone**④. Every year on the anniversary of the operation, he celebrated his recovery.

Pepys began his diary on 1 January 1660. It is written in a form of shorthand, with names in **longhand**⑤. It ranges from private remarks, including revelations of **infidelity**⑥ — to detailed observations of major events in 17th century England, such as the plague of 1665, the Great Fire of London and Charles II's **coronation**⑦; and some of the key figures of the era, including Sir Christopher Wren and Sir Isaac Newton. Fear of losing his eyesight **prompted**⑧ Pepys to stop writing the diary in 1669.

---

① Member of Parliament 下议院议员
② protectorate *n.* 摄政政体
③ Huguenot *n.* 胡格诺教徒
④ bladder stone 膀胱结石
⑤ longhand *n.* 普通书写法（和速写法相对）
⑥ infidelity *n.* 通奸
⑦ coronation *n.* 加冕礼
⑧ prompt *v.* 推动，促使

In June 1660, Pepys was appointed clerk of the acts to the navy board, a key post in one of the most important of all government departments. This is a position that brings a new house for him and his wife. Fiercely devoted to his wife, he nevertheless records many experiences where he looks at, kisses, and "**dallies with**①" other women, a trend that he will continue throughout *The Diary of Samuel Pepys*, and a trend that will slowly invoke the **ire**② of his wife, Elizabeth.

Most of his leisure he spent on his library. He intensified his search for books and prints, setting himself a target of 3000 volumes. Pepys and his library clerk devised a great three-volumed **catalogue**③. He **bequeathed**④ his library to the Magdalene College, Cambridge. His library contains a unique collection of 3,000 books and **manuscripts**⑤.

Pepys earned his place in history by his work for the navy, but perhaps these diary volumes, and the library containing them, are his most **eloquent**⑥ **memorials**⑦. They speak, as no other relics can, of the man himself.

塞缪尔·佩皮斯的日记

塞缪尔·佩皮斯是以他 1659 ～ 1669 年的日记而闻名于世的，同时他也是成功的英国海军官员和下议院议员。

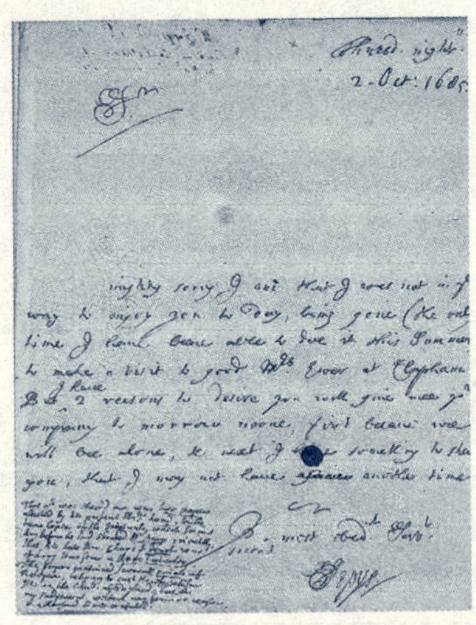

1633 年 2 月 23 日，塞缪尔·佩皮斯出生于伦敦的舰队街附近，是一个裁缝的儿子。他就读于伦敦的圣保罗学校和剑桥大学。毕业后，佩皮斯被雇为远房亲戚爱德华·蒙太古的秘书。爱德华·蒙太古是克伦威尔摄政和随后的查理二世执政时期的议员。1665 年，佩皮斯和 15 岁的伊丽莎白结婚，伊丽莎白是一个胡格诺教徒的女儿。1658 年，为了取出膀胱结石，佩皮斯做了一个危险的手术。此后每年他都会在手术纪念日举行活动，庆祝自己身

① dally with 调戏
② ire *n.* 愤怒
③ catalogue *n.* 目录
④ bequeath *v.* 将……遗赠给
⑤ manuscript *n.* 手稿
⑥ eloquent *adj.* 雄辩的，清楚表现出来的
⑦ memorial *n.* 纪念碑，纪念物

体康复。

1660 年 1 月 1 日，佩皮斯开始写日记。他是用速记法写的，但是名字用普通写法记录。他的日记内容广泛，包括从披露通奸的个人评论到 1665 年的瘟疫、伦敦大火和查理二世加冕的 17 世纪英格兰重大事件的细致观察，包罗万象。此外，佩皮斯的日记还记录了那个时代的重要人物，包括克里斯多弗·雷恩爵士和艾萨克·牛顿爵士。由于害怕失明，佩皮斯 1669 年停止了写日记。

1660 年 6 月，佩皮斯被任命为海军委员会的执行办事员，这是重要政府部门中的关键职位。这个职位给他和妻子带来了一座新房子。虽然佩皮斯对妻子很专一，但他却记录了很多自己关注、亲吻和调戏其他女人的经历。在《塞缪尔·佩皮斯日记》中，他继续这样记录，逐渐招致了妻子伊丽莎白的不满和愤怒。

闲暇时，佩皮斯一般待在自己创建的图书馆里。他加强对书籍和印刷品的研究，为自己制订了一个搜集 3000 卷书的目标。佩皮斯和他的图书馆助理还制作了一个大的三卷式目录。他把图书馆捐赠给了剑桥大学麦格达伦学院。他的图书馆收藏了珍贵的 3000 卷书和手稿。

对英国海军的贡献使得佩皮斯在历史上占有一席之地，但也许是这些日记册以及收藏日记册的图书馆才是佩皮斯功勋的最好纪念物。没有其他遗物能够像日记那样代表佩皮斯。

24 Nehru—India's Prime Minister

印度总理尼赫鲁

焦点对话

Jimmy and Catherine are visiting **Trinity College**[①], Cambridge together.

C: Catherine J: Jimmy

C: Wow, visiting the **picture-postcard**[②] Trinity College brings me enormous enjoyment.

J: And speaking of Trinity College, it's the most **aristocratic**[③] of the Cambridge colleges and it has generally been the academic institution of choice of the Royal Family.

C: Trinity College has more members than any other colleges in Cambridge, but it has the lowest state school **intake**[④] of any college. Trinity has a strong academic tradition, with members having won 32 Nobel Prizes.

J: And I heard that there are many famous alumni in the history of Trinity College.

C: Yes, you're quite right. Jawaharlal Nehru, the first Prime Minister of India, is a great example.

J: Nehru's father wanted Nehru to get a proper English education and to qualify him for the Indian Civil Services or I.C.S.. So Nehru was sent to **Harrow**[⑤], the elite Public school in England.

---

① Trinity College 三一学院，是剑桥大学中规模最大、财力最雄厚、名声最大的学院之一。
② picture-postcard *adj.* 风景如画的
③ aristocratic *adj.* 贵族的，高贵的
④ intake *n.* 吸收，录取
⑤ Harrow 哈罗公学，英国最著名的公学之一。公学是贵族化了的文法中学，是专门为名门贵族服务的私立学校。

C: But the young Nehru did not enjoy his schooling at Harrow. He found the school **syllabus**① **stifling**②and the residency conditions unbearable. All students of the school were forced to condition themselves to bath and wash in cold water.

J: After completing school, Nehru took the University of Cambridge entrance examinations in 1907. The same year, he got admission into the University.

C: Jawaharlal Nehru studied natural sciences at Cambridge University. His chosen subjects were physics, chemistry and botany.

J: He studied the three natural science subjects with only one aim, to pass the Indian Civil Services examination. Nevertheless, Jawaharlal Nehru enjoyed his stay at Cambridge.

C: Yes. The liberal atmosphere of the University encouraged him to do a host of non-academic activities. Jawaharlal Nehru passed the final Cambridge degree examinations successfully, where he stood second.

J: He then studied law at the **Inner Temple**③ in London. He returned to India in 1912 and practised law for some years.

C: In 1919, Nehru joined the Indian National Congress which was fighting for greater **autonomy**④ from the British. He was heavily influenced by the organisation's leader Mohandas Gandhi.

J: Gandhi set a great example of how to struggle for independence for Nehru. And by the end of World War Two, Nehru was recognised as Gandhi's successor.

C: But Nehru had suffered from a lot of disasters during the 1920s and 1930s. He was repeatedly **imprisoned**⑤ by the British for **civil disobedience**⑥.

J: He played a central role in the negotiations over Indian independence. He opposed the

① syllabus *n.* 教学大纲，课程提纲
② stifling *adj.* 沉闷的
③ Inner Temple 内殿法学院，英国的大律师组织之一，其余三个为林肯法学院、中殿法学院和格兰法学院。
④ autonomy *n.* 自治，自治权
⑤ imprison *v.* 下狱，监禁
⑥ civil disobedience 不合作主义，即以拒绝遵守政府法令，拒绝纳税等方式进行的非暴力反抗。

Muslim League's insistence on the division of India on the basis of religion.

C: On 15 August 1947, Nehru became the first prime minister of independent India. He held the post until his death in 1964.

J: By the way, Nehru's daughter Indira Gandhi was the prime minister of the Republic of India for fifteen years until her assassination in 1984.

C: She was India's first, and to date only, female prime minister.

C: 哇，游览风景如画的三一学院带给我极大的享受。

J: 说到三一学院，它是剑桥大学众学院中最高贵的，英国皇室成员通常在此就读。

C: 三一学院的人数比剑桥大学中的其他学院都要多，但是它的录取率却是众学院中最低的。三一学院有悠久的学术传统，该学院的成员获得过 32 个诺贝尔奖。

J: 而且我还听说在三一学院的历史上有很多著名的校友。

C: 是的，你说得很对。印度首任总理贾瓦哈拉尔·尼赫鲁就是一个很好的例子。

J: 尼赫鲁的父亲想让他接受正统的英国教育，让他有资格参加印度公务员考试（I.C.S.）。所以尼赫鲁被送进了英格兰顶尖公学——哈罗公学学习。

C: 但是年轻的尼赫鲁并不喜欢在哈罗公学上学。他发觉学校的教学大纲枯燥乏味，住宿条件难以忍受。学校的所有学生被迫用冷水洗澡。

J: 完成哈罗公学的学业后，尼赫鲁在 1907 年参加了剑桥大学入学考试，同年，他顺利考入剑桥大学。

C: 贾瓦哈拉尔·尼赫鲁在剑桥大学学习自然科学。他选的科目是物理、化学和生物。

J: 他学这三门自然科学课程只有一个目的——通过印度公务员考试。不过尼赫鲁还是喜欢待在剑桥大学的。

C: 是的，剑桥大学的自由氛围鼓励他进行了很多的非学术活动。尼赫鲁成功通过了剑桥大学毕业等级考试，排名第二。

J: 然后尼赫鲁在伦敦的内殿法学院学习法律。1912 年他回到印度，作了几年律师。

C: 1919 年，尼赫鲁加入了印度国大党，该党当时正向英国争取更大的自治权。尼赫鲁受国大党领导莫罕达斯·甘地的影响很大。

J: 甘地为尼赫鲁树立了一个如何争取独立的好榜样。二战结束时，尼赫鲁被认为是甘地的接班人。

C: 但是在 20 世纪 20 年代到 30 年代之间，尼赫鲁遭受了很多苦难。他因奉行不合作主义而多次被英国当局关进监狱。

J: 尼赫鲁在印度独立的谈判中扮演了主要角色。他反对穆斯林联盟的提议，不赞同以宗教为基础对印度进行分治。

C: 1947 年 8 月 15 日，尼赫鲁成为独立后的印度的首任总理，他一直担任总理直到 1964 年去世。

J: 对了，尼赫鲁的女儿英吉拉·甘地也当了 15 年的印度共和国总理，直到她 1984 年被刺杀。

C: 她是印度第一位也是至今唯一位女性总理。

1 And I heard that there are many famous **alumni** in the history of Trinity College.

alumni 意为“校友”，原型是 alumnus，alumni 是复数形式。alumnus 可以指校友，也可特指为男校友。如果要特指女校友的话，可以用 alumna，复数形式是 alumnae。

2 Nehru's father wanted Nehru to get a proper English education and to **qualify him for** the Indian Civil Services or I.C.S..

qualify sb. for sth. 意为“使具有资格，使合格”，也可以说 qualify sb. to do sth.。

- Fluency in three languages qualifies her for work in the European Parliament.
  她能流利的说 3 种语言，这使她能胜任在欧洲议会的工作。
- Our four-week course will qualify you to teach English overseas.
  我们为期 4 周的课程将使你有资格在国外教英语。

3 All students of the school were forced to **condition** to bath and wash themselves in cold water.

condition 意为“（通过训练或影响）使适应于，习惯于”常见的用法是 condition sb. to do sth.。

- The animals were conditioned to expect food at the sound of the bell.
  这些动物受训后一听到铃声就知道有食物可吃了。

4 Gandhi **set a great example** of how to struggle for independence for Nehru.

set an example 意为“树立榜样”。

➢ It's my duty as an officer to set an example to the troops.
作为军官，我有责任为士兵树立好榜样。

此外，be an example to 意为“是……效仿的好榜样”。

➢ Her courage is an example to us all.
她的勇气是我们所有人的榜样。

Nehru— India's Prime Minister

Jawaharlal Nehru was the first Prime Minister of India, as well as the father of the most famous Prime Minister—Indira Gandhi. He was a **patriot**[①], a freedom fighter as well as a highly regarded **statesman**[②].

Jawaharlal Nehru was born on November 14, 1889 in Allahabad, central India. His father was a prominent **advocate**[③] and early leader of the Indian independence movement. The younger Nehru graduated from Cambridge University, and returned to India in 1912.

Even though he had a brilliant academic record, the legal profession did not attract him. Instead, he wanted to join the freedom struggle under the influence of Gandhiji. For a while he was the Chairman of the Allahabad Municipal Committee as a member of the Congress and then he joined the Home Rule League established by Bal Gangadhar Tilak and Annie Besant.

During the freedom struggle, he courted arrest many a times, and had been jailed 14 years in all. He was elected Congress President 5 times, and it was under his influence that the Congress adopted complete freedom as its goal. In 1947, after India gained its independence, he was **automati-**

① patriot *n.* 爱国者
② statesman *n.* 政治家
③ advocate *n.* 提倡者，辩护律师

cally[①] elected first Prime Minister.

Nehru headed the Indian government for 17 long and brilliant years. He wanted India to develop into a **world-recognized**[②]nation. He supported technological and scientific progress encouraged art and literature, wanted to eliminate discrimination from the face of the world and encouraged peaceful **co-existence**[③]. Nehru did not believe in aligning himself with the military political blocks and wanted to end the cold war. He was awarded the **Bharat Ratna**[④] in 1955.

Nehru was a renowned **orator**[⑤]. He could give many **extemporaneous**[⑥] speeches in a single day. His most famous speech is the "Tryst with Destiny" addressing to the **Constituent Assembly of India**[⑦] in New Delhi on the night of August 14th, 1947.

Not only was he a brilliant orator, a charming, warm and noble thinker and philosopher, but also a fantastic writer. He has written a few wonderful books *Discovery of India*, *Glimpses of World History* and *Letters from a father to a daughter*. His autobiography, *Towards Freedom* (1936) ran nine editions in the first year alone.

印度总理尼赫鲁

贾瓦哈拉尔·尼赫鲁是印度首任总理，同时也是印度史上最出名的总理——英吉拉·甘地的父亲。尼赫鲁是一个爱国者，一个为自由而战的斗士，同时也是一位非常受人尊重的政治家。

1889 年 12 月 4 日，贾瓦哈拉尔·尼赫鲁出生在印度中部的阿拉哈巴德。他的父亲是一位杰出的辩护律师，同时也是印度独立运动的早期领导人。年轻的尼赫鲁毕业于剑桥大学，并在 1912 年回到印度。

虽然尼赫鲁学习成绩优异，但是他对法律并不感兴趣，在甘地的影响下迫切想加入旨在印度独立的运动。作为国会议员，尼赫鲁曾在一段时间内任阿拉哈巴德市政委员会主席，然后他加入了由巴尔·甘加达尔·提拉克和安妮·贝赞特创建的印度自治同盟。

---

① automatically *adv.* 自动地，自然而然地
② world-recognized *adj.* 世界知名的
③ co-existence *n.* 共存
④ Bharat Ratna 巴域·维那，印度最高荣誉奖
⑤ orator *n.* 演讲家
⑥ extemporaneous *adj.* 即兴的，即席的
⑦ Constituent Assembly of India 印度制宪会议

在争取印度独立的斗争中，尼赫鲁多次面临被捕的危险，总共做了14年牢。他5次当选国会议长。在他的影响下，国会把印度的完全自由和独立作为奋斗目标。1947年印度获得独立后，尼赫鲁理所当然地被选举为首任总理。

尼赫鲁领导印度政府长达17年，成绩斐然，在任期间，他一直致力于把印度发展成一个世界闻名的国家。尼赫鲁支持科技进步、鼓励艺术和文学发展；试图在全世界范围内消除歧视，鼓励和平共处；不赞成和军事、政治阵营联盟，支持结束冷战。1955年尼赫鲁获得印度最高荣誉奖——巴域·维那。

尼赫鲁是一位知名的演讲家，能在一天之内做出很多即兴演讲，其中最著名的是1947年8月14日晚在新德里的印度制宪会议上的演讲《命运之约》。

尼赫鲁不仅是一位卓越的演讲家，一位有魅力、热情的、高尚的思想家和哲学家，还是一位极其出色的作家。他的佳作包括：《印度的发现》、《世界历史一瞥》和《一个父亲给女儿的信》等。尼赫鲁的自传《走向自由》(1936年出版)在问世第一年就再版了8次。

Unit 7 Chinese in Cambridge

剑桥中国心

25 Xu Zhimo, the Romantic Poet

浪漫诗人徐志摩

Wen Fang is reading a book and Henry comes over to her.

H: Henry W: Wen Fang

H: Hi Fang. Every time I see you, you've **got your head stuck in a book**①!

W: I'm reading a poetry book by Xu Zhimo. It is so great.

H: I know him! Besides poetry, he also wrote some **prose**②.

W: True. I like his style very much, you know, he was the **pioneer**③ in Chinese modern poetry movement.

H: Does it mean that they write in the **vernacular**④ style?

W: Yes. I can't believe that you know so much about Chinese literature! Only a few people outside China know him.

H: It's a Chinese friend who introduced his works to me. I only wish I know Chinese better, thus I can understand more about his poetries.

① got your head stuck in a book 把头埋在书堆里，埋头读书

② prose *n.* 散文

③ pioneer *n.* 拓荒者，先锋

④ vernacular *adj.* 方言，白话

W: Actually, his story was **wide-spreading**① in China, especially his love stories with three women—Zhang Youyi, Lin Huiyin and Lu Xiaoman.

H: So that is part of the reason why he can write such great poems!

W: Definitely. His poems like "By chance" were loved by millions of people.

H: I think the most famous one is "Saying Good-bye to Cambridge Again"? The Cambridge even installed a white marble stone to **commemorate**② him with verses of this poem carved upon it.

W: True. He must have spent a wonderful time in Cambridge which enables him to produce beautiful verses like that.

H: I'm wondering since there are so many bridges over the Cam, which one is the bridge he mentioned in the poem?

W: I have no idea. It seems that there are many **disputes**③ over that. Some said that it is the Byron Bridge; some said it is the Mathematical Bridge and some said it must be the Bridge of Sighs.

H: This poem is loaded with love and romance.

W: Yes, the rhythm and words are so **delicate**④. Some said that he wrote this for Lin Huiyin.

H: One of the three women Xu has ever involved himself in?

W: Yes. By chance Zhimo met Lin Huiyin in a London International Union and fell in love with her. Both Zhimo and Huiyin were interested in literature and they often met to discuss about literature after they first met.

H: Miss Lin must be charming girl.

W: That's for sure. She was beautiful, elegant and smart and later became a famous **architect**⑤ as well as a writer in China. Zhimo was so in love with Huiyin that he request to divorce with Zhang Youyi.

H: He has already got married then?

W: He was married when he was 18 years old. The marriage was arranged by his parents. In

① wide-spreading *adj.* 广为流传的
② commemorate *vt.* 纪念
③ dispute *n.* 辩论，争吵，争端
④ delicate *adj.* 精美的，精致的
⑤ architect *n.* 建筑学家，建筑师

old China, children had no say in that.

H: He must be unhappy then.

W: Definitely. The two then **divorced**[①] in Berlin in March 1922. At the same time, Huiyin left for China with her father. When Zhimo knew that, he went back to China immediately.

H: What happened next? Have they met each other then?

W: Yes. But by the time he found her, she had become the wife of Liang Sicheng, the son of Zhimo's teacher Liang Qichao. Zhimo felt desperate and experienced the hardest period of time in his life.

H: How about the third woman in his life?

W: She was called Lu Xiaoman. Originally, she was the wife of Xu's friend, who was very popular in the Beijing upper class society. I can tell you the details next time.

H: OK. Xu died in a plane **crash**[②] when he was young, is that true?

W: Yes, at age 34. He never stopped pursuing truth, beauty and freedom until he died. His death was a great loss for Chinese literature. If he did not die so early, he might have done much more for Chinese literature as well as the world literature.

H: 你好，芳。每次看到你，你都在埋头读书。

W: 我正在读一本徐志摩的诗集，他的诗真不错。

H: 我知道他！除了诗，他也写散文吧。

W: 对。我非常喜欢他的风格。你知道吗，他是中国现代诗歌运动的先驱。

H: 就是说他们用白话创作对吧？

W: 对。真不敢相信，你对中国文学有如此多的了解！其实国外知道他的人很少。

H: 是一位中国朋友介绍他的诗作给我的。真希望自己的汉语水平再高一些，这样我就能读懂更多他的诗歌了。

W: 实际上在中国，他的故事广为流传，特别是他和三位女性的爱情故事——张幼仪、林徽因和陆小曼。

H: 他能写出这么棒的诗，肯定也和这个有关！

W: 肯定的。很多人都很喜欢他的诗歌，比如说《偶然》。

H: 我想他的诗中最著名的应该是那首《再别康桥》吧？为了纪念他，剑桥大学竖起了一座白色石碑，上面刻的就是《再别康桥》中的名句。

---

① divorce *vt.* 与……离婚

② crash *n.* 碰撞，堕落

W: 对啊。他肯定在剑桥度过了一段十分美好的时光，要不然他也写不出这么好的诗句。

H: 我在想，既然康河上有那么多的桥，他诗中提到的究竟是哪一座呢？

W: 我也不知道。对于这一点，好像有很多争议。有些人说是拜伦桥，有些人说是数学桥，还有些人说肯定是叹息桥。

H: 这首诗充溢着爱和浪漫。

W: 对啊。这首诗辞藻华丽，朗朗上口。有人说，这是特别为林徽因作的。

H: 是那三个女人中的一位吗？

W: 对。徐志摩在伦敦国际联盟遇到了林徽因，之后就爱上了她。他们两人都对文学感兴趣，之后就常常相约一起谈论文学。

H: 这位林小姐一定是位有魅力的女子。

W: 当然啦，她美丽优雅又冰雪聪明，之后成为了中国著名的建筑设计师。徐志摩十分爱慕林徽因，甚至向张幼仪提出了离婚。

H: 他那个时候已经结婚了吗？

W: 他 18 岁的时候就结婚了，是由父母安排的。在旧社会，子女们通常无权作主婚姻大事。

H: 他那时候肯定不幸福。

W: 肯定的。1922 年，他们在柏林离了婚。同时，林徽因和她父亲回到了中国。徐志摩一听说这个，马上赶了回去。

H: 之后呢？他们见面了吗？

W: 见了。但是当他见到林徽因的时候，她已经成为了梁思成的妻子。梁思成是徐志摩的老师梁启超的儿子。徐志摩非常的绝望，好长一段时间都十分沮丧。

H: 那另外一个女人是怎么回事？

W: 她叫陆小曼，开始是徐志摩一位朋友的妻子，是当时北京的社交名媛。我以后再详细跟你讲吧。

H: 好的。徐志摩死于一次飞机事故，那时他还很年轻，对吗？

W: 是的，他那时只有 34 岁。他的一生从未停止过对真理、美好和自由的追求。他的死对中国文学来说是一个巨大的损失。如果不是英年早逝，他肯定能为中国文学乃至世界文学的发展作出更大的贡献。

1 This poem **is loaded with** love and romance.

（1）意为“使承载，使负荷”。

➢ Have you finished loading (up)?
你们装完货了没有？

➢ Load up the van!
把（货物）装车吧！

（2）意为“把子弹上膛，把胶卷装入（相机）”。

➢ Don't move! This gun is loaded.
别动！这支枪是上了膛的。

2 One of the three women Xu has ever **involved** himself in?

（1）与介词 in, with 搭配，意为“使（别人或自己）卷入，使介入”。

➢ Don't involve other people in your mad schemes!
不要把别人卷入你的疯狂计划中去！

（2）与介词 in 搭配，意为“包含，需要，使成为必要部分（必然结果）”。

➢ I didn't realize that so much work was involved in putting on a play.
我那时不了解演一场戏竟要做那么多的工作。

➢ The job involves travelling abroad for three months each year.
这份工作需要每年去国外 3 个月。

3 **By chance** Zhimo met Lin Huiyin in a London International Union and fell in love with her.

（1）by chance 意为“偶然地，意外地”。

➢ It happened quite by chance.
这完全是偶然发生的。

➢ Have you got a spare stamp by any chance?
你也许碰巧有张多余的邮票吧？

（2）另外还有一些关于 chance 的常用词组和用法，如下：

➢ There is an outside chance that he will win.
他获胜的可能性很小。

➢ The theatre was almost fully booked, but he went on the off chance.
剧院的座位几乎已经预定一空，但他还是怀着一线希望去了剧院。

➢ You don't stand a chance of winning the case.
你没有胜诉的可能。

➢ Chances are that she's already heard the news.
很可能她已经听到这个消息了。

Xu Zhimo, the Romantic Poet

Xu Zhimo (January 15, 1897—November 19, 1931) born in a town called Xia shi in Zhejiang province, was an early 20th century Chinese famous poet, who dedicated his life to the development of literature.

In the 1918 of summer, Zhimo acknowledged Liang Qichao, a well-known Chinese writer at that time who Zhimo had admired for a long time. With the encouragement of Liang Qichao, Zhimo decided to go the U.S. to continue his education. After graduating from Peking University, Xu went to the United States to study economics and political science. While there, he changed his **courtesy name**① to Zhimo. In 1920 he received an M.A. in political science from Columbia University in New York City. Later he left for Britain and entered London Economic College. One of the reasons Zhimo went to Britain was to consult **Bertrand Russell**②, a person known to many as a great **philosopher**③, but he left for China just before Zhimo came. Zhimo later went to Cambridge University, where he became **fascinated**④ with English Romantic poetry and decided upon a literary career.

Returning to China in 1922, Xu began writing poems and essays in the vernacular style. He fell under the influence of the Indian poet Rabindranath Tagore while serving as interpreter for him during a lecture tour of China. The foreign literature to which Xu had been exposed shaped his own poetry and helped establish him as a leader in the modern Chinese

① courtesy name 中国文人称谓中的“字”
② Bertrand Russell 伯特兰·罗素，系第三代罗素伯爵。是20世纪英国哲学家、数学家、逻辑学家、历史学家、无神论者，也是上世纪西方最著名、影响最大的学者和和平主义社会活动家。1950年，获得诺贝尔文学奖。
③ philosopher *n.* 哲学家，哲人
④ fascinated *adj.* 着迷的，被……深深吸引的

poetry movement. He served as an editor (1925–26) of the literary **supplement**[1] of the Chenbao ("Morning Post")—the most important literary supplement in Beijing at that time—and as a professor of literature and law at various universities. In 1927 he helped organize the Xinyue Shudian (Crescent Moon Book Company), and the following year he began editing Xinyue ("Crescent Moon"), a literary monthly featuring liberal ideas and Western literature.

In 1931, Xu died in an airplane crash when he was flying from Nanjing to Beijing, ending his brilliant life as a poet. To commemorate Xu Zhimo, in July, 2008, a white **marble**[2] stone has been **installed**[3] at the back of King's College, University of Cambridge, on which is **inscribed**[4] a verse from Xu's best-known poem, "Saying Goodbye to Cambridge Again".

浪漫诗人徐志摩

徐志摩出生于浙江省硖石镇，是中国 20 世纪早期著名诗人，他将自己的一生都献给了文学。

1918 年夏，徐志摩结识了他仰慕已久的著名作家梁启超。在梁的鼓励之下，徐志摩决定去美国继续深造。从北京大学毕业后，徐志摩前往美国学习经济和政治学。就是在那里，他改名志摩。1920 他取得了纽约的哥伦比亚大学政治学的硕士学位，之后又前往英国，进入伦敦经济学院学习。他来到英国的目的之一，是从师于著名的哲学家罗素。但罗素刚好在徐志摩到英国前去了中国。之后，他就进入剑桥学习。也正是在剑桥大学的学习期间，他开始对欧美浪漫主义诗歌产生浓厚兴趣，并作出了走文学道路的决定。

1922 年回国后，徐志摩开始以白话创作诗歌和散文。英国诗人泰戈尔访华期间，徐志摩作为翻译，陪同左右，之后他创作的风格也深受泰戈尔影响。正是因为深受异域文学的影响，徐志摩逐渐形成了自己的风格，这使他得以成为中国现代诗运动中的领袖人物。1925 ~ 1926 年间，他在当时北京最有影响力的文学增刊《晨报》当编辑，同时也在国内多所知名大学教授文学和法律。1927 年，他组织成立了新月书店，之后，又创办了文学月刊《新月》，传播西方文化和自由主义思想。

1931 年在从南京飞往北京的路上，徐志摩因飞机失事而亡，结束了他光辉灿烂的一生。为了纪念徐志摩，2008 年 7 月，剑桥大学国王学院的后面，竖起了一座白色大理石碑，上面刻着徐志摩最著名的诗《再别康桥》中的名句。

---

① supplement *n.* 补充，增刊
② marble *n.* 大理石，大理石制品
③ install *vt.* 安装，安顿
④ inscribe *vt.* 题写，铭记，雕

26 Hua Luogeng
数学巨匠华罗庚

焦点对话

Zheng Jun and Vicki are talking about Hua Luogeng.

Z: Zheng Jun V: Vicki

V: I heard that the first contact of Cambridge University with China dates back over 100 years.

Z: Yes. Over these years, many Chinese scholars have traveled long distances to study in Cambridge, and among them was the **outstanding**① Chinese mathematician Hua Luogeng.

V: I've heard about him. He was a world-famous mathematician.

Z: Yes. Now mathematics in China enjoys high popularity in public esteem, that is due in large measure to the leadership Hua Luogeng gave his country, as scholar and teacher, for 50 years.

V: He was really smart. No wonder that someone praised Hua as "China's Einstein".

Z: Though he had a **humble**② origin, he never gave up his interest and kept working hard on it.

V: Oh, really? Could you please tell me more, I'm really interested in him.

Z: Ok. Hua was born in 1910 in Jintan in the southern Jiangsu Province of China. Jintan is now a flourishing town, with a high school named after Hua.

V: They want to remember him.

Z: True. There is a **memorial**③ building celebrating his achievements; but in 1910 it was little more than a village where Hua's father managed a general store with mixed

① outstanding *adj.* 杰出的，显著的
② humble *adj.*（地位，身份，等级等）低下的
③ memorial *adj.* 纪念的，追悼的

success. The family was poor throughout Hua's **formative**① years.

V: Many famous people in history were **born in poverty**②.

Z: Hua's formal education was brief and, on the face of it, hardly a preparation for an academic career.

V: He must have been working hard on mathematics, or he would never have made such great contribution.

Z: Yes. The Jintan Middle School that opened in 1922 just when he had completed **elementary**③ school had a well-qualified and demanding mathematics teacher who recognized Hua's talent and **nurtured**④ it.

V: He was really lucky to have someone realize his talent.

Z: Yes. Next, Hua gained admission to the Chinese Vocational College in Shanghai, and there he distinguished himself by winning a national **abacus**⑤ competition; although tuition fees at the college were low, living costs proved too high for his means and Hua was forced to leave a term before graduating.

V: That was pitiful. A genius like him should have a good education.

Z: After failing to find a job in Shanghai, Hua returned home to help in his father's store. In that same year also, Hua got married.

V: He did not end up as a sales man but was a famous mathematician which as I see was a miracle.

Z: Yes, though life was not easy, he continued with his studies on mathematics. Hua showed in a short note in the same journal that a certain paper claiming to have solved the **quintic**⑥ was fundamentally **flawed**⑦.

V: I can't believe that a man with limited education could find the fault of a scholar!

Z: It happens. Hua's **lucid**⑧ analysis caught the eye of a **discerning**⑨ professor at Tsing

① formative *adj.* 形成的，造型的，格式化的
② born in poverty 出身贫寒
③ elementary *adj.* 基本的，初级的
④ nurture *vt.* 养育，鼓励，培植
⑤ abacus *n.* 算盘
⑥ quintic *adj.* 五次的
⑦ flawed *adj.* 有缺陷的，有裂纹的
⑧ lucid *adj.* 易懂的，清晰的
⑨ discerning *adj.* 有辨识能力的，有眼光的

Hua University in Beijing, and then Hua was invited, despite his lack of formal qualification, he joined the mathematics department there.

V: This man developed a sharp eye for discovering able people!

Z: He began as a clerk in the library, and then moved to become an assistant in mathematics. Then, years later he received an invitation to come to Cambridge.

V: That's a good opportunity for him to **enhance**[①] his studies.

Z: He did make some achievements there.

V: 我听说剑桥大学与中国的交往始于 100 多年前呢。

Z: 是啊，许多中国学者曾不远万里到剑桥求学，如中国杰出的数学家华罗庚。

V: 我听说过他，他可是位闻名世界的大数学家呢。

Z: 对啊。现在数学学习在中国如此普及，很大程度上还要感谢华罗庚作为一位学者和一名教师 50 年来对中国数学事业发展所起的引领作用。

V: 他真的很聪明，怪不得有人称他为“中国的爱因斯坦”呢。

Z: 尽管他出身平凡，却从来没有放弃过自己的兴趣，一直都十分努力。

V: 真的吗？你可以跟我多讲讲吗，我对他很感兴趣。

Z: 好的。华罗庚 1910 年出生于中国江苏南部的金坛。金坛现在是一个繁荣的城镇，还有一所以华罗庚命名的高中。

V: 那肯定是为了纪念他。

Z: 是啊。那里还有一座为纪念他的成就而设立的纪念堂；但是在 1910 年的时候，金坛只不过是一个小村庄，华罗庚的父亲开了间杂货店，生意时好时坏。华罗庚整个少年时代，家庭都比较清贫。

V: 历史上许多有名的人士都出身贫寒。

Z: 华罗庚早期的教育很简单，而且乍看起来，这根本就不足以使他走上之后的学术道路。

V: 他肯定非常用功的学习数学，要不然，他绝对不可能有这么大的成就。

Z: 是啊。金坛中学成立于 1922 年，那时候他刚刚小学毕业。金坛中学有位很好的

① enhance *vt.* 提高，增强

数学老师，他发现了华罗庚的才华，并且很用心地培养他。

V: 能有这样一位赏识自己的人，华罗庚很幸运。

Z: 对，之后，华罗庚被上海一所职业学校录取，在校期间因为一次全国珠算比赛脱颖而出。尽管学费并不是很高，但对于他来说，生活费还是很成问题，华罗庚只好中途辍学了。

V: 真可惜，像他那样的天才应该接受高质量的教育才对。

Z: 在上海找工作失败后，他就回到家乡，帮父亲打点店铺，也是在那一年，他结了婚。

V: 他没有沦落到只做一个小商贩，而成为了一位著名的教学家，在我看来还真是个奇迹。

Z: 是啊，尽管生活艰难，他还是一如既往的研习数学。他在一本杂志上发表了一篇短文，指出此前发表在同一本杂志上的一篇论文有错误，文中代数的五次方程的解法根本不能成立。

V: 真是难以置信，一个并没有受过很好教育的人居然能挑出一位学者的错！

Z: 可事情就是发生了。华罗庚清晰的分析论证引起了清华大学一位目光锐利的教授的注意。之后，没有正规教育背景的华罗庚成为了清华大学数学系正式的一员。

V: 这位教授还真是慧眼识人啊。

Z: 刚开始的时候，他在图书馆当管理员，之后就以助教身份去了数学系。几年之后，他又获邀前往剑桥访问学习。

V: 这对他提高自己的学术水平来说是个很不错的机会。

Z: 他也确实在那里取得了一些成就。

1 Now mathematics in China enjoys high popularity in public esteem,that is **due** in large measure to the leadership Hua Luogeng gave his country, as scholar and teacher, for 50 years.

（1）应得的，应归于

➤ Any money that is due to you will be paid before the end of the month.
欠你的钱将在月底之前全部支付给你。

（2）约定的，预期的，该发生的，应到达的

➤ The next train to London is due at 4 o'clock.
下一班去伦敦的火车应在 4 点钟到站。

2 Next, Hua gained admission to the Chinese Vocational College in Shanghai, and there he **distinguished** himself by winning a national abacus competition

（1）辨认出，认明，看（听）清楚

➢ Can you distinguish the different buildings at such a distance?
你能在这么远的地方看清那些不同的建筑物吗？

（2）与介词 between 或 from 搭配，意为“辨别，分清，把……与……加以区别”。

➢ It's important to distinguish between compound interest and simple interest.
分清复利与单利很重要。

➢ Small children can't distinguish right from wrong.
小孩子不能明辨是非。

3 He did not **end up** as a sales man but a famous mathematician which as I see was a miracle.

end up 意为“最后成为（处于）”。

➢ He ended up (as) head of the firm.
他最后成了公司的主管人。

➢ We set off for Newcastle but ended up in Scotland.
我们动身去纽卡斯尔，可后来却去了苏格兰。

Hua Luogeng

Hua Luogeng was the first world-famous scholar returned from overseas upon the founding of the People's Republic of China. He **fostered**① and educated many mathematicians of New China, his influence lasting several generations. He was a fellow of the Third World Academy of Sciences and the first Chinese member of the American Academy of Arts and Sciences since its foundation in the late 19th Century. English mathematician Harry Bateman once praised Hua as "China's Einstein", saying he was worthy to be a member of any famous science academy around the world. Mathematical accomplishments named after him include Hua's **theorem**②, Weil-Hua **inequation**③, Hua's inequation, Brauer-Cartan-Hua theorem and

① foster *vt.* 培养，抚育
② theorem *n.* 定理，原理
③ inequation *n.*（数）不等式

Hua **matrices**①.

In 1936, Hua went to Cambridge University to study. During the following two years, he wrote 18 articles, of which "Hua's theorem" actually persuaded the famous English mathematician G.H. Hardy to revise one of his works just before its publication. Hua also solved the problem of a complete triangle sum **estimation**② put forward by **Johann Carl Friedrich Gauss**③, arousing a sensation in the university and becoming regarded as the "glory of Cambridge". After returning to China, he became a professor in Southwest Associated University and an academician of Academia Sinica (predecessor to Chinese Academy of Sciences in the PRC). His greatest work Additive Theory of Prime Numbers finished in 1942 won him First-Class honors in natural science. Later, he went to the Soviet Union and the United States to give lectures and was invited to be a researcher at Princeton Research Institute and **tenured**④ professor of Illinois University. He was the first chair of the Department of Mathematics and vice president of University of Science and Technology of China (USTC), head of Mathematics Institute and later Institute of Applied Mathematics of Chinese Academy of Sciences (CAS), academician and vice president of CAS. In 1957, his work Harmonic analysis of functions of several complex variables in the classical domains won the first prize of State inventions.

In the beginning of the 1960s, he applied mathematics to the national economy in a creative way, sorting out **optimization**⑤ aiming at improving craftsmanship and overall planning to handle the organization and management of production. He led a team to promote the two new methods in more than 20 provinces and municipalities around the country, achieving obvious economic profit. Early in 1964, he wrote to Chairman Mao Zedong, Mao then wrote back to him cherishing his "high aspirations" and offering his congratulations. He died of a heart attack in 1985 while giving a lecture in the University of Tokyo in Japan.

---

① matrice *n.* 矩阵，真值表
② estimation *n.* 估计
③ Johann Carl Friedrich Gauss 约翰·卡尔·弗里德里希·高斯，生于布伦瑞克，卒于哥廷根，是德国著名的数学家、物理学家、天文学家、大地测量学家。他有"数学王子"的美誉，并被誉为历史上伟大的数学家之一，和阿基米德、牛顿、欧拉同享盛名。
④ tenured *adj.* 享有终身职位的
⑤ optimization *n.* 最佳化，最优化

数学巨匠华罗庚

华罗庚是新中国成立后，从海外归来的第一位国际知名学者。他为新中国培养了一大批数学人才，影响了好几代人。他是第三世界科学院院士，也是美国科学院自19世纪末成立以来的第一位中国院士。英国数学家哈利·贝特曼曾把华罗庚誉为“中国的爱因斯坦”，并说他足以成为全世界所有著名科学院的院士。在国际上以华氏命名的数学科研成果就有“华氏定理”、“怀依—华不等式”、“华氏不等式”、“普劳威尔—加当华定理”、“华氏算子”等。

1936年，华罗庚前往剑桥大学学习。在接下来的两年时间里，他写了18篇论文，其中关于“华氏定理”的那篇甚至说服了英国著名数学家哈代亲自操刀对其进行发表前的修改。他解决了高斯完整三角和估计的历史难题，曾在剑桥引起轰动，并被称作“剑桥的荣光”。回国后，他在西南联合大学执教，并当选为中国中央研究院院士（中国科学院前身）。在1942年完成的《堆垒素数论》为他在自然科学领域赢得了很高的声誉。之后，他前往原苏联和美国访问讲学，期间曾任美国普林斯顿高等研究院研究员，并被伊利诺伊大学聘为终身教授。华罗庚还曾担任中国科学院数学研究所第一任所长，中国科技大学副校长，中国数学会理事长，中国科学院应用数学研究所所长，中国科学院副院长等职。1957年，他的《多复变数函数论中的曲型域的调和分析》为他赢得了国家发明奖的一等将。

20世纪60年代初，他创造性地把数学应用于促进国家经济发展。他发现数学中的统筹法和优选法是在工农业生产中能够被普遍应用的方法，可以提高工作效率，改变工作管理方式。他带领了一个小分队前往全国20多个省市去推广统筹法和优选法，结果取得了明显的经济成效。1964年初，他给毛主席写信，之后毛主席亲笔回函道：“诗和信已经收读。壮志凌云，可喜可贺。”1985年，他在日本东京大学讲学时因突发急性心肌梗塞而倒在了讲台上。

27 Louis Cha in Cambridge
金庸80岁拜师学艺

焦点对话

Lucy and Jin Ming are talking about the famous kung fu novelist Louis Cha in China.

L: Lucy　　　　J: Jin Ming

L: Do you know the kung fu novelist Louis Cha?

J: Oh, you mean Jin Yong. Of course, I've known him since I was in middle school. He is my favorite writer, and I have read all of his 14 most famous novels. What about him?

L: When he was 81years old, he decided to go to study for a master's degree in Cambridge University.

J: Really? I heard that he had already got an **honorary doctoral degree**[1] of Cambridge University. Was it still necessary for him to study there at such an old age?

L: The university also thought it unnecessary, too.

J: He was very sincere on this. But how did he get into Cambridge?

L: Cha owed this **opportunity**[2] to the president of Cambridge University at that time, Alison Richard who had read and **favored**[3] the English version of one of his famous works ***The Deer and the Cauldron***[4].

J: What did she do to help him?

---

① honorary doctoral degree 荣誉博士学位

② opportunity *n.* 时机，机会

③ favor *vt.* 喜欢，赞成

④ *The Deer and the Cauldron*《鹿鼎记》，长篇武侠小说，当代著名作家金庸著，作于1969～1972年，小说以清代康熙年间的社会历史为背景，描写了一个出身于社会最底层的少年韦小宝的传奇经历。

L: As the president of Cambridge Degree **Recommendation**[①] Committee, Ms. Richard suggested that the university should award Cha an honorary doctoral degree.

J: Yes. I've already talked about that before. What happened then?

L: No matter what, Cha applied to study in Cambridge until he could get a doctoral degree. Cha insisted on his **request**[②] and said that he would like to study for more knowledge rather than simply for a degree.

J: Cambridge must be persuaded by his **sincerity**[③] and admitted him into the university.

L: You're right.

J: As an old saying goes, it's never too old to learn. How is he doing in Cambridge?

L: Very good. He got his master's degree two years ago, and now he is pursuing his doctoral degree in Oriental Studies. It will not be long before he succeeds in getting it.

J: Impressive. He has set a very good example for us Chinese young people, encouraging us to exert ourselves to learn.

L: Yes, I can't agree with you more. Do you know what the most popular way is for people in Cambridge to commute?

J: What is it? Bike? Why did you mention this?

L: I want to tell you an **anecdote**[④] of Cha. When Mr. Cha saw that many students in Cambridge commute by bikes, he wanted to ride bike to school too.

J: I'm worried about his safety since he was not young and perhaps had no experience in riding at all.

L: His wife worried about him, too, and she wanted to persuade Cha to give up riding, but he won't listen.

J: He is stubborn.

L: Yes. But after some time, he felt that commuting by bike was not really suitable for him, but he felt **embarrassed**[⑤] to tell his wife that he did not want to ride bike anymore.

J: He was cute. What happened then? How did he commute from then on?

L: His wife was so smart that she sensed that Mr. Cha did not want to ride bike, and bought him a car at last. From then on, he drove to school. Later, he dropped driving and commuted by taxi apain.

J: That's interesting.

---

① recommendation *n.* 推荐，建议
② request *n.* 请求，需要
③ sincerity *n.* 真实，诚挚
④ anecdote *n.* 奇闻轶事
⑤ embarrassed adj 尴尬的，不好意思的

L: By the way, I'd like to read one of Mr. Cha's kung fu novels. Do you have one?

J: Yes, here is *The Deer and the Cauldron*, my favorite one.

L: Thank you very much.

J: You are welcome.

L: 你知道武侠小说家查良铮吗?

J: 哦，你是说金庸吧，当然，我上初中的时候就知道他了。他是我最喜欢的作家，我读过他最著名的 14 本小说。他怎么了?

L: 他 81 岁的时候，决定去剑桥攻读硕士学位。

J: 真的? 我听说他已经拿到了剑桥大学荣誉博士学位。还有必要在如此高龄前去求学吗?

L: 剑桥大学也如此认为。

J: 看来他在这件事情上面十分认真啊。但是他是如何进入剑桥学习的呢?

L: 这多亏了剑桥校长理查德女士。她阅读了金庸的著作《鹿鼎记》的英译本后，非常喜欢。

J: 她是怎样帮助金庸的呢?

L: 时任学位推荐委员会主席的她，向剑桥提名授予金庸荣誉文学博士称号。

J: 是啊，这个我们前面已经讲过了，后来又怎样了呢?

L: 不管怎样，金庸先生坚决请求入校就读，他表示求学并非为了学位，而是感到自己学问不够。

J: 最后剑桥肯定被他的诚意感动，最终才同意他入学的吧。

L: 你说的对。

J: 正如一句古话所说，活到老学到老。他在剑桥过得怎样?

L: 很棒。他于两年前获得硕士学位，现在攻读东方研究博士学位，不久便可获得学位。

J: 了不起。他为我们年轻人树立了很好的榜样，鼓励我们努力学习。

L: 的确，我非常赞同你的看法。你知道在剑桥，最流行的交通方式是什么吗?

J: 是什么? 自行车吗? 你为什么提到这个呢?

L: 我想跟你讲一件金庸的轶事吧。当他看到许多剑桥的学生都骑自行车上学时，他也想骑车上学。

J: 我担心他会不安全啊，他年纪大了，再说可能以前根本就没有骑过车。

L: 他的夫人也很担心他，她还劝金庸不要骑车了，但是他不肯听。

J: 他真固执。

L: 是啊。但是过了一段时间，他感觉到骑车对他来说还是不合适，但是又不好意思跟夫人讲自己不想再骑车上学了。

J: 他真可爱，之后怎么样？他之后怎么去上学的？

L: 他的夫人很聪明，看出来他不想再骑车了，就为他买了一辆车。之后他就开车上学。过了不久，他又开始坐计程车上学。

J: 真有趣。

L: 对了，我想借一本金庸的武侠小说，你有没？

J: 有，这是《鹿鼎记》，我最喜欢的一本。

L: 十分感谢！

J: 不客气。

1 Cha **owed** this opportunity to the president of Cambridge University at that time, Alison Richard who had read and favored the English version of one of his famous works *The Deer and the Cauldron.*

（1）与介词 to，for 搭配，意为“对……负有……的义务”。

➢ I still owe the garage for those repairs.
我还没有付给汽车修理厂那笔修理费呢。

➢ We owe loyalty to our country.
我们对国家负有尽忠的义务。

（2）与介词 to 搭配，意为“感激”。

➢ We owe a lot to our parents.
我们非常感激自己的父母。

2 I'm worried about his safety **since** he was not young and perhaps had no experience in riding at all.

（1）作连词，与现在完成时或过去完成时连用，意为“从……以来”。

➢ When we met him last week, it was the first time we had seen each other since we were at school.
我上星期遇见了他，那是我们从学校离别后第一次见面。

（2）因为，既然

➢ Since you can't answer the question, perhaps we'd better ask someone else.
既然你不能回答这个问题，我们也许该问问别人。

3 His wife worried about him, too, and she wanted to **persuade** Cha to give up riding, but he won't listen.

（1）说服，劝说

➢ He persuaded her out of going to the party.
他说服她不参加这次聚会。

（2）使相信，使信服

➢ She was not persuaded of the truth of his statement.
她不相信他的话是真的。

➢ He was unable to persuade the police that he had been elsewhere at the time of the crime.
他不能使警察相信案发时他在别处。

Louis Cha in Cambridge

Louis Cha, famously known as Jin Yong, went to Cambridge University to study for a non-honorary master's degree after receiving his honorary **doctorate**[①] from the university in 2005. Aged 81, he became one of the oldest students to enroll in the university's history. Since two years ago, Cha has been studying for his PhD in **Oriental**[②] Studies, Chinese History, at **St John's College**[③], Cambridge.

While in Cambridge, Cha and his wife has rented a house near the university, which is much **shabbier**[④] compared to their house in Hong Kong. It is interesting that after a careful discussion they have decided to hire an Italian chef to cook meals for them so that they can

① honorary doctorate 荣誉博士
② oriental *adj.* 东方人的，东方的
③ St John's College 圣约翰学院，创办于 1511 年，是剑桥大学第二大学院，在学生人数上仅次于三一学院，学院的创办人是王太后玛格丽特·博福特（Margaret Beaufort）女士。
④ shabby *adj.* 破旧的，低劣的

eat Chinese food in **Italianate**[①] style.

Every day, Cha carries a **slanting**[②] **satchel**[③] which contains all the books and material he needs for class that day. As a renown kung fu novelist, he has a lot of fans. Whenever some of his fans ask him for his **signature**[④], he would refuse them politely and tell them jokingly that if he was taking a walk or having a coffee instead of going to class, he would sign for them.

In the beginning, Cha used to go to class by bike. However, he no longer rides a bike now because his wife is afraid that the cars in the campus might knock him down. Then, the bike was replaced by a car, but Cha called himself an old man with little sense of direction and before long gave up the car too. Then how does he go to school? The best way is to take a taxi.

Why would Cha want to study at Cambridge while he was in his eighties? Some people think that it is because his cousin Xu Zhimo had studied in this university. When Cha was very young, his mother once praised his cousin for going to Cambridge University. Of course, Cha was a little jealous, determining[⑤] that one day he would study in Cambridge too. However, the most important reason is his strong thirst for knowledge. In an interview, Cha told a reporter: "Some people said that I am not **qualified**[⑥] to be the dean of school of literature in Zhejiang University. I could not **retort**[⑦] upon them and the only thing I can do is to increase my own knowledge." His willingness to learn deserves our, especially young people's, admiration. As Cha once said, he wants to set an example for the young, showing them it's never too late to learn and people should **exert**[⑧] themselves to learn.

---

① Italianate *adj.* 意大利风格的
② slanting *adj.* 倾斜的
③ satchel *n.* 小背包，书包
④ signature *n.* 署名，签名
⑤ determine *vi.* 决定，确定
⑥ qualified *adj.* 有资格的，合格
⑦ retort *vt.* 反驳，反击
⑧ exert oneself 努力，尽力

金庸80岁拜师学艺

查良镛，即著名的金庸先生，于2005年获得剑桥大学荣誉博士学位后，前往剑桥攻读硕士学位。81岁高龄的他，成为剑桥历史上年龄最大的学生之一。两年前，他开始在圣约翰学院攻读东方研究及中国历史博士学位。

在剑桥的时候，金庸夫妇在学校附近租了一套住房。与在香港的住所相比，他在剑桥的住所显得十分简陋。有趣的是，“大侠”和太太商量，请了一位意大利厨师解决一日三餐，能吃到意大利式的“中国菜”。

金大侠每天斜背着一只书包，书包中装着当天上课要用的书和资料。遇到有“金迷”上前请求签名，他每次都婉言拒绝，并补充一句：“我在散步或者在喝咖啡时，可以给你们签名。”

开始金大侠还曾骑车上学，不过现在单车是不骑了，因为太太担心校园里穿梭的汽车很容易把人撞倒。后来改为开汽车，但金庸又自称是个“没有方向感的老头儿”，所以没开几次也放弃了。如何上课呢？最终的办法只好是每天搭出租车。

80多岁的金庸为什么要去剑桥读书呢？有人说因为他的表哥徐志摩曾在剑桥读书。金庸的妈妈就跟他说，你看你的表哥徐志摩多厉害，读的是剑桥大学。金庸当然不服气，便说自己长大也要读剑桥大学！然而，最主要的原因是金庸先生对于学问的渴求。金庸先生在接受媒体记者采访时说，“在浙江大学担任文学院院长，有人说我学问不好，不够做院长。别人指责，我不能反驳，唯一的办法就是增加自己的学问。”金庸先生的求学精神，值得我们大家尤其是年轻人敬佩和学习。正如金庸先生所说，他想为现在的年轻人树立一个榜样，活到老、学到老，人人都应该努力地学习。

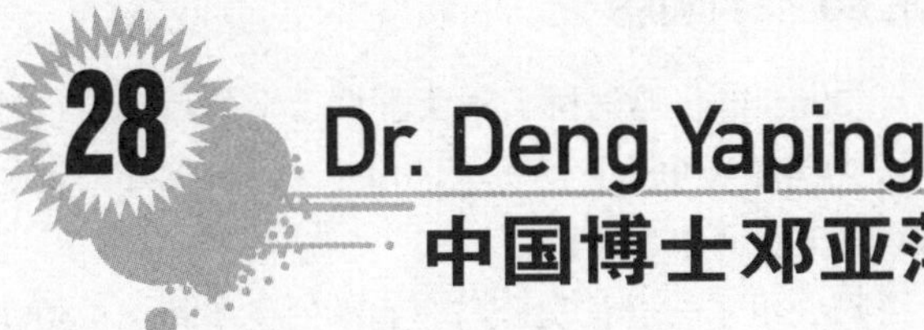

28 Dr. Deng Yaping
中国博士邓亚萍

焦点对话

Kate is watching TV, and Jim comes over to her.

J: Jim　　K: Kate

J: Hey, Kate, what are you watching?

K: Oh, it's Yang Lan's interview of Deng Yaping. Deng is the **top-notch**[①] athlete in my mind. Do you like her?

J: Yes. Deng is remembered by the world for her outstanding performance in the playing table tennis in so many important matches, especially in the Olympic Games.

K: That's right. She was the champion in the 25th and 26th Olympic Games held in Barcelona in 1992, as well as in Atlanta in 1996.

J: You are really **a die-hard fan**[②] of her! It seems to me that she have altogether won 18 world championship, only second to Wang Nan and Zhang Yining. Is that right?

① top-notch *n.* 顶级的，最优秀的

② a die-hard fan 铁杆粉丝

K: Yeah. But I set her as my idol not only because of her excellence in the sports field, but also outside the **stadium**[①]. Do you know the reason?

J: Let me see, you must refer to the fact that she acts as the Deputy Director of Olympic Village Department of Beijing Organizing Committee of Olympic Games. Am I correct?

K: Partly. Besides this, she is also the Spokeswoman of Olympic (Paralympics) Village Department.

J: Really! I didn't know that! She is **fabulous**[②]!

K: Of course. But do you have any idea about how she made these achievements?

J: Now you do **arouse my curiosity**[③]. You will **elaborate**[④] the story for me, won't you?

K: Sure. I'd like to do that. After she retired in 1997 and entered Tsinghua University, Deng was just a **greenhand**[⑤] in learning English. She could not even write all the 26 letters at first. But at that time, Deng has already been nominated by president Samaranch as the member of the International Olympic Committee Athletes Commission.

J: Whoa, that must be hard, as far as I know, the official languages in the Committee are English and French…

K: Indeed, it is unimaginable for an English **rookie**[⑥] to accomplish her duty in such working environment. But where there is a will, there is a way. After **back-breaking**[⑦] work, she managed to get her bachelor's degree.

J: Sounds amazing. That's all?

K: Of course not. Then she was admitted by the University of Nottingham, a famous university in Britain, to gain a master's degree. She continued to chase her dream.

J: This lady is charming enough!

K: You bet it. What amazes me most is her experience in the University of Cambridge, one of the best higher education institutions in the world. She became a doctor there!

J: That's really beyond my imagination. Which major does she study?

K: I guess it's about economy.

---

① stadium *n.* 体育馆
② fabulous *a.*（口语）极好的，特别棒的
③ arouse one's curiosity 激起某人的好奇心
④ elaborate *v.* 详细阐述，仔细说明
⑤ greenhand *n.* 新手，初学者
⑥ rookie *n.* 新手，初学者
⑦ back-breaking *a.* 艰苦的，艰难的

J: Cool! I guess it can play an **indispensable**[①] role in her work in the Beijing Organizing Committee of Olympic Games.

K: What she has done proves that as long as we have perseverance and determination, a dream-chaser can finally be a dream-catcher.

J: 嘿，凯特，你在看什么呢？

K: 哦，是杨澜对邓亚萍的采访录。邓亚萍在我心目中是最出色的运动员。你喜欢她吗？

J: 喜欢。她在众多重要赛事，尤其是奥运会中都表现得十分精彩，人们都对她印象深刻。

K: 对。邓亚萍是1992年在巴塞罗那举办的第25届奥运会及1996年在亚特兰大举办的第26届奥运会的连续两届世界冠军。

J: 你真是她的铁杆粉丝！我记得她好像总共夺得了18个世界冠军，仅次于王楠和张怡宁，对吗？

K: 的确如此。但是我把她当成我的偶像，不仅是因为她在体育领域的成就，而且也是因为她在运动场外所作出的成绩。你知道我指的是什么吗？

J: 让我想想，你肯定是在说她担任了北京奥组委奥运村部副部长这件事吧，是吗？

K: 这只是一部分。除此以外，她也是北京残奥村的新闻发言人。

J: 真的吗！我不知道这个，她真棒！

K: 当然了。那你知道她是怎么取得这些成就的吗？

J: 现在你把我的好奇心都激发起来了。给我仔细讲讲她的故事好吗？

K: 没问题，我十分乐意。邓亚萍1997年退役进入清华大学学习时，她在英语学习方面还仅仅是个新手，一开始甚至不能写全26个英文字母。但当时她已经被国际奥委会萨马兰奇主席提名为国际奥委会运动委员会的委员了。

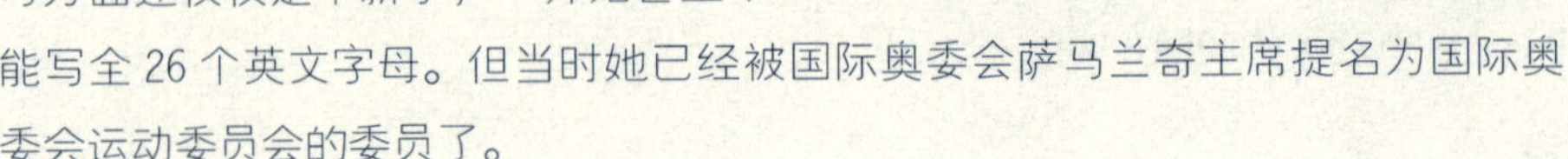

J: 哇，那她学习的难度肯定不小。据我所知，国际奥委会的工作语言是英语和法语……

K: 正是这样。对于一个英语学习刚刚入门的学生来说，在这样的工作环境里要完成

① indispensable *a.* 不可或缺的，十分重要的

工作任务是难以想象的。但是，有志者，事竟成。在刻苦学习以后，邓亚萍顺利取得了学士学位。

J: 听起来真不错。全部事情就是这样?

K: 当然不是了。然后，邓亚萍又被英国著名的诺丁汉大学录取为硕士研究生。她继续追寻她的梦想。

J: 这位女士真是充满了魅力!

K: 没错。最让我惊叹的是她在剑桥这所世界顶级的高等学府里的经历。她在那儿成为了一名博士!

J: 这真是不可思议。她学习的专业是什么?

K: 我记得大概是经济学。

J: 太酷了! 我想这些经历在帮助她完成北京奥组委的工作上是不可或缺的吧。

K: 她所做的证明了一个道理：只要有毅力和决心，一个追梦人最终会成为一个梦想实现者。

1 But I set her as my idol **not only** because of her excellence in the sports field, **but also** outside the stadium. Do you know the reason?

“not only … but also …”是一个并列连词词组，其意思基本等于“both … and …”，但侧重点放在“but also”上。另外该词组使用时须遵守一定的规则，如要求对称，倒装及主谓一致等。注意，not only 放在句首，后接句子时要用倒装结构。

- Not only you but also she has to attend the ceremony.
  不仅你而且她也得参加典礼。
- They completed the project not only punctually but also perfectly.
  他们不仅准时完成工程，而且完成得很出色。
- Not only should proletarians emancipate themselves but also the whole mankind.
  无产者不仅要解放他们自己，而且要解放全人类。

2 But at that time, Deng has already been **nominated** by president Samaranch as the member of the International Olympic Committee Athletes Commission.

（1）与 for 和 as 搭配，意为“提名，推荐”。

➢ I wish to nominate Jane for/ as president of the club.
我想提名简为俱乐部的主席。

（2）与介词 as 搭配，意为“任命，指定”。

➢ The director nominated me as his official representative at the conference.
那位董事指定我作为他的正式代表出席会议。

3 That's really **beyond** my imagination.

beyond one's imagination 指出乎某人的意料，意想不到；beyond 的意思是“超过，超出”。

➢ The book on the shelf is beyond my reach.
我够不着架子上的那本书。

➢ This question is beyond my knowledge.
这个问题超出了我的知识范围。

Dr. Deng Yaping

Deng Yaping, known as a **world-class**[①] table tennis athlete, has won many important sports games including the 25th and 26th Olympic Games held **respectively**[②] in Barcelona in 1992 and Atlanta in 1996.

After she retired at the end of the 1997 season, Deng became an English major student of Tsinghua University and gained **a bachelor's degree**[③] in 2001. In the same year, she was admitted to the **University of Nottingham**[④]in Britain and accomplished the study of her master's degree there. Eventually, in 2008 she received **a PhD degree**[⑤] in **Land Economy**[⑥] at the Jesus College in University of Cambridge.

At the end of 1996, Deng Yaping was recommended by Juan Antonio Samaranch, who then was the president of the International Olympic Committee, for the appointment of its

---

① world-class *a.*. 世界级的，世界一流的
② respectively *ad.* 分别地，各自地
③ bachelor's degree 学士学位
④ University of Nottingham 诺丁汉大学建于 1881 年，是英国著名的重点大学，以其出色的教学质量赢得了国际声誉，一直是全英报考学生的首选。
⑤ PhD degree 博士学位
⑥ Land Economy 土地经济学

members of the **International Olympic Committee Athletes Commission**[1]. Though Mr. Samaranch helped her build a good platform in the field of international sports development, Deng gradually realized that she was confronted with a great **obstacle**[2]—English. The working languages of the Olympic Committee are English and French. However, at that time, Deng had just **started learning English from scratch**[3], let alone French. She felt quite anxious for her **incompetence**[4], and decided to catch up as soon as possible.

During the learning process, she led a boring life. After four hours of classes every day, she had to spend four hours more to finish her professors' assignments.

A year later, a miracle happened. Facing the strict professors of Cambridge, Deng read her doctoral thesis, which is over 35,000 words, on the research of "The Impact of the Olympic Games on Chinese Development". This article gained **unanimous**[5] approval! Mr. Samaranch praised her for "having the key to open the world".

Her coverage of **conquering**[6] difficulties in one of the best higher education institutions in the world inspires lots of people. We admire her **perseverance**[7] and **determination**[8]. Her success proves that where there is a will, there is a way.

中国博士邓亚萍

作为一名大家熟知的世界级乒乓球运动员，邓亚萍曾在多项重要赛事中夺得冠军，其中包括 1992 年在巴塞罗那举办的第 25 届奥运会及 1996 年在亚特兰大举办的第 26 届奥运会。

在 1997 年赛季结束后，邓亚萍结束了她的运动生涯，成为了清华大学英语专业的一名学生，并于 2001 年顺利获得了学士学位。 同年，她被英国诺丁汉大学录取，

---

① International Olympic Committee Athletes Commission 运动员委员会是国际奥委会下设的 21 个专门委员会之一，定期召开会议，讨论运动员的权利和义务并向国际奥委会执委会提出建议。
② obstacle *n.* 障碍，阻碍
③ start from scratch 从头开始
④ incompetence *n.* 缺乏能力，不适当
⑤ unanimous *a.* 意见一致的，无异议的
⑥ conquer *v.* 征服，克服
⑦ perseverance *n.* 毅力，不屈不挠
⑧ determination *n.* 决心，果断

在该校取得了硕士学位。最终在2008年，她在剑桥大学的耶稣学院获得了土地经济学专业的博士学位。

1996年底，邓亚萍被时任国际奥委会主席的胡安·安东尼奥·萨马兰奇先生提名为国际奥委会运动委员会委员。尽管这为她在国际体育领域提供了一个良好的发展平台，但她逐渐意识到英语成为制约她顺利开展工作的一个重要因素。因为国际奥委会的两种工作语言分别是英语与法语，然而，当时邓亚萍的英语学习刚刚起步，更不用说法语了。她感到十分焦急，决定尽快地学好这两门语言，迎头赶上。

从开始学习英语到最终取得博士学位这一期间，她都是过着一种枯燥的生活。在每天上完4小时课后，她还要另外花4个小时来完成教授布置的作业。

一年之后，奇迹出现了。面对着严格的剑桥大学的考官，邓亚萍用英语宣读了长达3.5万字的博士论文，文章讨论的是关于“奥运会对中国未来发展的影响”，并获得一致通过！萨马兰奇先生称赞她“拥有了打开世界大门的钥匙”。

邓亚萍战胜困难的勇气激励了许许多多的人。我们钦佩她的毅力和决心。她的成功证明：有志者，事竟成。

Unit 8 Women in Cambridge
巾帼胜须眉

29 Emma Thompson
奥斯卡最佳女演员

Tom and Kelly are discussing how to choose the perfect date movie.

T: Tom K: Kelly

T: Okay, Kelly, if you were me, would you take your date to a **violent action flick**① or a romantic movie?

K: A romance, of course.

T: Well, there might be some scientific basis for why romantic movies make for good dates. In one study, participants were asked to watch a romantic movie and a violent movie, and watching the romance **stimulated**② the viewers, "implicit **affiliation**③ motives."

K: What are those?

T: Their unconscious desire for close friendships. Plus, in men, watching the romance decreased their power motives, or their unconscious desire for dominance.

K: I'll bet the opposite was true for the violent movie.

T: That's the neat part. Changes in implicit affiliation and power motives are associated with changes in **hormone**④ levels. For example, the viewers who watched the romantic

---

① violent action flick 暴力的动作片
② stimulate *v.* 刺激，鼓舞
③ affiliation *n.* 亲和力，友好关系
④ hormone *n.* 激素，荷尔蒙

movie experienced a temporary increase in **progesterone**① levels.

K: Um…It's so complicated.

T: Yes, but with the violent movie, things were more complicated. So as far as the ideal date movie goes, until you check out your partner's video collection, it's probably safest just to go with a romance.

K: Do you have any good romances to recommend?

T: Have you ever watched *Love Actually*? It is a romantic and warm movie.

K: Yes, I've watched it before and I like it very much too. The screenplay **delves**② into different aspects of love as shown through ten separate stories involving a wide variety of individuals, many of whom are shown to be interlinked as their tales progress.

T: Yes, and the **ensemble**③ cast is composed predominantly of British actors. Which part is your favourite?

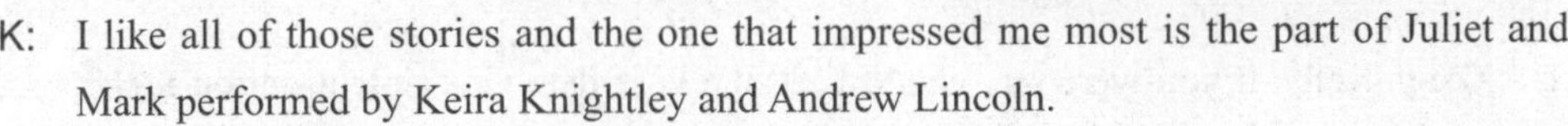

K: I like all of those stories and the one that impressed me most is the part of Juliet and Mark performed by Keira Knightley and Andrew Lincoln.

T: I love that part too. However, my favorite one is the story about the couple named Harry and Karen. You know, I am a big fan of Emma Thompson.

K: I felt heart-broken when I saw that part. She was an excellent actress.

T: I agree with you. As an **Oscar**④ winner for best actress, her performance is so natural that you can't say that she is acting.

K: She is so talented that she can play all kinds of roles. Have you ever seen *Nanny Mcphee* ? Thompson's **appearance**⑤ in that movie is very funny.

T: Of course. But still I think it is not as fun as that in *Harry Potter and the Prisoner of Azkaban*. She acts as Professor Sybil Trelawney, do you remember?

K: I think so. Is she the one who is constantly being looked down upon by Professor

① progesterone *n.* 黄体酮，孕酮
② delve *vt.* 钻探，探究
③ ensemble *n.* 全体
④ Oscar *n.* 奥斯卡金像奖，其正式名称是“电影艺术与科学学院奖 (Academy of motion picture Arts and Sciences)”，1927 年设立，每年一次在美国洛杉矶举行。80 多年来一直享有盛誉。它不仅反映美国电影艺术的发展进程和成就，而且对世界许多国家的电影艺术有着不可忽视的影响。
⑤ appearance *n.* 外貌，外观

McGonagall, but showed her ability by making the **prediction**[①] about the escape of Peter Pettigrew?

T: Right!

K: How about Thompson's life, Is she married?

T: Yes. After divorcing with Branagh in, I guess it's, 1994, Thompson is now married to actor Greg Wise, who had played Willoughby in Ang Lee's *Sense and Sensibility*. They have one daughter, Gaia, born in 1999.

K: I see. You're really a great fan of Thompson!

T: 好吧，凯利，如果你是我的话，你约会时会去看暴力的动作片还是浪漫温情的电影？

K: 当然是浪漫温情的啦。

T: 嗯，浪漫的电影对约会起了良好作用，这是有科学依据的。在一次调查中，参与者被要求看一个浪漫电影和一个暴力动作片，结果表明观看浪漫电影刺激了观看者“含蓄的亲和力动机”。

K: 这是什么东西？

T: 他们潜意识中对亲密友谊的欲求。此外，观看浪漫电影还削减了男性的权利欲和他们潜意识中的支配欲。

K: 我打赌暴力的动作片正好相反。

T: 差不多是这样。亲和力和权利欲的改变与体内荷尔蒙的改变也有着密切的关系。例如，观看浪漫电影的人会经历短暂的黄体酮的上升。

K: 嗯……好复杂啊。

T: 对啊，但是对于观看暴力动作片而言，情况更为复杂。所以呢，根据这个理想约会电影的原则，在你弄清楚你的约会对象都收藏什么类型的电影前，去看一场浪漫电影才是最保险的。

K: 你有什么好的浪漫电影推荐吗？

T: 你看过《真爱至上》没有？这是个浪漫温情的电影。

K: 嗯，我原来看过这个电影，也非常喜欢。它通过10个独立的故事向我们展示了爱的不同层面，这些故事涉及到形形色色的人，随着故事情节的发展，你会发现这些人又相互联系。

T: 对，而且演员班底主要由英国演员组成。你最喜欢哪个部分？

K: 所有的故事我都喜欢，但我印象最深的是茱丽叶和马克的故事，由凯拉·奈特莉

① prediction *n.* 预言，预报

和安德鲁·林肯主演。

T: 我也喜欢那个故事。不过，我最喜欢的还是那对叫哈利和凯伦的夫妇的故事。你知道，我可是爱玛·汤普森的影迷。

K: 是啊，看得我都心痛不已。她真是个很棒的演员。

T: 我同意你的说法。作为奥斯卡最佳女主角奖的得主，她的表演真是天衣无缝，你完全都看不出来她是在表演。

K: 她很有天赋，无论表演起什么角色来都游刃有余。你看过《魔法保姆麦克菲》吗？汤普森在里面的扮相真的很搞笑。

T: 当然看过啦。但是我还是觉得她在《哈利波特与阿兹卡班的囚徒》里的扮相更加滑稽。她在里面演的是西比尔·特里劳尼教授，你还记得吗？

K: 也许吧。是不是那个老被麦格教授看扁的人啊？但是她成功预言了彼得·佩迪鲁的逃跑。

T: 对啦！

K: 现实中汤普森的生活怎样，她结婚了没有？

T: 结了。 1994 年和莱纳格离婚后，她又和演员格雷格·怀斯结了婚，就是在《理智与情感》里扮演威勒比的那个演员。 他们有一个孩子，名叫盖亚，出生于 1999 年。

K: 哦，你真不愧是汤普森的铁杆影迷！

1 Okay, Kelly, if you **were** me, would you take your date to a violent action flick or a romantic movie?

这里用"were"是英语中的虚拟语气。虚拟语气用来表示说话人的主观愿望或假想，所说的是一个条件，不一定是事实，或与事实相反。这里的条件句可分为两类，一类为真实条件句，一类为非真实条件句。非真实条件句表示的是假设的或实际可能性不大的情况，故采用虚拟语气。非真实条件句的基本特点是时态退后。在这句话中，叙述的是非真实的条件，故采用 were(不使用 was 是因为英语中惯用 were)，而不用 am。

➢ If he were here, everything would be all right.
如果他在这儿，一切都会好的。

➢ If I were a boy again, I would practice perseverance more often, and never give up a thing because it was difficult or inconvenient.
假如我又回到了童年，我做事要更有毅力，决不因为事情艰难或者麻烦而撒手不干。

2 Well, there might be some scientific basis for why romantic movies **make for** good dates.

（1）make for 在文中意为“有助于，促进”。

➢ Bright colours make for good mood.
明亮的颜色让人心情舒畅。

（2）make for 还可以理解为“趋势，走向”。

➢ The TV legal programs make for mature and flourish in China and have Chinese character.
电视法制节目在我国逐步走向成熟和繁荣，并具有中国特色。

3 Changes in implicit affiliation and power motives **are associated with** changes in hormone levels.

be associated with 意为“和……相关”，和 be related to 相近。

➢ This new source should somehow be associated with the solar system.
这个新的来源与太阳系应有某种程度的关联。

4 **In contrast**, women with higher pre-movie testosterone levels and power motives experienced a drop in both, while women with lower testosterone levels became downright uncomfortable.

in contrast 意为“对比之下，与此相反”；in sharp contrast 意为“形成鲜明对比”。

➢ For humans, in contrast, imitation is a very important means by which we learn and transmit skills, language and culture.
与此相反，就人类来说，在学习以及传递技能、语言和文化上，模仿是一个非常重要的途径。

Emma Thompson

Emma Thompson was born in London on April 15, 1959, into a family of actors—her father was Eric Thompson, who has passed away; and her mother, Phyllida Law, has **co-starred**① with Thompson in several films; her sister, Sophie Thompson, is an actor as well. She attended Cambridge University, studying English Literature, and was part of the university's Footlights Group.

① co-star *vt.* 与某人联合主演

Thompson graduated in 1980 and **embarked**① on her career in entertainment, beginning with **stints**② on BBC radio and touring with comedy shows. She soon got her first major break in television on the comedy skit program "Alfresco" (1983). She also worked on other TV comedy review programs in the mid-1980s, occasionally with some of her fellow Footlights alums, and often with actor Robbie Coltrane. Thompson found herself **collaborating**③ again with Fry in 1985, this time in his stage adaptation of the play "Me and My Girl" in London's West End, in which she had a leading role, playing Sally Smith. The show was a success and she received favorable reviews, and the strength of her performance led to her casting as the lead in the BBC television miniseries "Fortunes of War" (1987), in which Thompson and her co-star, Kenneth Branagh, play an English ex-patriate couple living in Eastern Europe as the Second World War erupts. Thompson won a **BAFTA**④ award for her work on the program. In the late 80s and early 90s, she starred in a string of well-received and successful television and film productions, most notably her lead role in the Merchant-Ivory production of Howards End (1992), which confirmed her ability to carry a movie on both sides of the Atlantic and appropriately showered her with trans-Atlantic honors—both an Oscar and a BAFTA award.

Since then, Thompson has continued to move effortlessly between the art film world and **mainstream**⑤ Hollywood, though even her Hollywood roles tend to be in more up-market productions. She continues to work on television as well, but is generally very **selective**⑥ about which roles she takes. She writes for the screen as well, such as the screenplay for Ang Lee's *Sense and Sensibility* (1995), in which she also starred as Elinor Dashwood, and the **teleplay**⑦ **adaptation**⑧ of Margaret Edson's acclaimed play *Wit* (2001), in which she also starred.

---

① embark *vt.* 从事，着手
② stint *n.* 定量
③ collaborate *vi.* 合作
④ BAFTA 英国电影和电视艺术学院奖（British Academy of Film and Television Arts）是一个英国的机构，每年颁发奖项给杰出的电影、电视、儿童电影和电视以及互动媒体。
⑤ mainstream *n.* 主流
⑥ selective *adj.* 选择性的
⑦ teleplay *n.* 电视剧
⑧ adaptation *n.* 改编本

奥斯卡最佳女演员

爱玛·汤普森于1959年4月15日出生于伦敦的一个演艺世家。她的父亲是艾里克·汤普森(已故),母亲是费莉达·洛,曾与爱玛共同主演过数部影片。她的妹妹苏菲·汤普森也是一个演员。她进入剑桥大学的时候，学习的是英国文学，并且是学校戏剧小组的一员。

爱玛在1980年毕业后便开始了她的舞台生涯。起初，她在BBC广播节目中做定额演出，跟着一些喜剧节目组到处跑。很快她就在电视剧上有了重要突破，1983年她编写并出演了讽刺剧《在户外》。1980年代中期，她还为其他电视评论节目工作。

1985年，汤普森与斯蒂芬·佛莱再次合作，出演他的舞台改编剧《我和我的姑娘》，演出地点在伦敦西区。她出演主角萨莉·史密斯。这出舞台剧大获成功，爱玛的表演也受到了好评。凭借这次成功，爱玛获得了主演BBC电视剧《战争财》(1987)的机会。在《战争财》中，爱玛和肯尼思·布莱纳格共同主演了一对二战爆发时移居东欧的英国夫妇。爱玛凭借此片赢得了英国电影和电视艺术学校奖。

20世纪80年代末90年代初，她出演了一系列大受欢迎的电视和电影。她在莫吉安特一伊沃里制片公司的电影《霍华德庄园》(1992)里的角色尤为突出。这个角色确立了她在大西洋两岸的影响力，并为她赢得了盛誉—— 奥斯卡和英国电影和电视艺术学院双料影后。

此后，不管是出演文艺片，还是好莱坞主流片，爱玛都游刃有余，虽然她的好莱坞角色更为商业化。她仍会出演电视剧，只不过对角色总是精挑细选。她也写剧本，比如1995年的《理智与情感》(李安导演)，同时她出演了片中埃莉诺·达什伍德一角。还有一部改编自玛格丽特·埃德森广受好评的同名舞台剧的电视剧《深知我心》(2001),也是由她撰写的剧本，在剧中她同样担当主演。

Sylvia Plath
为爱而死的美国女诗人

Tom is walking on the compus alone, and then he comes across Kerry who is sitting on the bench holding a book in her hands.

T: Tom　　K: Kerry

T: Hi, Kerry. What are you reading?

K: Oh, these are just some books I picked up at a local poetry festival that took place a couple of weeks ago. It was nice to see that there are so many people who appreciate poetry here.

T: I didn't know you were such a poetry lover, Kerry. Personally, I've always found that stuff a little bit boring and hard to understand. All that **flowery language**[①] gives me a headache! I'd rather read a nice long novel any day.

K: I'll admit that poetry's an **acquired**[②] taste. But once you learn more about it, you'll find that poems aren't all flowery and **incomprehensible**[③] they don't even have to **rhyme**[④]!

T: Fine, but if there is no rhyme in a poetry, I'm wondering whether we can call it poetry.

K: Next time I'll find you some belonging to that category. I'm sure you'll be **enchanted**[⑤] by the words.

---

① flowery language 花哨的语言
② acquired *adj.* 后天获得的
③ incomprehensible *adj.* 难以理解的，晦涩难懂的
④ rhyme *vi.* 押韵
⑤ enchanted *adj.* 被施魔法的，着迷的

T: Ok. Why do you love poetry so much?

K: The words, the feelings in it...Besides, I think they often provide us with the **essence**[1] of life.

T: Great. Which is your favorite poet?

K: One of my favorite poets is Sylvia Plath, who is a **confessional**[2] poet. Have you ever read her poetry?

T: I'm not sure. The name sounds familiar to me. Perhaps the high school American literature teacher ever introduced her to us. But to tell you the truth, most of the names of the poets have just **slipped from my memory**[3].

K: Understandable. Her fame is not so great as those of other top American poets.

T: Wait. Is she the one who killed herself in her thirties by turning on the gas?

K: You are right. That's a tragedy. She must have been heart-broken and felt hopeless then.

T: Why? Because of her unhappy marriage?

K: Yes, this is the most important reason. She suffered from depression when she was a junior student in college. Plath was briefly committed to a mental institution where she received **electroconvulsive therapy**[4].

T: She must have spent a miserable time there.

K: Yes, then Plath seemed to make an acceptable recovery and graduated from Smith with honors. Then she obtained a Fulbright scholarship to Cambridge where she met Ted Hughes.

T: Wow, she was a lucky girl.

K: Not at all. Plath's marriage to Hughes **was fraught with**[5] difficulties, particularly surrounding his **affair**[6] with Assia Wevill, the wife of one colleague, Plath's mental problem became more severe after that.

T: Gosh, what happened next?

K: Finally, the couple separated in late 1962. In 1963, Plath killed herself by turning the gas on. She was then only 30 years old.

T: What a tragedy! She was a poor woman.

K: There is a film named *Sylvia* telling us the life story of her, especially the love story

① essence *n.* 实质，本质，精华
② confessional *adj.* 自白的，忏悔的
③ slipped from my memory 从我的记忆中溜走，忘记
④ electroconvulsive therapy 电休克治疗法
⑤ be fraught with 充满……的
⑥ affair *n.* 私事，风流韵事

between she and the later **England's Poet Laureate**[①] Ted Hughes . If you are interested, you can go and have a look. I'm sure that you will have a further understanding of her and her poetry.

T: Who is the leading actress?

K: Gwyneth Paltrow. And Daniel Craig is the leading actor.

T: I have to watch it. Say, have you ever written any poetry of your own? Some love **sonnets**[②], perhaps?

K: No love sonnets, but I did try to write some poems a long time ago. They were all really bad. Once I spent three hours trying to come up with a word that rhymes with "panda"!

T: Silly Kerry! How could you not think of "Sylvia"?

T: 嗨，凯瑞。你在读什么呢？

K: 哦，这是我在几周前的诗歌节上买的书。真高兴看到这儿有这么多人都喜欢诗歌。

T: 凯瑞，我还不知道你是个诗歌迷呢。就我个人而言，我总觉得诗歌枯燥无味，晦涩难懂。花哨的词藻让我头疼！还不如哪天读本有意思的长篇小说呢。

K: 我承认欣赏诗歌需要慢慢品味。不过，如果你多接触诗歌，就会发现诗歌并不都是花哨、难懂的，它们甚至都不需要押韵！

Smith College Archives

T: 好吧。不过如果一首诗连韵脚都没有，那还能叫诗吗？

K: 下次我给你找一些这样的诗。你肯定会被它的词句迷住的。

T: 好的。你为什么这么喜欢诗歌啊？

K: 嗯，它的语言，它给人的感觉……此外，我觉得诗歌总是向我们展示生命的真谛。

T: 太棒了。那么你最喜欢的诗人是谁？

K: 我最喜欢的诗人之一是西尔维亚·普拉斯。她是自白派诗人。你读过她的诗吗？

T: 也许吧。这个名字听起来很耳熟。或许高中美国文学的老师曾经向我们介绍过她。但跟你说句实话，我都不记得几个诗人的名字了。

K: 这也可以理解。她并不像美国顶尖的诗人那么有名。

T: 等等，她是不是那个在 30 岁开煤气自尽的诗人？

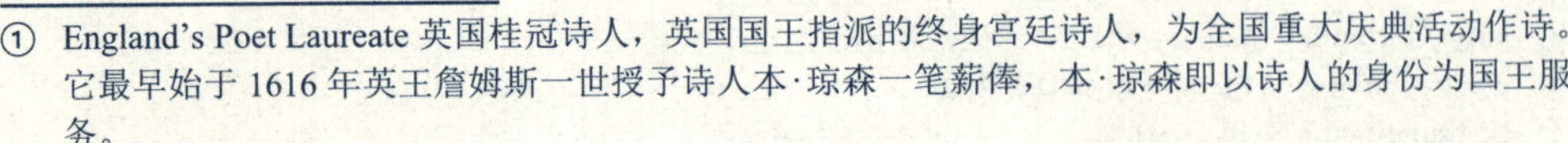
① England's Poet Laureate 英国桂冠诗人，英国国王指派的终身宫廷诗人，为全国重大庆典活动作诗。它最早始于 1616 年英王詹姆斯一世授予诗人本·琼森一笔薪俸，本·琼森即以诗人的身份为国王服务。

② sonnet *n.* 十四行诗

K: 对。那真是个悲剧。她那个时候肯定是伤心绝望至极。

T: 为什么呢？家庭生活不幸福吗？

K: 对，这是主要原因。她在大三的时候就曾经得过抑郁症，尝试自杀未遂。曾被送进精神病院进行治疗，进行电休克治疗。

T: 她那段时间一定特别难熬。

K: 是啊。她似乎康复得还不错，之后顺利从史密斯学院毕业，并获得富布赖特奖学金到剑桥大学深造。在那里她遇到了当时在诗坛小有名气的泰德·休斯。

T: 哇，她真幸运。

K: 一点也不。后来普拉斯和休斯的婚姻因为休斯和同事的妻子阿西亚发生婚外情而愈加困难重重，普拉斯的精神疾病也因为休斯的婚外情而加重。

T: 天啊，他们后来怎么样了呢?

K: 终于，1962 年底他们分手了。1963 年，她在厨房里开煤气自尽，年仅 30 岁。

T: 太悲剧了。她真是个可怜的女人。

K: 有个电影就叫做《西尔维亚》，讲述了西尔维亚的一生，尤其是她和后来成为英国桂冠诗人的泰德·休斯的爱情故事。如果你感兴趣的话，可以找来看看。你肯定会对她和她的诗有进一步的了解。

T: 谁是女主演?

K: 格温妮丝·帕特洛。男主演是丹尼尔·克雷格。

T: 我一定得看看这部电影。你自己写过诗没有？比如说关于爱情的十四行诗?

K: 没写过这个。 但很久以前我的确尝试过写诗，只是写得很糟糕。我曾经花了 3 个小时来想可以和“panda”押韵的词!

T: 盖瑞你真笨，你怎么没想到“Sylvia”？

1 Oh, these are just some books I picked up at a local poetry festival that took place **a couple of** weeks ago. It was nice to see that there are so many people who appreciate poetry here.

a couple of 意为“一两个，两三个，几个，一些”，注意不要受 couple 意思的影响而理解为“两个”。

➢ A couple of them had decided they wanted the bill to pass and our office to enforce it.
有两三个人已经下了决心，希望看到议案通过，并让我们的办公室来负责执行。

2 The name **sounds familiar to** me.

sound 在这里是“听起来”的意思，是系动词。系动词 +familiar to sb. 意为“为……所熟悉，为……所了解”。注意 be familiar with，意为“对……熟悉”。

- Those restaurants are very familiar to Jack.
- Jack is very familiar with those restaurants.
  杰克对这些餐馆很熟悉。

以上两句话都可以表示某人对某物或者某地很熟悉，但要注意主体和客体的位置不要颠倒。

3 Is she the one who killed herself **in her thirties** by turning on the gas?

in her thirties 的意思是“在她三十多岁的时候”。同样地，in sb's forties 就是“在某人四十多岁的时候”。

- She became very famous in her fifties.
  她在五十多岁的时候就非常有名了。

4 Once I spent three hours trying to **come up with** a word that rhymes with “panda”!

come up with 意为“提出，提供，想出，找到或提出（答案、办法）”，而 come up to 则意为“接近，走近”，应该注意介词的使用，不同的介词意义差别很大。

- I'm sure if we work on it together we'll be able to come up with the correct answer.
  我相信只要我们一起努力，就一定会想出正确的答案。
- He came up to us in the street.
  他在街上向我们走来。

Sylvia Plath

Sylvia Plath was an American poet, novelist, children's author, and short story author. Known primarily for her poetry, Plath also wrote a **semi-autobiographical**[①] novel, *The Bell Jar*, under the **pseudonym**[②] Victoria Lucas. Plath, along with Anne Sexton, was credited

① semi-autobiographical *adj.* 半自传体的
② pseudonym *n.* 假名，笔名

with advancing the genre of **confessional poetry**[①].

She was born in Massachusetts to Aurelia Schober Plath, a first-generation American of Austrian descent, and Otto Emile Plath, an immigrant from Germany. At age eight, Plath published her first poem in the Boston Herald's children's section.

Plath has suffered from Depression for several times in her lifetime. In 1950, she attended Smith College. After her third year of college Plath made her first medically documented **suicide**[②] attempt. She wrote about that in *The Bell Jar*.

After her suicide attempt, Plath was briefly committed to a mental institution where she received electroconvulsive therapy. Plath seemed to make an acceptable recovery and graduated from Smith with honors in June 1955. In the same year, she won the prominent Glascock Prize with *Two Lovers and a Beachcomber* by the Real Sea.

She obtained a Fulbright scholarship to Newnham College, Cambridge where she continued actively writing poetry, occasionally publishing her work in the student newspaper Varsity. Then she met the later English Poet Laureate Ted Hughes. After a **tempestuous**[③] **courtship**[④], they were married on June 16, 1956.

Plath and Hughes spent from July 1957 to December 1959 living and working in the United States. The couple then moved to Boston. Upon learning Plath was pregnant the couple moved back to the United Kingdom. In 1960 Plath published her first collection of poetry, *The Colossus*. Plath's marriage to Hughes was fraught with difficulties, particularly surrounding his affair with Assia Wevill. Plath's mental problem became more severe since then. Finally, the couple separated in late 1962.

She returned to London with their children and rented a house where W. B. Yeats once lived. However, in February, 1963, Plath took her own life. She placed her head in the oven while the gas was turned on. She was then only 30 years old.

Plath's gravestone in Heptonstall churchyard bears the inscription "Even amidst fierce flames the golden lotus can be planted."

Two years after her death, Ariel , a collection of some her last poems was published, that was followed by Crossing the Water and Winter Trees in 1971 and in 1981 The Collected Poems was published, edited by **none other than**[⑤] Ted Hughes.

① confessional poetry 自白诗。自白诗派兴起于上世纪 60 年代的美国。它在彻底反叛新批评学派的基础上对个体生命经验予以了充分肯定，并对自我的隐秘世界进行了深入开掘。“自白诗派”的标签最早由美国文学评论家 M. L. 罗森塔尔创立。

② suicide *n.* 自杀，自杀者

③ tempestuous *adj.* 暴乱的，剧烈的

④ courtship *n.* 恋爱阶段

⑤ none other than 不是别的而正是

In 1982 Plath became the first poet to win a **Pulitzer Prize**① **posthumously**② for The Collected Poems.

美国女诗人

西尔维亚·普拉斯，美国诗人、小说家、儿童作家与短篇故事作家。除了较为著名的诗作外，普拉斯也以笔名维多利亚·卢卡斯创作了半自传小说《瓶中美人》(又译《钟形罩》)。同安·塞克斯顿一样，普拉斯被公认是自白诗的重要推动者之一。

普拉斯生于美国马萨诸塞州波士顿市，父亲是德国人，母亲是德裔美籍奥地利人。她很早就展露天赋，8 岁时在《波士顿先驱报》的儿童版上发表了第一首诗。

普拉斯一生经历了多次发作的严重抑郁症。她 1950 年进入史密斯学院就读。大三课程结束后不久，她第一次(医学上有记录的)尝试自杀。后来她在小说《瓶中美人》描述了此事。自杀未遂后，普拉斯被送进精神病院并接受电休克治疗。她似乎恢复得不错，并于 1955 年以优异成绩从史密斯学院毕业。同年，她的诗《真实海滨的两个情人和一个游荡者》获得名望极高的 Glascock Prize 诗人奖。普拉斯赢得富布赖特奖学金到剑桥大学深造。她继续写诗，偶尔在学生报刊上发表作品。在剑桥，她认识了后来成为英国桂冠诗人的泰德·休斯经过短暂的相处后，两人于 1956 年结为连理。

1957 至 1959 年，普拉斯和休斯在美国居住及工作，然后迁居到波士顿。1960 年，因为普拉斯的怀孕，他们搬回英国。同年，普拉斯出版了她的第一本诗集《巨人》。 普拉斯和休斯的婚姻因为休斯和同事的妻子阿西亚发生婚外情而愈加困难重重，普拉斯的精神疾病也因为休斯的婚外情而加重。终于，1962 年底他们分手了。

普拉斯带孩子们回到伦敦，住在诗人叶慈曾经住过的房子里。但是，1963 年 2 月，她却在厨房里开煤气自尽，年仅 30 岁。

普拉斯被葬在西约克郡，墓碑上写着："即使在激烈燃烧的火焰中，我们仍能种下金色的莲花。"

她死后两年，最后的诗作被整理成诗集《爱丽尔》出版，之后《渡湖》和《冬天的树》也分别在 1971 和 1981 年出版了。这些诗集都是由休斯编辑和整理的。

1982 年，普拉斯以遗作《诗集》成为在死后获得获普利策奖的第一个作家。

---

① Pulitzer Prize 普利策奖。美国著名报人约瑟夫·普利策将自己的财产捐献给美国的哥伦比亚大学，由他们建立一个新闻学院。这笔高达 200 万美元的款项中，有四分之一被用来设立奖项，后来这笔钱成了普利策奖的基金。1917 年，该奖的第一届颁奖仪式举行，此后每年颁发一次。普利策奖中最重要的组成部分是新闻类奖项，文学奖是众多分支中的一个。

② posthumously *adv.* 于著作者死后出版地，于死后

31 Germaine Greer
女权主义者的声音

焦点对话

Bob and Cathy come across each other in a book store several days after the International Women's day.

B: Bob　　　C: Cathy

B: This is a small world! Nice to meet you.

C: Nice to see you, too. What kind of book are you looking for?

B: Nothing special, just looking around. How about you?

C: I want to have a look at Germaine Greer's book.

B: Germaine Greer, the **feminist**[1]? I don't like her.

C: I'm afraid I cannot agree with you. I think she is **courageous**[2] and interesting. You know, she is one of the **pioneers**[3] of women's movement.

B: Yes, her book *The Female Eunuch* is very influential.

C: Oh, I'm very interested in the book. Have you read it?

B: No, I haven't. I get to know it from the Australian magazine *Monthly* of this month and Germaine Greer is the cover woman of *Monthly.*

C: I know. They made a special topic to **commemorate**[4] the 100th **anniversary**[5] of International Women's Day and the 40th anniversary of the publication of *The Female*

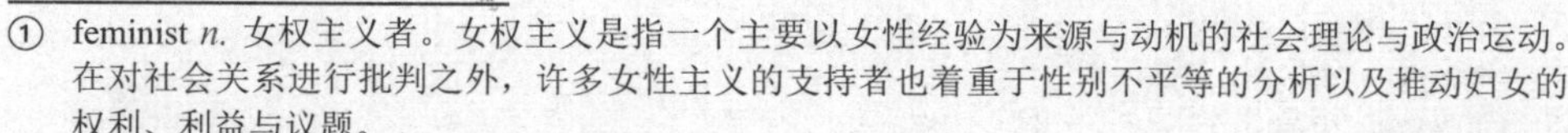

① feminist *n.* 女权主义者。女权主义是指一个主要以女性经验为来源与动机的社会理论与政治运动。在对社会关系进行批判之外，许多女性主义的支持者也着重于性别不平等的分析以及推动妇女的权利、利益与议题。

② courageous *adj.* 有胆识的，勇敢的

③ pioneer *n.* 先驱

④ commemorate *vt.* 庆祝，纪念

⑤ anniversary *n.* 周年纪念日

Eunuch. I find that is interesting, so I decided to have a look at this book.

B: I don't think it is appealing at all.

C: I see. Since you are a man, you don't have the same kind of feeling as I do. *The Female Eunuch* explores the idea of continual female oppression arguing that society seeks to impose certain **norms**[①] onto women's expected behavior.

B: True. See, things changed nowadays. You women even got a special day to celebrate your female identity.

C: Yes. There are some changes and this book actually serves as a **catalyst**[②] in the popularization of ideas about women's liberation.

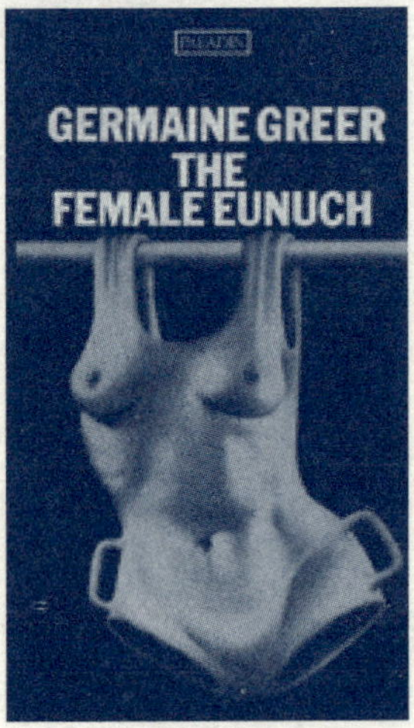

B: It seems that women's status in the society has been changed a lot, but an Australian **playwright**[③] named Louise Nora said in his article that Greer must be very disappointed in women's life style nowadays.

C: Why is that?

B: He held that instead of choosing the life style she **advocated**[④], most of the women just be content with being a housewife.

C: I don't think so. There are more and more career women now. However, **the glass ceiling**[⑤] has not been broken yet. It's still not easy for a woman to get promoted. What else did this Mr. Nora say?

B: I bet you don't want hear that. He even **sneer** at Greer that she can only remind him of his mad grandmother.

C: Not surprised. Greer has been a controversial figure ever since she **leaped into fame**[⑥] in her thirties. Have you heard that On Easter weekend 2000, a 19-year-old student at the University of Bath tied Greer up in her home and proceeded to smash her belongings with a **fire poker**[⑦]?

B: Really? What happened to Greer next, has she been hurt?

C: No. Greer's colleagues eventually came looking for her as they had been expecting her

---

① norm *n.* 规范，基准

② catalyst *n.* 催化剂，刺激因素

③ playwright *n.* 剧作家

④ advocate *vt.* 鼓吹，宣扬

⑤ the glass ceiling 玻璃天花板，喻指女性在职场遇到的升职瓶颈。

⑥ leap into fame 一夜成名

⑦ fire poker 火钳

for dinner. The student had apparently been **stalking**[①] Greer for some time after reading her books.

B: Fortunately, she is safe. It seems that she continues advocating her principal that it is time for women to get angry again and pursue greater independence away from the social pressures that exist.

C: Yes. Greer is known as an "angry" feminist, and most people have no idea that she received her Ph.D. in Cambridge. If it is not the feminist movement in the 1960s, it's very possible that she would spend the rest of her life teaching in a University.

B: 这世界真小，碰到你真高兴！

C: 见到你我也很高兴。你在找什么书呢？

B: 没什么特别的，随便转转。你呢？

C: 我想看看杰曼·格里尔的书。

B: 杰曼·格里尔，那个女权主义者吗？我不喜欢她。

C: 恐怕我和你看法不同。我觉得她很勇敢也很有趣。你也知道，她是女权主义运动的先驱之一。

B: 是啊。她的《女太监》影响力不小呢。

C: 我对那本书很感兴趣，你读过吗？

B: 没有。我只是在这个月的澳大利亚的杂志《月刊》中才知道这本书的，而且杰曼·格里尔就是这期《月刊》的封面女郎。

C: 这我知道。他们为国际妇女节的百周年纪念和《女太监》出版40周年而做了一个专题。我觉得挺有趣的，所以过来看看这本书。

B: 我觉得这本书一点意思也没有。

C: 我能理解。你们男的不能理解我们的感受。《女太监》指出当前妇女在社会中仍然饱受压迫，社会总是想把一定的行为准则强加于女性。

B: 对。但是你看，现在情况已经改变了许多。你们甚至都有一个专门的节日来庆祝你们的女性身份了。

C: 是啊。情况确实有了一些变化。这本书就是妇女解放思想得以广泛传播的催化剂。

B: 看起来女性的社会地位的确改变了不少，但是一个叫路易斯·诺拉的澳大利亚剧作家在他的一篇文章中指出，格里尔肯定对当代女性的状况感到特别失望。

C: 为什么呢？

① stalk *vt.* 潜近，偷偷接近

B: 他认为，绝大多数妇女都满足于当一个家庭主妇，而不是选择格里尔所鼓吹的生活模式。

C: 我不这么认为。当今社会中职业女性越来越多了。不过，女性的职场瓶颈还是没被打破。女性想要晋升仍然不容易。这位诺拉先生还说了什么?

B: 我敢打赌你不想听。他还讽刺格里尔只能让他想起他那疯疯癫癫的老祖母。

C: 我一点也不觉得奇怪。格里尔自从30多岁一夜成名以来就一直是个有争议的人物。你听说过没，在2000年的复活节，一个19岁的巴斯大学女生闯进了格里尔家，把她绑了起来，还用火钳打碎了好多东西。

B: 真的吗? 后来格里尔怎样，有没有受伤?

C: 没有。格里尔的同事们一直都在等她吃晚饭，见她没来就到她家去找。这个女生明显是在读过格里尔的书后，一直试图接近她。

B: 幸好这位奇怪的老太太没出什么事儿。好像后来她还是一直在宣扬自己的原则，女性应该再次愤怒起来，去追求社会重压之外的更大程度的独立性。

C: 嗯。其实许多人只知格里尔是位“愤怒的”女权主义者，却不知她拥有剑桥大学的文学博士学位，如果不是20世纪60年代风生水起的女权运动，或许她会一直安静地在大学里教书直至终老。

1 There are some changes and this book actually **serves as** a catalyst in the popularization of ideas about women's liberation.

serve as 意为“担任……，充当……，起……的作用”。

➢ He was served as a general.
他被任命为将军。

➢ Newspaper serves me as a curtain.
我用报纸充当窗帘。

2 He even sneer at Greer that she can only **remind** him of his mad grandmother.

remind sb. of sth. 意为“提醒，使记起，使回想起”。也可以使用 remind sb. of doing, remind sb. that。

➢ The old picture reminds me of the summer I spent in the house of my grandmother.
这张老照片让我想在奶奶家度过的那个夏天。

➢ Please remind me of sending an e-mail to Jane.
请提醒我给简发一封电子邮件。

➢ She reminds that I should not make the same kind of mistake again.
她提醒我不要再犯同一个错误。

3 Have you heard that On Easter weekend 2000, a 19-year-old student at the University of Bath tied Greer up in her home and **proceeded to** smash her belongings with a fire poker?

（1）proceed to do. 意为"继续做某事"，也可以说 proceed with sth.。

➢ He paused to consult his notes, and then proceeded with his question.
他停了下来看了看笔记，然后继续提问。

（2）法律用语中用 proceed against 表示"起诉"。

➢ Are you sure that you want to proceed against your neighbor over such a trifling matter?
你确定要因为这么点小事而起诉你的邻居？

（3）proceed from 意为"发出，出自"。

➢ Many diseases proceed from negligence of hygiene.
许多疾病源于不讲卫生。

4 **If it is not** the feminist movement in the 1960s, it's very possible that she would spend the rest of her life teaching in a University.

if it is not 意为"假如不是（没有）……，如果不是这样"。

➢ If it is not too troublesome, I would like to go with you.
如果不是太麻烦的话，我倒愿意和你一起去。

Germaine Greer

Germaine Greer (born 29 January 1939) is an Australian-born writer, academic, journalist and scholar of early modern English literature, widely regarded as one of the most significant feminist voices of the later 20th century.

Germaine Greer spent her **formative**① years in an all-girl **Catholic**② Academy. Then she was educated at Melbourne and Sydney Universities in Australia and in 1964 she left to England where she studied at Newnham College, Cambridge. In 1968 she received her Ph.D. and accepted a **lectureship**③ in English at the University of Warwick in Coventry. The same year, in London, she married Australian journalist Paul du Feu, but the marriage lasted only three weeks, during which, as she later admitted, Greer was unfaithful several times.

With the publication of *The Female Eunuch*, she became a highly influential figure in the sexual liberationist and feminist movements. *The Female Eunuch* explores the idea of continual female oppression arguing that society seeks to impose certain norms onto women's expected behavior. In the book Germaine argues it is time for women to get angry again and pursue greater independence away from the social pressures that exist. The book relates women's sexual passivity of the day with that of a **castrate**④, essentially sexless and it also turns her into a household name and bringing her both **adulation**⑤ and opposition. Greer resigned her post at **Warwick University**⑥ in 1972 after travelling the world to promote her book. The media saw Germaine Greer as the high priestess of "women's lib" and her book as its bible. During the seventies, Greer remained in the public eye, encouraging women to seek out their own sexuality. In her sixties, Greer has published another book, *The Whole Woman*. Greer certainly does not avoid confrontation, she once said: "The more people we annoy, the more we know we're doing it right."

Greer had attracted controversy in the Southern Hemisphere before. In 1972 she was fined in New Zealand $40 for offensive language. The incident surrounded a speech she gave attacking anti-**abortion**⑦ campaigners at Auckland's Town Hall. She was arrested for swearing during the speech.

She has ever posed nude for the underground London magazine *Oz* on the understanding that the male editors would do likewise, but they did not.

① formative *adj.* 形成期的，成长期的
② Catholic *adj.* 天主教的
③ lectureship *n.* 讲师职务
④ castrate *n.* 阉割
⑤ adulation *n.* 谄媚，奉承
⑥ Warwick University 华威大学。英国的一所校园式大学，创建于 1965 年，作为一所年轻的大学，在英国乃至全球都有享有良好的学术声誉，近年来一直都保持在全英前十所顶尖高校的行列。
⑦ abortion *n.* 流产

Greer is now retired but retains her position as **Professor Emeritus**① in the Department of English Literature and Comparative Studies at the University of Warwick, Coventry. She has defined her goal as "women's liberation" as distinct from "equality with men".

女权主义者的声音

杰曼·格里尔，出生在澳大利亚，她既是作家、学者和记者，也是早期现代英国文学的著名学者，并被广泛认为是20世纪后半叶最杰出的女权主义运动家之一。

她在一所天主教女校里度过了成长时期。之后，她曾在澳大利亚的墨尔本和悉尼大学求学，1964年前往剑桥大学纽纳姆学院深造。1968年，她顺利拿到了博士学位，并获得了一个考文垂华威大学的讲师职位。同年，她与澳大利亚记者保罗在伦敦结婚，但这场婚姻只持续了3周。此后她承认，在这3周时间里，她曾经红杏出墙过几次。

随着《女太监》的出版，她成为在女性解放和妇女运动中一个十分有影响力的人物。《女太监》指出当前妇女在社会中仍然饱受压迫，社会总是想把一定的行为准则强加于女性。格里尔认为女性应该再次愤怒起来，去追求社会重压之外的更大程度的独立性。这本书把当时妇女在性方面的被动性与阉割联系在一起，使她的名字家喻户晓，也给她带来了不少赞誉和批评。1972年，在前往世界各地对新书进行宣传后，格里尔辞去了华威大学的职位。媒体把杰曼·格里尔誉为妇女解放运动的祭司，她的书就是整个运动的圣经。60多岁的时候，格里尔出版另一本书，名为《完整的女人》。格里尔从不回避争议，她曾经说过："被我们惹恼的人越多，就更说明了我们行为的合理性。"

她曾经在南半球遭到了反对。1972年她在新西兰演讲的时候因为"不雅之辞"被罚款40美金。这件事与她在奥克兰市政厅发表攻击反堕胎组织的言论有关。之后，她又因为在演讲中说脏话而被逮捕。

她还曾为伦敦的地铁杂志《奥兹》做过裸体模特。她认为男性编辑也会这么做，但他们没有。

格里尔现在已经退休了，但仍在华威大学的英语文学和比较研究中心保留名誉教授的职位。她曾说过，自己的目标是"女性的解放"，这和"与男性平等"明显不同。

① Professor Emeritus 名誉退休教授

32 Margrethe II of Denmark
丹麦王室才女

Wendy is reading a newspaper, Adam comes over to her.

A: Adam W: Wendy

A: Hi, Wendy. Who are those people on the paper?

W: Oh, these are the Denmark royal family.

A: Let me have a look. Is the old lady in the middle the Queen of Denmark?

W: You are right. She is Margrethe II, and her sons, **daughter-in-law**① and grandchildren.

A: It is a happy family and all of them are good-looking.

W: Yes. From left to right, this is Prince Joachim, his two sons, the Queen, Prince Frederik and his wife.

A: Is this their baby? It is so cute!

W: Yes, it is a little prince.

A: The Queen is so elegant. How old is she now?

W: She is nearly seventy now.

A: I cannot believe it! She still looks beautiful and she is just lucky to be a Queen.

W: Yes. But you know, she was not born to be Monarch. At the time of her birth, only males could **ascend**② the **throne**③ of Denmark.

A: Really? How did she become the Queen at last?

W: The Denmark **constitution**④ has been amended. The process of changing the constitution started in 1947, when it became clear that Queen Ingrid would have no

① daughter-in-law *n.* 儿媳
② ascend *vt.* 上升
③ throne *n.* 王位，宝座
④ constitution *n.* 宪法

more children. At this time, Margrethe's uncle Prince Knud was the Heir Presumptive.

A: What happened next?

W: The new Act of **Succession**[①] permitted female succession to the throne of Denmark, according to **cognatic**[②] **primogeniture**[③], where a female can ascend to the throne only if she does not have a brother. Princess Margrethe therefore became the Heiress Presumptive.

A: That's cool. How long has she been the Queen?

W: After King Frederik IX died in 1972. Queen Margrethe II became the first female Danish **Sovereign**[④] under the new Act of Succession.

A: She must be very busy since then. What's her task?

W: The Queen's main tasks are to represent the Kingdom abroad and to be a unifying **figurehead**[⑤] at home. The queen performs the latter task by accepting invitations to open exhibitions, attending anniversaries, **inaugurating**[⑥] bridges, etc.

A: It is more or less the same as things in other countries like Britain. I heard that as an unelected public official, the Queen takes no part in party politics and does not express any political opinions.

W: That's true. Well, let me tell something else about Margrethe II of Denmark. She is a **chain smoker**[⑦], and she is famous for her tobacco habit. However, a Danish newspaper reported an **announcement**[⑧] from the Royal Court stating that the queen would never again be seen smoking in public.

A: She likes smoking, that's bad.

W: Absolutely. Still, the queen does continue to smoke but in the future she will do so only privately. The announcement is probably due to the fact that the Danish parliament recently has decided on strict rules concerning smoking.

A: Smoking is difficult to quit.

---

① succession *n.* 继位，继承权
② cognatic 是 cognate 的变形，同族的，同祖先的
③ primogeniture *n.* 长子身份，长子继承权
④ sovereign *n.* 君主，最高统治者
⑤ figurehead *n.* 有名无实的领袖
⑥ inaugurating *vt.* inaugurate 的现在分词形式，意为举行就职典礼。
⑦ chain smoker *n.* 烟瘾大的人
⑧ announcement *n.* 通告，宣告

W: Anyway, she is a smart woman and has a gift for art. She has even studied **prehistoric archaeology**① at **Girton College**②, Cambridge.

A: Wow, that's great. But, I bet she has no time in doing the archeology work.

W: Maybe. In addition, the Queen is an **accomplished**③ painter, and has held many art shows over the years. It is said that were she not the queen, she could make a living as a professional artist.

A: 嗨，温迪。报纸上的人都是谁啊？

W: 哦，这是丹麦皇室的合照。

A: 让我看看。中间这个年迈的女士是丹麦女王吗？

W: 你说对了。她就是玛格丽特二世，还有她的儿子，儿媳和孙子。

A: 真是个幸福的家庭，而且他们都相貌出众。

W: 是啊。从左到右分别是约阿希姆王子，他的两个儿子，女王，腓烈特王子和他的王妃。

A: 这是他们的孩子吗？

W: 是啊，是个小王子。

A: 女王看起来好优雅。她现在多大年纪了？

W: 她现在大约有 70 岁了。

A: 真不敢相信！她看起来还是很漂亮。她能当女王真是幸运啊。

---

① prehistoric archaeology 史前考古学

② Girton College, Cambridge 剑桥大学格顿学院，于 1869 年建立，是英格兰第一所寄宿制女子学院。1977 年学院开始招收男性院士，1979 年学院开始招收男性本科生，现在男性本科生约占学院人数的一半。

③ accomplished *adj.* 熟练的，有技巧的，有学问的

W: 嗯。但是你知道吗，她并不是生来就能当女王的。她出生的时候，丹麦只有男性子嗣才有资格继承王位。

A: 真的吗？为什么她还是当上了女王？

W: 丹麦修改了宪法。宪法的修改开始于 1947 年，那个时候，英格丽王妃明显不可能再生育了。这时，玛格丽特的叔叔努德王子是王位的假定继承人。

A: 后来怎么样了呢？

W: 新的继承法允许女性继承丹麦王位，根据血亲长子继承的原则，女性在没有兄弟的情况下，有继承王位的资格。所以，玛格丽特公主就成为了假定继承人。

A: 太棒了。她登基多久了？

W: 1972 年，她的父亲弗雷德里克九世去世之后，根据新的继承法，玛格丽特二世成为了丹麦历史上第一位执政女王。

A: 从那时候开始她一定很忙吧。她的主要职责是什么？

W: 女王的主要职责就是在国外代表她的王国，在国内维护统一，是个象征性的国家元首。女王常常会参加一些公开的展览，出席周年庆典、就职典礼等等，来履行她的职责。

A: 这和英国的情况差不多嘛。我听说，作为一个非民选的公职人员，女王不参与党派政治，也不发表任何政治观点。

W: 你说的对。好吧，我再跟你讲一些关于玛格丽特二世的事情。她烟瘾很大，人们都知道她有抽烟的习惯。但是，一个丹麦报纸曾经发表过一篇皇室的声明，宣布女王将不会再在公众面前吸烟。

A: 她喜欢抽烟啊，这可不好。

W: 就是。不过女王还是会再抽烟，只是她以后只会在私人空间这么做。这个声明可能是因为丹麦议会最近决定要制定严格的条列来管制吸烟。

A: 烟很难戒掉的。

W: 不过，她还是一位聪明的女性，在艺术上很有天分。她曾经在在剑桥大学格顿女子学院学习史前考古。

A: 哇，她太厉害了！但我敢打赌，她没时间去考古。

W: 也许吧。此外，女王还是一位颇有成就的画家，过去几年还办过不少画展。有人说，如果不是女王的话，她肯定会是一位富有成就的艺术家。

难点解析

1 But you know, she was not **born** to be Monarch.

born to be 意为"生来就是……"，还有可以说born to do sth.，如：born to win(生而为赢)，born to try(生为拼搏)。

➢ Believe in yourself because you are born to win.
请相信自己，因为你是天生的赢家。
常见的相关词组还有：born to the purple(出身贵族)，born with a silver spoon in one's mouth(生在富贵人家)。

2 Anyway, she is a smart woman and **has a gift for** art.

has a gift for 意为"有……的天赋"，还可以用 be talented in 和 have talent for 来表示相同的意思。

➢ The boy has a gift for painting.
这男孩有绘画天赋。

➢ Lily has a gift for music.
这个小姑娘有音乐的天赋。

➢ Not everyone is born to be talented in all areas.
不是所有人生来就具备各种才能。

➢ Each human being has talent for creative thinking.
每个人都拥有创造性思维的天赋。

3 She is a chain smoker, and she is **famous** for her tobacco habit. However, a Danish newspaper reported an announcement from the Royal Court stating that the queen would never again be seen smoking in public.

famous 意为"著名的，惊人的"，相关词组有 be famous as, be famous for。

➢ She was famous as a post-modernism artist.
她是一位著名的后现代主义艺术家。

➢ Yao Ming was famous for playing basketball.
姚明因为打篮球而出名。

Margrethe II of Denmark

Margrethe II (born 16 April 1940) is the Queen **regnant**① of Denmark. In 1972 she became the first female monarch of Denmark, and meanwhile she is a talented artist. Margrethe's name can be heard everywhere in Denmark, in people's chat or on TV. Every Wednesday, she will receive the Danish who comes to visit. She is more famous than any pop stars and enjoys a high prestige among the Danish people.

Margrethe received an all-around and strict education since she was a child. She learnt from her **tutors**② coming from Britain or France as the **formative**③ education. Then She studied prehistoric archaeology at Girton College, Cambridge during 1960–61, political science at Aarhus University between 1961–1962, at the Sorbonne in 1963, and at the London School of Economics in 1965. In order to be a **competent**④ monarch, she joined the army for a while to learn military affairs. King Frederik IX died in 1972. On the occasion of her accession to the throne on 14 January 1972, Queen Margrethe II became the first female Danish Sovereign under the new Act of Succession when she was 31.

Besides being a monarch, she is an accomplished painter, set designer, translator and she is also interested in archaeology. The Queen's talent in art can be tell from her works: her watercolours and oil paintings were highly praised when exibited in Denmark; she made **book illustrations**⑤ for several fairy tale books; she designed the costums for pantomimes based on Anderson fairy tales. In addition, she has ever designed the costum and set for the Denmark Royal Ballet. When the master introduced her to the audiences, they applaused **enthusiastically**⑥ for her artistic contribution.

She is a master of several foreign languages, French, English, Swedish, German and good at writing. Every new

① regnant *adj.* 统治的，在位的
② tutor *n.* 家庭教师
③ formative *adj.* 形成期的，初期的
④ competent *adj.* 胜任的，有能力的
⑤ book illustrations *n.* 图书插画
⑥ enthusiastically *adv.* 热心的，满心热忱的

year's eve, she would give a speech on TV to her people. What makes it special is that the Queen will draft and revise it by herself to present her own style and show her **cordiality**[①].

On 10 June 1967, Princess Margrethe of Denmark married a French **diplomat**[②], Henrik, now the Prince Consort of Denmark. They have two sons, Prince Frederik and Prince Joachim.

丹麦王室才女

玛格丽特二世是现任丹麦女王，她于 1972 年成为了丹麦第一位执政女王。同时，她也是一位才华横溢的艺术家。在丹麦，闲谈中、电视上都可听到女王玛格丽特二世的名字。每个星期三女王都会接见前来探访的丹麦人，倾听他们的心声。她不是明星胜似明星，在丹麦人心中享有很高的威望。

玛格丽特自幼便接受了全面而严格的教育。来自英国和法国的家庭教师对她进行了启蒙。之后她进入哥本哈根女子中学，1960 ～ 1961 年在剑桥大学格顿学院学习史前考古、1961 ～ 1962 年奥尔胡斯大学学习政治学，1963 在索邦大学，之后 1965 年又在伦敦经济学院学习。为了做一个称职的君王，她还曾进入丹麦军队服役，学习军事。1972 年，腓特烈九世因心脏病去世，同年 1 月 14 日玛格丽特根据丹麦的新继承法，继承了父亲的王位，时年 31 岁。

她不仅是丹麦女王，而且还是出色的画家、舞台设计师、翻译家，她还对考古学感兴趣。在众多的艺术领域里，女王都显露出难能可贵的艺术天赋：她的水彩画和油画在丹麦展出，博得一片赞誉；她为童话故事绘制插图，为《安徒生童话剧》设计戏服；还为丹麦皇家芭蕾舞团出演的剧目制作了服装和布景。当芭蕾舞团团长向观众介绍这位女士时，观众对她的艺术贡献报以热烈的掌声。

玛格丽特精通法语、英语、瑞典语、德语等多门外语。她还擅长写作，每年除夕下午 6 时，她都要通过电视向全国发表新年祝辞，与众不同的是，对于这种文字要求很高的特殊演讲稿，女王一般都是亲自起草和修改，突显她的个人风格，以便更贴近百姓。

1967 年 7 月 10 日，当时还是公主的玛格丽特嫁给了一位法国的外交官，就是现在的丹麦亲王亨里克。他们育有两个孩子，腓烈特王子和约阿希姆王子。

---

① cordiality *n.* 热诚，诚挚

② diplomat *n.* 外交官，外交家

Unit 9 Competitor and Partner

牛桥恩仇录

33 Oxbridge

牛津剑桥如影随形

Julie and Mark are talking about Cambridge and Oxford, the most famous universities in Britain.

J: Julie M: Mark

J: Mark, which university is better, Oxford or Cambridge?

M: It's hard to say. Both of them rank the top in the world.

J: Well, which one is older?

M: Both were founded more than 800 years ago, and continued as England's only universities until the 19th century. Let me see…Oxford was first mentioned in 12th century records, while Cambridge was found in 1209.

J: Is there any relationship between them since they were the only universities that time?

M: Yes. It was said that Cambridge grew out of an association of scholars in the city of Cambridge that was formed, early records suggest, in 1209 by scholars leaving Oxford after a dispute with townsfolk.

J: That's interesting! No wonder it is said that Oxford is the mother of Cambridge.

M: The two “ancient universities” have many common **features**① and are often **jointly**② referred to as Oxbridge.

J: Oxbridge? Oh, I see. It is a **combination**③ of the name of the two universities—the former part of Oxford and the latter part of Cambridge.

M: You are right!

J: Who invented this name?

M: **William Thackeray**④. In his novel *Pendennis*, published in 1849, the main character *Pendennis* wants to attend the fictional College, Oxbridge, but failed. According to the Oxford English Dictionary, this is the first recorded **instance**⑤ of the word.

J: I never read his works, but I bet he is full of imagination.

M: Yes, he is. Actually, *Pendennis* also introduced the term Camford as another combination of the university names, but this term has never achieved the same degree of usage as Oxbridge.

J: Since both of them are the top universities in Britain and even in the world, I'm wondering whether they want to slug it out for who is the best.

M: Many annual competitions are held between Oxford and Cambridge, including the famous **annual**⑥ Boat Race. The first Boat Race was won by Oxford, but Cambridge lead the overall series with 79 wins to Oxford's 75, with one dead heat in 1877.

J: I know the boat race, and I heard that the boat race for this year will be held on Saturday, 3 April.

M: Yes. It is a big event in Britain.

J: Anything else besides this competition?

M: The other major Oxbridge competitons are the **Rugby**⑦ union and Rugby League Varsity Matches.

J: I don't think they are as popular as the Boat Race since I never heard about that.

M: The Boat Race and the two **Varsity Matches**⑧ are **notable**⑨ in the UK in that they are

---

① feature *n.* 容貌，特征

② jointly *adj.* 共同的，连带的

③ combination *n.* 联合，组合

④ William Thackeray 英国小说家，最著名的作品是《名利场》，与狄更斯齐名，为维多利亚时代的代表小说家。此外还有《班迪尼斯》等等。1863 年 12 月 24 日，在写《丹尼斯·狄万》的时候死去，享年 52 岁。他被葬在伦敦的肯萨尔园公墓。

⑤ instance *n.* 实例

⑥ annual *adj.* 年度的，每年的

⑦ rugby *n.* 英式橄榄球

⑧ Varsity Match 大学对抗赛

⑨ notable *adj.* 著名的

the only university sports events that have any public **profile**① outside the universities themselves; all three are screened live on national television and are widely covered in the national media.

J: Despite the impassioned rivalry between the two universities, there is also much **cooperation**② when the need arises.

M: That's true. Most Oxford colleges have a sister college in Cambridge. Some Oxford and Cambridge colleges with the same name are "sisters", for example, Jesus College, Cambridge and Jesus College, Oxford. Trinity College, Oxford is the sister college of Churchill College, Cambridge, while Trinity College, Cambridge is the sister college of Christ Church, Oxford.

J: 马克，牛津大学和剑桥大学哪个比较好？

M: 这不好说。两所都是世界顶尖的学校。

J: 那么哪一所的历史更久远呢？

M: 两所大学都有超过 800 年的建校历史，直至 19 世纪仍然是英国仅有的两所大学。让我想想……公元 12 世纪的记录中有了对牛津的最早记录，而剑桥成立于 1209 年。

J: 既然他们是那时候仅有的大学，他们之间有没有什么特殊关系呢？

M: 有啊。据早期文献记载，那个时候一些牛津学者为了躲避反对他们的市民而来到剑桥，建立了剑桥大学。

J: 这太有趣了！难怪人们总是说，牛津是剑桥的母亲。

M: 这两所“古老的大学”有很多的共同点，通常被合称为“牛桥”。

J: 牛桥？哦，我明白了。这是用他们的名字组合而成的，也就是牛津的前半部分和剑桥的后半部分。

M: 你说的对。

J: 是谁发明了这种叫法？

M: 英国作家威廉·萨克雷。他 1849 年完成的小说《潘登尼斯》中的主人公想到一所叫“牛桥”的大学求学却没有被录取。根据牛津英语词典，这是关于这个词的最

① profile *n.* 侧面轮廓
② cooperation *n.* 合作，协作

早记载。

J: 我从来没有读过他的书，不过我想他一定是个充满想象力的人。

M: 他的确是。实际上，《潘登尼斯》中还创造了这两所大学的另外一个合成词“剑津”，但这个词从来就没有“牛桥”的使用频率高。

J: 既然两所都是英国乃至世界最顶尖的学府，我在想，他们有没有想过要决一胜负，看看谁是最好的呢?

M: 他们会举行许多各种各样的年度比赛，其中就有著名的赛艇。第一届赛艇，牛津获胜。但是剑桥以获胜 79 次的总成绩超过了获胜 75 次的牛津，除了 1877 年出现了一次平局。

J: 我知道那个赛艇，听说今年的比赛会在 4 月 3 日（星期六）举行。

M: 对。这在英国可不是件小事啊。

J: 除了这个，还有别的比赛吗?

M: 其他的主要赛事有，英国橄榄球联赛和橄榄球联盟大学对抗赛。

J: 这两个比赛应该不像赛艇那么有名吧，我从来都没有听说过。

M: 赛艇和两个对抗赛在英国都很有名，因为他们不仅是大学内部的体育比赛，还受到公众的广泛关注。这三项比赛都会对全国观众进行直播，也会受到全国媒体的广泛关注。

J: 两所大学之间除了这些激烈的比赛以外，在需要的时候，还会进行合作。

M: 这倒是真的。牛津大学的大多数学院都在剑桥大学有兄弟学院。有一些学院的名字都一样，例如剑桥大学耶稣学院和牛津大学耶稣学院。而剑桥大学三一学院和牛津大学基督学院就是兄弟学院。

1 Both of them **rank** the top in the world.

rank 作动词用，意思有细微的差别，具体如下：

（1）（被认为）具有……等级和地位

➢ This result ranks as one of their most successful election performances of the last ten years.
这次选举结果被视为他们最近 10 年来最成功的竞选成绩之一。

（2）排列，常用被动语态

➢ The cups were ranked neatly on the shelf.
那些杯子在架子上排得整整齐齐。

2 It was said that Cambridge **grew out of** an association of scholars in the city of Cambridge that was formed, early records suggest, in 1209 by scholars leaving Oxford after a dispute with townsfolk.

此句话中 grow out of 意为“由什么发展而来”，但 grow out of 还有其他的意思，具体如下：

（1）因长大而穿不下（衣服、鞋子等）

➢ My daughter has grown out of all her old clothes.
我的女儿长大了，所有的旧衣服都穿不了了。

（2）（因年龄的增长而）戒除，改掉（幼时的缺点）

➢ He will soon grow out of wetting the bed.
他大些就会很快改掉尿床的毛病的。

3 Since both of them are the top universities in Britain and even in the world, I'm wondering whether they want to **slug it out** for who is the best.

slug 原本的意思为“（用拳头）猛击，打昏”，slug it out 意为“凶猛地战斗到底，决一胜负”。

➢ They decided to slug it out for the crown of England.
他们决定为英格兰皇冠而一决雌雄。

4 **Despite** the impassioned rivalry between the two universities, there is also much cooperation when the need arises.

despite 意为“不管，尽管，任凭”，后面可以接名词，也可以接名词性的词组。

➢ He came to the meeting despite his illness.
尽管生病，他还是来参加会议。

➢ Demand for cars is high, despite the fact that the price of them keep rising.
尽管汽车的价格不断上涨，人们对洗车的需求仍然很高。

Oxbridge

Oxbridge is a **composite**[1] of the University of Oxford and the University of Cambridge which are most famous in England and the term is now used to refer to them collectively,

① composite *n.* 合成物，合成词

often with implications of perceived superior intellectual or social **status**[①]. Oxbridge can be used as a noun referring to either or both universities or as an adjective describing them or their students.

Although both universities were founded more than seven centuries ago, the term Oxbridge is relatively young. In William Thackeray's novel *Pendennis*, published in 1849, the main character Pendennis wants to attend the fictional College, Oxbridge, but failed. According to the Oxford English Dictionary, this is the first recorded instance of the word. Virginia Woolf used it, citing Thackeray, in her 1929 essay *A Room of One's Own*. By 1957 the term was used in the Times Educational Supplement and in Universities Quarterly by 1958. Thackeray's *Pendennis* also introduced the term Camford as another combination of the university names, but this term has never achieved the same degree of usage as Oxbridge.

Oxbridge is often used as **shorthand**[②] for characteristics that the two institutions share. Firstly, they are the two oldest universities in continuous operation in England. Both were founded more than 800 years ago, and continued as England's only universities until the 19th century. Between them they have educated a large number of Britain's most **prominent**[③] scientists, writers and politicians, as well as noted figures in many other fields. Besides, they have established similar institutions and facilities such as printing houses, **botanical**[④] gardens, museums, and debating societies. In addition, both universities comprise many buildings of great beauty and antiquity, sited on level **terrain**[⑤] ideal for cycling, near slow-moving rivers suitable for rowing and punting. At each of the universities there is a college which has a "Bridge of Sighs", although neither **resembles**[⑥] the original Bridge of Sighs in Venice.

Oxford and Cambridge also share a common **collegiate**[⑦] structure: each university is **composed**[⑧] of more than 30 autonomous colleges, which provide the environments in which groups of students live, work and sleep. Applicants must choose a specific college when applying to Oxford or Cambridge, or allow the university to select one for them, as all undergraduate and graduate students must be a member of one of the university colleges. All Oxbridge colleges are part of the university, and students studying the same subject are given

① status *n.* 地位，身份
② shorthand *n.* 速记，速记法
③ prominent *adj.* 突出的，杰出的
④ botanical *adj.* 植物的，植物学的
⑤ terrain *n.* 地势，地带，领域
⑥ resemble *vt.* 类似，像
⑦ collegiate *adj.* 学院的，大学的
⑧ compose *vt.* 组成，构成

lectures together, **irrespective**[①] of which college they attend.

Competition between Oxford and Cambridge also has a long history, dating back to around 1209 when Cambridge was founded by scholars **taking refuge from**[②] hostile townsmen in Oxford.

牛津剑桥如影随形

“牛桥”是一个合成词，是英国两所最知名的大学牛津大学和剑桥大学的合称。现在这个词常用来代指这两所大学，通常寓示着更高等的教育或社会地位。“牛桥”可以作为一个普通名词使用，指代两所大学里任何一个学校，也可以用作一个形容词来修饰这两所大学或它们的学生。

尽管两所大学都建成于 7 个多世纪以前，“牛桥”这个说法却相对年轻。英国作家威廉·萨克雷 1849 年完成的小说《潘登尼斯》中的主人公想进入一所叫“牛桥”的大学求学却没有被录取。根据牛津英语词典，这是关于这个词的最早记载。弗吉尼亚·伍尔夫曾经在她 1929 年的散文《一个人的屋子》中引用了这个词。1957 年，泰晤士报的教育增刊用到了这个词，1958 年大学季刊也使用了这个词。萨克雷在《潘登尼斯》中还创造了这两所大学的另外一个合成词“剑津”，但这个词从来就没有“牛桥”的使用频率高。

牛桥通常被用来指代两所大学共有的特征。首先，他们是英国历史最为久远的两所大学。他们都有超过 800 年的建校史，直至 19 世纪，他们仍是英格兰仅有的两所大学。英国最著名的科学家、作家和政治家及其他各界几乎所有的知名人士都出自这两所大学。 此外，他们还有相似的机构和设施，比如出版社、植物园、博物馆、辩论社等。两所大学还都有许多漂亮的古建筑，坐落在地势平坦的地方，旁边有静静流淌的河流，在这里骑车、划船，撑篙十分惬意。两所大学各有一座“叹息桥”，尽管和威尼斯的叹息桥重名，但它们截然不同。

牛津和剑桥有着相似的组织结构：它们都由 30 多所独立学院组成。学生们可以在这样的氛围中一起住宿、工作和休息。申请人在申请这两所大学的时候必须选择一个特定的学院，或者让校方为学生选择学院，因为所有的本科生和研究生必须成为某个学院的一员。牛桥的每个学院都是大学的一部分，不管在哪个学院，选择同样课程的学生都在一起上课。

牛津和剑桥之间有很长的竞争史，可以回溯到 1209 年左右，那个时候一些牛津学者为了躲避反对他们的人而来到剑桥，建立了剑桥大学。

---

① irrespective *adj.* 不顾，不管

② take refuge from 避难，逃离

34 Art and Science

文科牛津和理科剑桥

Amy and Tom are talking about Cambridge and Oxford.

A: Amy T: Tom

A: If you are going to apply for University, which one will you choose, Cambridge or Oxford?

T: I think I will choose Oxford.

A: Why?

T: Because I heard that the two have their own **strengths**①. Cambridge is good at science and has produced more scientists while Oxford is good at art and almost all the British Prime Ministers come from it.

A: Is that true? I remember that Prime Minister Walpole graduated from Cambridge.

T: Yes, he is one of the three ministers graduated from Cambridge. The other two are Prime Ministers Baldwin and William Pitt.

A: How about Oxford? Has Oxford produced any country leaders?

T: Definitely. Twenty-five British prime ministers have attended Oxford and At least thirty other international leaders have been educated at Oxford.

A: So do you want to be another prime minister in the future since you are so fond of Oxford?

T: Maybe. I'm really interested in politics.

A: That's great! I never knew that you are an **ambitious**② boy, Tom! Now I understand that

① strength *n.* 长处，力气

② ambitious *adj.* 有雄心的，野心勃勃的

why it was said that **you can never judge a person by his or her looks**[①]!

T: That's for sure.

A: You've mentioned just now that Cambridge produced more scientists? Can you give me some examples?

T: That's easy. Many world-famous scientists have spent part of their life in Cambridge, such as Newton, Darwin and so on.

A: I think Oxford produced some important scientists, too, for example, the inventor of the World Wide Web, Tim Berners-Lee.

T: Yes, besides, there are Edmond Halley, Robert Hooke and Dorothy Crowfoot Hodgkin. But generally speaking, Cambridge produced more Nobel winners.

A: The University of Cambridge has won 87 Nobel prizes as of 2010, more than any other **institution**[②] according to some **counts**[③].

T: Yes. Former undergraduates of the university have won a **grand**[④] total of 61 Nobel prizes, more than the undergraduates of any other university.

A: They are really great.

T: In addition, designer of the world's first computing system, discoverer of **Hydrogen**[⑤], discoverer of the **neutron**[⑥], inventor of the atomic bomb, inventor of the jet engine, inventor of the camera and so on all come from Cambridge.

A: It seems what you said just now is true. However, I do know some **acclaimed**[⑦] writers who have spent some time in Cambridge, for example, E. M. Forster, Virginia Woolf.

T: And Christopher Marlowe, W. M. Thackeray.

A: Furthermore, at least nine of the Poet Laureates graduated from Cambridge, and it keeps producing excellent writers now.

T: Yes. There are many actors and directors such as James Mason, Emma Thompson and Stephen Fry who have studied at Cambridge.

A: The University is also known for its **prodigious**[⑧] sporting reputation and has produced many fine athletes, including more than 50 Olympic medalists.

---

① You can never judge a person by his or her looks. 人不可貌相。
② institution *n.* 公共机构
③ counts *n.* 计数，统计
④ grand *adj.* 宏伟的，豪华的
⑤ Hydrogen *n.* 氢
⑥ neutron *n.* 中子
⑦ acclaimed *adj.* 受到赞扬的
⑧ prodigious *adj.* 巨大的，惊人的，异常的，奇妙的

T: Yes, 6 in 2008 alone. I can name some of those athletes, for example the **legendary**① Chinese six-time world table tennis champion Deng Yaping, the **sprinter**② and **athletics**③ hero Harold Abrahams.

A: And the inventors of **the modern game of Football**④, Winton and Thring; and also George Mallory, the famed mountaineer and the first man ever to reach the summit of Mount Everest.

T: Well, you haven't told me, which university do you prefer?

A: Since we have talked about so many advantages of Cambridge, of course Iwould choose Cambridge.

A: 如果你要申请大学的话，剑桥大学和牛津大学你会选哪一个?

T: 我想我会选择牛津大学。

A: 为什么呢?

T: 因为我听说，这两所大学各有所长。剑桥的优势在理科，那里出了很多著名的科学家而牛津的优势在文科，大多数的英国首相都来自牛津。

A: 真的吗? 我记得沃波尔首相就毕业于剑桥啊。

T: 对。他是出自剑桥的三位首相之一，其他两位是首相鲍尔温和威廉·皮特。

A: 那牛津呢? 牛津是不是产生了很多的国家领袖?

T: 绝对的。有 25 位英国首相都上过牛津，至少还有 30 余位世界其他国家的领导人在牛津念过书。

A: 你对牛津这么感兴趣，是不是也想将来成为一位首相呢?

T: 也许吧。我真的对政治很感兴趣。

A: 太棒了！汤姆，我从来不知道你这么有抱负呢！现在我知道，人们为什么说“人不可貌相”了。

T: 那是当然。

A: 你刚才说剑桥培养了很多的科学家? 能举几个例子吗?

---

① legendary *adj.* 传说的，传奇的

② sprinter *n.* 短跑选手

③ athletics *n.* 体育运动，竞技

④ the modern game of Football 现代足球，起源于英国。据史料记载，中世纪时在英国就出现了类似今天这种足球活动。到 19 世纪初，足球运动在英国已经相当普及。

T: 这太容易了。许多世界著名的科学家都在剑桥待过，比如牛顿、达尔文等等。

A: 牛津也培养了很多重要的科学家，比如万维网的发明者——蒂姆·伯纳斯·李。

T: 对。此外，还有埃德蒙·哈雷、罗伯特·胡克和多萝西·霍奇金。不过总的来说，剑桥出了更多的诺贝尔奖获得者。

A: 截止到 2010 年初，剑桥大学赢得了 87 个诺贝尔奖项，这比其他任何一个机构都要多。

T: 对啊。之前剑桥的本科生赢得了 61 个诺贝尔奖项，比任何大学的本科生获得的都要多。

A: 他们真是太棒了。

T: 此外，世界上第一个计算机系统的设计者，氢气的发现者，中子的发现者，原子弹的发明者，喷射发动机的发明者，照相机的发明者也都出自剑桥。

A: 看来你刚才说的很有道理。不过，我还知道一些著名的作家也在剑桥待过。比如，福斯特、伍尔夫。

T: 还有克里斯托弗·马洛、萨克雷等等。

A: 至少有 9 位桂冠诗人都毕业于剑桥，现在仍有很多优秀作家都出身剑桥。

T: 是。许多著名的演员和导演也曾经在剑桥就读，比如，詹姆士·梅森、艾玛·汤普森、还有史蒂芬·弗莱。

A: 剑桥在体育方面也很有名气，产生过很多优秀的运动员，其中包括 50 多位奥运会的奖牌获得者。

T: 对啊，仅仅在 2008 年就有 6 位获奖。我都能说出几位运动员的名字，比如蝉联世界乒乓球赛冠军 6 次的传奇中国人物邓亚萍，短跑和田径运动员哈罗德·亚伯拉罕斯等等。

A: 发明现代足球运动的温顿和斯林，还有第一个登上珠峰山顶的著名的登山家乔治·马洛里。

T: 对了，你还没告诉我如果是你的话，你会选哪所大学？

A: 你看我们刚才谈了好多剑桥的优势，我当然会选剑桥啰。

1 Cambridge is good at science and produced more scientists **while** Oxford is good at art and almost all the British Prime Ministers come from it.

while 除了作名词用，表示一段时间，还可以作连词，又作 whilst, 用法如下：

（1）当……的时候，和……同时

➢ They arrived while we were having dinner.
他们来的时候我们正在吃晚饭。

（2）尽管

➢ While I understand what you say, I can't agree with you.
尽管我能理解你所说的，但却无法赞同。

（3）但是，却，反之，表示一种对比的关系

➢ Their country has plenty of oil, while our country has none.
他们国家盛产石油，我们国家却一点也没有。

2 So do you want to be another prime minister in the future since you are so **fond** of Oxford?

（1）喜欢的，喜爱的

➢ She has many faults, but we're all very fond of her.
她虽然有许多缺点，但我们都很喜欢她。

（2）多情的，温柔的

➢ It is a fond farewell.
这是个深情的告别。

3 Furthermore, at least nine of the Poet Laureates graduated from Cambridge, and it **keeps producing** excellent writers now.

keep doing sth. 意为“一直不停地做某事”。

➢ Keep repeating this tongue twister. It's a good practice for your oral speaking.
一直重复这个绕口令吧，对提高口语来说是个很好的练习。

Art and Science

It is easy to **stereotype**① the two institutions as having different strengths, for example, Oxford with politics and Cambridge with science. However, Cambridge has also produced

① stereotype *n.* 陈腔滥调，老套

distinguished[①] politicians including Prime Ministers Walpole, Baldwin and William Pitt, and Oxford graduates include noted scientists such as Edmond Halley, Robert Hooke and Dorothy Crowfoot Hodgkin (and more recently Tim Berners-Lee, the inventor of the World Wide Web).

Affiliates[②] of the University of Cambridge have won 87 Nobel prizes as of 2010, more than any other institution according to some counts. Former undergraduates of the university have won a grand total of 61 Nobel prizes, more than the undergraduates of any other university. Perhaps most of all, the university is renowned for a long and distinguished tradition in mathematics and the sciences.

Among the most famous of Cambridge **polymaths**[③] are Sir Isaac Newton. Besides, Sir Francis Bacon also spent part of his life there with pioneering mathematicians John Dee and Brook Taylor soon followed. Other ground-breaking mathematicians include Hardy, Littlewood and De Morgan, three of the most **renowned**[④] pure mathematicians in modern history. Perhaps most importantly of all, James Clerk Maxwell, who is also considered to have brought about the second great unification of Physics (the first being accredited to Newton) with his classical **electromagnetic**[⑤] theory.

Another Cambridge scholar responsible for major developments in scientific understanding was Charles Darwin, the biologist who first suggested the theory of evolution. Later Cambridge biologists include Francis Crick and James D. Watson developed a model for the three-dimensional structure of DNA whilst working at the university's **Cavendish Laboratory**. More recently, Sir Ian Wilmut, the man who was responsible for the first cloning of a mammal with Dolly the Sheep in 1996, was an undergraduate at Darwin College.

In addition to those big names, there are numerous famous scientists who have studied or taught in Cambridge, for example, physicist Stephen Hawking, economist John Maynard Keynes. Besides, there are designer of the world's first computing system, discoverer of Hydrogen, discoverer of the neutron, leader of the **Manhattan Project**[⑥], inventor of the atomic bomb, astronomers, inventor of the jet engine, inventor of the camera and so on.

---

① distinguished *adj.* 著名的，高贵的，卓越的
② affiliate *n.*（隶属的）机构，联号
③ polymath *n.* 博学的人
④ renowned *adj.* 著名的，有声望的
⑤ electromagnetic *adj.* 电磁的
⑥ Manhattan Project 曼哈顿计划。美国陆军部于 1942 年 6 月开始实施的利用核裂变反应来研制原子弹的计划，亦称曼哈顿计划。

Different from Cambridge, Oxford produced more politicians. Twenty-five British prime ministers have attended Oxford and At least thirty other international leaders have been educated at Oxford.

文科牛津和理科剑桥

人们常常认为牛津和剑桥有着各自的优势，例如，牛津在政治上优于剑桥，而剑桥在科学上胜过牛津。尽管如此，剑桥也出了不少有名的政治家，其中就包括三位英国首相：沃波尔、鲍尔温和威廉·皮特；牛津也出了不少著名的科学家，如：埃德蒙·哈雷、罗伯特·胡克和多萝西·霍奇金（更近一点的，还有万维网的发明者蒂姆·伯纳斯·李）。

据统计，截止到2010年初，剑桥大学赢得了87个诺贝尔奖项，这比其他任何一个机构都要多。之前剑桥的本科生赢得了61个诺贝尔奖项，比任何大学的本科生获得的都要多。也许是因为，这所大学长久以来都在数学和科学领域有出色的表现。

剑桥最有名气的学者要算是艾萨克·牛顿了，此外还有弗朗西斯·培根。此后，还有数学界的先驱约翰·迪和布鲁克·泰勒。此外，三位对数学界有着开拓性贡献的数学家，哈代，利特伍德和摩根也曾在剑桥大学学习。这三位是现代历史中最著名的理论数学家。也许最重要的还有詹姆士·麦克斯韦，他的经典电磁理论通常被认为带来了物理学的第二次大一统（第一次是牛顿）。

另外一位被认为对当今科学发展有着突出贡献的是首次提出了生物进化论的生物学家查尔斯·达尔文。之后，剑桥的其他生物学家，如弗兰西斯·克里克和詹姆士·沃森在卡文迪什实验室工作的时候，建立了DNA的三维结构模型。更近一些的还有1996年第一只克隆哺乳动物“多利羊”的负责人，在达尔文学院获得了学士学位伊恩·维尔穆特爵士。

除了这些知名人士之外，还有许多著名的科学家也曾经在剑桥学习或任教。例如，物理学家史蒂芬·霍金，经济学家约翰·凯恩斯。此外，世界上第一个计算机系统的设计者、氢气的发现者、中子的发现者、曼哈顿计划的负责人、原子弹的发明者、天文学家，喷射发动机的发明者、照相机的发明者也都出自剑桥。

和剑桥不同，牛津出了更多的政界名人。有25位英国首相都出自牛津，至少还有30余位世界其他国家的领导人在牛津留过学。

35 Oxford and Cambridge Club
共同的俱乐部

Danny is showing Hanna his photos taken last weekend.

D: Danny　　H: Hanna

H: This building is beautiful, what is it?

D: It is the Oxford and Cambridge Club. See, these are flags of the two universities.

H: I thought the two most famous universities in Briton don't get along well, but they even build up a Club together. Where is it located? Is it far from here?

D: Yes, a little bit far from here. It is at 71 Pall Mall, London. The clubhouse was designed for the **membership**[①] by **architect**[②] Sir Robert Smirke and completed towards the end of 1837.

H: I guess it was founded especially for members of the universities of Oxford and Cambridge?

D: Not really. Graduates from the two universities, students in other universities, graduates of any university, whether in Britain or overseas, are **eligible**[③] for membership.

H: Does it charge any fee?

D: As of 2009, the membership **subscription**[④] costs 900 pounds per year, with a 480 pounds **rate**[⑤] for younger members. However, the club does not charge an entrance fee.

---

① membership *n.* 成员资格，会员身份
② architect *n.* 建筑师
③ eligible *adj.* 合格的，符合条件的
④ subscription *n.* 会费
⑤ rate *n.* 费用

H: If I'm not mistaken, there was an old club of this kind in Briton named United University Club.

D: Let me tell you. Eight years after the foundation of the original United University Club in 1821, the waiting list had become **inconveniently**[①] long; so it was decided to form a second club.

H: So I guess that is the Oxford and Cambridge Club now?

D: Yes. But it was only in 2001 that it **reverted**[②] to the Oxford and Cambridge Club.

H: Have you entered the Club building?

D: Yes. We even dined there! Actually when I sit in the grand coffee house, I felt like a **toff**[③], yet I still want to share my experience with you.

H: Go ahead please.

D: As the taxi drove down this road on Pall Mall on a dark December evening, I could see into the tall grand windows of the buildings.

H: What did you see then?

D: There were 8 feet tall oil paintings of important men in **Renaissance-style**[④] **wigs**[⑤] in **tails**[⑥], parties of men in black tie and tails gathered around holding **champagne flutes**[⑦]…

H: It is just like scene in **Jane Austen**[⑧]'s novels! How romantic! How was when you entered the hall?

D: Inside, having undressed our multiple coats and layers in the **cloakroom**[⑨], we then made our way to the Coffee Room. It was really grand.

H: What do they serve there? Is the food nice?

D: Looking at the menu, you can find things are as traditionally British as you could get! The food was just pleasant, and plentiful. I finished nearly everything on my plates.

---

① inconveniently *adv.* 不方便地
② revert *vi.* 归还，是恢复原状
③ toff *n.* 有钱人，花花公子
④ Renaissance-style *n.* 文艺复兴时期款式的。文艺复兴是一场发生在14世纪至17世纪的思想文化运动，在中世纪晚期发源于佛罗伦萨，后扩展至欧洲各国。
⑤ wig *n.* 假发
⑥ tail *n.* 燕尾服
⑦ champagne flute *n.* 喝香槟的高脚杯
⑧ Jane Austen 简·奥斯汀，英国著名女性小说家，她的作品主要关注乡绅家庭女性的婚姻和生活，以女性特有的细致入微的观察力和活泼风趣的文字真实地描绘了她周围世界的小天地。
⑨ cloakroom *n.* 衣帽间

Furthermore, I should say that the service was **impeccable**[①].

H: Really? I should go and have a look.

D: If you ever have the chance, I would recommend a visit to the Oxford and Cambridge club. It will be a moment where you remember how **posh**[②] we British really are.

H: Great! I think I'll go there with some friends next time.

H: 这个房子真漂亮，是哪儿的房子？

D: 这是牛津剑桥俱乐部。看，这是这两所大学的旗帜。

H: 我还以为这两所英国最著名的大学关系不好呢，谁知道它们还共同成立了一所俱乐部。在什么位置啊，距离这里远吗？

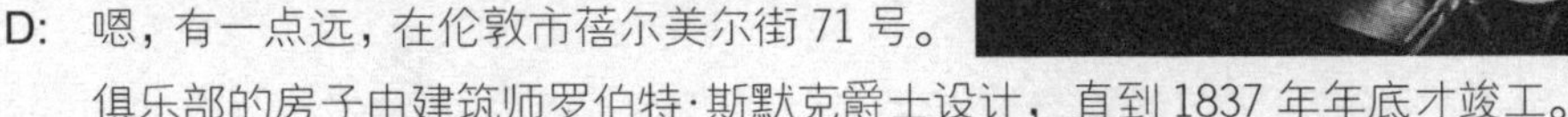

D: 嗯，有一点远，在伦敦市蓓尔美尔街 71 号。俱乐部的房子由建筑师罗伯特·斯默克爵士设计，直到 1837 年年底才竣工。

H: 我想这个俱乐部应该是为牛津和剑桥的学生特别建造的吧？

D: 不是。这两所大学的毕业生，别的大学的毕业生，和其他任何无论在英国还是外国念书的大学生都有加入这个俱乐部的资格。

H: 这俱乐部收费吗？

D: 就拿 2009 年来说吧，每位会员需要交纳 900 英镑的年费，年轻一些的成员只要交 480 磅就可以了。但是，这个俱乐部是不收门票的。

H: 如果我没搞错的话，之前英国就有一个类似的俱乐部，叫做联合大学俱乐部。

D: 让我来告诉你吧。1821 年，在联合大学俱乐部成立 8 周年之后，申请加入的人出奇的多，所以人们决定再成立一个类似的俱乐部。

H: 就是现在的牛津剑桥俱乐部啰？

D: 是啊。直到 2001 年，它才改名叫做牛津剑桥俱乐部的。

H: 你进这栋楼了吗？

D: 进了啊，我们还在里面吃了一顿饭呢！实际上，当我坐在那个装潢华丽的咖啡厅时，感觉自己像个纨绔子弟，不过我还是愿意和你分享一下我的经历。

H: 快讲讲吧。

D: 那是 12 月的一个晚上，当计程车开到蓓尔美尔街，缓缓地停下来时，我都能透过高大的窗户看到里面。

---

① impeccable *adj.* 无瑕疵的，无可挑剔的

② posh *adj.* 时髦的，讲究的，奢侈的

H: 你看见了什么?

D: 里面挂着几幅长约 8 英尺的油画，有重要人物穿着文艺复兴时期流行的燕尾服，戴着假发的肖像，也有聚会上系着黑色领结，身着燕尾服的男士，端着高脚香槟酒杯，来往应酬，谈笑风生。

H: 就像简·奥斯汀在小说描绘的场景那样！太浪漫了！那个大厅里面怎么样?

D: 一进去，我们就在衣帽间脱去了厚重的外套，然后走到了咖啡厅。这咖啡厅真的非常漂亮。

H: 那里有什么吃的? 味道如何?

D: 你能在菜单上找到所有传统的英国食物。味道很好，分量也很足。我几乎把盘子里的东西吃了个精光。还有，那里的服务真是无可挑剔。

H: 真的吗? 我真应该去看看。

D: 如果有机会，我建议你有时间去一趟。你绝对能感受到我们英国人的生活有多么精致。

H: 太棒了！我决定下次和朋友一起去看看。

1 I thought the two most famous universities in Briton don't **get along well** with each other, but they even build up a club together.

(1) (勉强) 过活，对付

➢ He didn't even offer to help us, but I'm sure we can get along quite well without him.
他甚至没向我们提供帮助，不过我确信没有他我们也能生活得很好。

(2) 前进，进展

➢ How is the work getting along?
工作进展得怎样?

(3) 与介词 with 搭配，意为“与人相处”。

➢ Do you get along well with your aunt?
你和姑母相处得好吗?

2 Does it **charge** any fee?

(1) charge 要价，(向……) 收费，索取（金额）

➢ How much do you charge for a double room?
双人房你们收费多少？

（2）把……记在某人的账上

➢ Charge the purchases to my account.
把购货款记在我账上。

（3）控告，指控

➢ He was charged with the robbery.
他被指控抢劫。

3 **If I'm not mistaken**, there was an old club in this kind in Briton named United University Club.

mistaken 是形容词，意为“弄错的，理解错误的”。

➢ I think you must be mistaken about seeing him at the theatre. I'm sure he's been abroad all week.
你说在戏院里见到他了，一定是弄错了。我敢肯定他整个星期都在国外。

Oxford and Cambridge Club

The Oxford and Cambridge Club is at 71 Pall Mall, London, England. The clubhouse was designed for the membership by architect Sir Robert Smirke and completed towards the end of 1837. The Club effortlessly combines the historic charm of its nineteenth century **roots**① with all that makes life in the twenty-first century convenient and **efficient**②. The Oxford and Cambridge Club provides alumni from both universities an exclusive home away from home in the heart of London.

The Club is the result of a number of **amalgamations**③ of university clubs, the most recent being in 1972 between the United University Club, founded in 1821 and the Oxford and Cambridge University Club, founded in 1830.

At the time of its creation the Club had 2,897 members as well as 563 lady associates. In February 1996, the Club voted by an **overwhelming**④ majority to allow women full mem-

① root *n.* 根源，祖先
② efficient *adj.* 有效率的，节能的
③ amalgamation *n.* 融合，混合，联合，合并
④ overwhelming *adj.* 压倒性的，势不可挡的

bership with **unhindered**① access to all areas of the Club house. Then, Queen Margarethe II of Denmark became the first Honorary Lady Member.

The foundation of the Oxford and Cambridge University Club dates from a meeting of members from the two Universities held at the British Coffee House, 27 Cockspur Street on 17 May 1830, with Lord Palmerston in the chair. The meeting resolved that a Club consisting of members of both universities should be formed "for the association of gentlemen educated at those universities and for promoting and continuing a mutual interest and fellowship between them."

Various kinds of sports activities are provided by this club, for example, **Squash**②, **fitness**③ facilities, running group, bridge, **billiards and snooker**④, golf, chess and backgammon. The Oxford and Cambridge Club **boasts**⑤ one of the best club libraries in London, and even with some sales of unwanted **accumulations**⑥, over 20,000 volumes remain to form a well-balanced and very usable collection. The Club hosts a variety of events throughout the year for members and their guests. These include a diverse calendar of discussion dinners, evening lectures and musical evenings that offer entertainment on a weekly basis.

All in all, the Club is well appointed to accommodate your leisure or business interests in a sophisticated setting with a unique charm. The central location, **inimitable**⑦ **ambience**⑧ and first class facilities make it an ideal meeting place for friends and business associates alike. When you join the Club you enter into a worldwide network of alumni and **luminaries**⑨ containing over 3,700 other Oxford and Cambridge University Graduates, including more than over 1,000 who live overseas.

共同的俱乐部

牛津剑桥俱乐部坐落于英格兰伦敦市蓓尔美尔街 71 号。俱乐部的房子由建筑师

---

① unhindered *adj.* 不受阻碍的
② squash *n.* 壁球
③ fitness *n.* 健康
④ billiards and snooker *n.* 台球，桌球
⑤ boast *vt.* 以有……而自夸
⑥ accumulation *n.* 积累，累计，堆积物
⑦ inimitable *adj.* 独特的，无比的，无法仿效的
⑧ ambience *n.* 气氛，布景，周围人物
⑨ luminary *n.* 杰出人物

罗伯特·斯默克爵士设计，直到1837年年底才竣工。它很自然地将19世纪的历史风情和21世纪的便利生活设施结合在了一起。这个俱乐部为两所大学的校友在伦敦市中心提供了一个独一无二的第二故乡。

它由几所大学的俱乐部合并而成，最近的一次在1972年，1821年成立的联合大学俱乐部和1830年成立的牛津剑桥俱乐部合并为一体。

俱乐部刚成立的时候，有2897个成员，其中只有563位女士。1996年2月，俱乐部以压倒性的多数票通过了允许女性参加俱乐部的决定，此后女性可以没有障碍的享受完全会员待遇。此后，丹麦女王玛格丽特二世成为了第一位荣誉女性会员。

1830年5月17日，来自牛津和剑桥的学生在鸡距街27号的一家英国咖啡屋会集，从此牛津剑桥俱乐部就成立了。那个时候，帕默斯顿勋爵是会长。这次会议决定，由两所大学的学生共同组成的俱乐部的宗旨应该是“为了在这两所大学受教育的绅士联盟，为了他们共同的利益和他们之间的友谊”。

俱乐部还提供各种体育运动。例如，壁球、健身器械、跑步队、桥牌、台球、高尔夫、国际象棋和十五子棋。牛津剑桥俱乐部拥有伦敦最好的俱乐部图书馆，那儿还有一些旧书出售。超过20,000册的图书品类齐全，极具实用价值。俱乐部常年为会员们准备各式各样的活动。其中包括了各种晚宴，演讲和音乐剧，通常每周进行一次。

总而言之，不管是休闲方面还是商务方面。这个俱乐部精致的装潢和独特的魅力，可以很好地满足你的需要，中央单元独特的氛围和一流的设施使其成为了会见亲朋好友或商业伙伴的理想场所。加入了这个俱乐部你就相当于走进了一个由3700余名牛津和剑桥大学的毕业生组成的庞大的全球社会关系网，其中来自海外的会员就多达1000余位。

36 Oxford and Cambridge Boat Race

牛桥赛艇比赛

Tony and Jane are talking about the coming boat race between Oxford and Cambridge.

T: Tony   J: Jane

T: Hi, Jane! Have you heard that the boat race this year is scheduled to start on Saturday, 3 April at 4:30pm?

J: Yes, of course. I learned of the race yesterday on TV.

T: I plan to go and have a look, would you like to come with me?

J: No, thanks. I'll watch that on TV.

T: But don't you think that it will be more exciting if we go the **spot**①? You know, I've never been to the spot before. Have you?

J: I went to the spot last year with Harry.

T: You must have spent a very wonderful time there.

J: Yes. I do think it is more excting than watching it on TV. Large crowds of people join together just to enjoy the same event.

T: It must be fun. I will go this Saturday.

J: Get there earlier and find a **vantage point**② in advance. When we arrived 2 hours before the competition start last year, there were so many people there already that we could not get to a good point to view the race. At first, I saw nothing but the backs of other people.

① spot *n.* 地点，现场

② vantage point 有利位置

T: That's awful, I'll be there as early as possible. So what happened to you next, did you find a better spot?

J: Yes. Harry and I tried our best to find a better spot amid the crowds. Wasn't good enough but better.

T: I see. I heard that this is the 155th race between the two. I cannot believe that it has such a long history.

J: You're wrong. It is the 156th race! Do you know which university won more times than the other?

T: I have no idea who won more, but I guess it might be Oxford. They were really good last year. I saw their victory on TV.

J: Actually the answer is Cambridge. It won 79 times, 4 times more than Oxford.

T: Wow, they are almost neck and neck. I'm wondering who will be the winner this time. Is there any **dead-heat**[①]?

J: Yes, ever since the race **initiated**[②] in 1829, there was one dead-heat in 1877.

T: Can women join the crew?

J: Yes, women first took part in the competition in 1981 when Sue Brown served as the **wheelwoman**[③] of Oxford. Oxford won that time. In 1989, both teams had women as their wheelwoman, and Oxford won again.

T: Cambridge must be very upset.

J: It doesn't matter since Cambridge won more times than Oxford in total.

T: Are the Boat Race crews up to the standard of international crews?

J: It is difficult to judge. since the Boat Race crews train for a long-distance race early in the season, so their training schedule is quite different for crews training for international regattas.

T: I see from the TV that the course follows an S shape. How long is the course?

J: The course is 4 miles from Putney to Mortlake, passing Hammersmith and Barnes; it is sometimes referred to as the Championship Course, and follows an S shape, east to west. The start and finish are marked by the University Boat Race Stones on the south bank.

T: Well, thanks for your information.

---

① dead-heat *n.* 平局
② initiate *vt.* 开始，创始
③ wheelwoman *n.* 女舵手

T: 嗨，吉米！你听说了吗？今年的赛艇在 4 月 3 日星期六下午 4:30 举行。

J: 当然啦，我昨天从电视上知道的。

T: 我打算去看看，你愿意和我一起去吗？

J: 不了，谢谢。我还是看电视吧。

T: 但是你不认为如果去现场看的话会更有趣吗？我还从来没去过呢。你呢？

J: 我去年和哈利一起去过。

T: 你们在那里肯定玩得很开心吧。

J: 是啊。在那里看确实比在电视上看要过瘾。你想，那么多的人聚集在一起就只是为了看一个比赛。

T: 肯定很有趣，我这周六一定要去。

J: 你要去早一点，占个好位置。去年，我们提前两小时到达的时候，那儿已经有好多人了，根本就找不到一个观看的好地方。刚开始的时候，我只能看到别人的后背。

T: 那样的话就太糟糕了。我会尽早过去的。你们后来怎么样，找到好一点的地方了吗？

J: 嗯，找到了。我们在人群中挤来挤去，费了很大力气。那地方还是不够好，不过比原来的好。

T: 我知道了。听说这是两所大学第 155 次比赛？真不敢相信这个赛艇有这么长的历史。

J: 你错了，这是第 156 次！你知道哪所大学赢的次数比较多吗？

T: 我不知道。可能是牛津吧，他们去年的表现真的很棒，我从电视上都看到了。

J: 实际上，剑桥赢的次数比较多。剑桥赢了 79 次，比牛津要多 4 次。

T: 哇，他们还真是不相上下。我在想，谁会是这届比赛的赢家呢。对了，他们有没有打过平手？

J: 有啊。从 1829 年这个比赛开始以来，只在 1877 年出现过一次平局。

T: 女性可以参加比赛吗？

J: 可以。在 1981 年首次出现了女性参加比赛，那年苏·布朗担任牛津队的舵手，牛津赢了。而 1989 年，两个队都由女性担任舵手，还是牛津赢。

T: 剑桥肯定很伤心。

J: 不过没关系，总数上，剑桥还是暂时领先的。

T: 赛艇队的成员们是不是已经达到国际比赛运动员水准了？

J: 这很难说。参加赛艇的选手，在赛季之前就开始了长距离的赛艇训练，而国际赛舟会选手的训练计划和他们的很不一样。

T: 我从电视上看到，赛道呈 S 形，它到底有多长?

J: 赛道从普特尼到莫特湖大约有 4 英里，经过汉默斯密和巴尔内斯。有时人们称它为冠军河道，从东到西呈 S 形。起始点的南岸都有大学赛艇的标志。

T: 好，谢谢你提供的信息。

1 Have you heard that the boat race this year **is scheduled to** start on Saturday, 3 April at 4: 30 pm?

be scheduled to do 意为"预期，计划做"。类似的用法还有 be scheduled for sb., 意为"为某人安排做什么事情"。

➢ If I were elected to chair the student union, the most brilliant scholars home and abroad will be scheduled to lecture here to feast out ears and eyes and update our knowledge.
如果能当选学生会主席，我会安排最著名的国内外学者在这里为我们讲学，丰富我们的知识。

➢ Concerning your time, we are willing to schedule for you again.
考虑到您的时间，我们愿意为您重新安排。

2 You **must have spent** a very wonderful time there.

must have done 表示对过去已经做过的事情的推测，语气十分肯定，类似的用法 might have done，语气比较不确定。

➢ Linda must have quarrelled with her husband last night.
琳达昨晚肯定和她丈夫吵架了。

➢ Linda might have quarrelled with her husband last night.
琳达昨晚可能和她丈夫吵架了。

3 Are the Boat Race crews **are up to** the standard of international crews?

be up to 意为"胜任，从事，忙于，轮到……，该由……负责"。

➢ They said it could be up to a month.
他们说可能要去将近一个月。

➢ Our goods must be up to export standards before going into the market.

我们的货物只有在符合出口标准后才能投入市场。

- In order to be up to the evolution demand of Computer Interlocking System, we successfully exploit a set of Automatic Testing Simulation System of Computer Interlocking Software.
  为了适应计算机联锁系统的发展需要，我们成功开发了一套微机联锁软件模拟自动测试系统。

- She must be up to something.
  她一定在搞什么鬼花招。

4 It is difficult to judge. since the Boat Race crews train for a long-distance race early in the season, so their training schedule is quite different for crews training for international regattas over 2000 metres that **take place** later in the year.

take place 意为“发生”，而 take place of 则意为“代替”，注意两者的区别。

- Could Marx predict that the October Revolution would take place in backward Russia?
  马克思能预料到在一个落后的俄国会实现十月革命吗？

- Nothing in the world can take place of persistence.
  世上没有任何东西能够代替坚持。

Oxford and Cambridge Boat Race

Each spring in west London, the Oxford University Boat Club and the Cambridge University Boat Club will hold a rowing race on the **Thames**[①]. Members of both teams are traditionally known as blues, with Cambridge in light blue and Oxford dark blue.

The tradition was started in 1829 by Charles Merivale, a student at St John's College, Cambridge, and his schoolfriend Charles Wordsworth who was at Oxford. Cambridge challenged Oxford to a race at Henley-on-Thames. The second race occurred in 1836, with the **venue**[②] moved from Westminster to Putney. Over the next couple of years, there was disagreement over where the race should be held, with Oxford preferring Henley and Cambridge preferring London. Cambridge therefore raced Leander Club in 1837 and 1838. Following

① Thames *n.* 泰晤士河。英国第二长的河流，也是最重要的水路，又是英国的母亲河。它发源于英格兰西南部的科茨沃尔德山，沿途汇集了英格兰境内的诸多细流，河水从西部流入伦敦市区，伦敦下游河面变宽，形成一个宽度为29千米的河口，最后经诺尔岛注入北海。

② venue *n.* 发生地点，集合地点

the formation of the Oxford University Boat Club, racing between the two universities **resumed**① and the tradition continues to the present day, with the loser challenging the winner to a re-match **annually**② with the exception of the two world wars.

The event is a popular one, not only with the alumni of the universities, but also with rowers in general and the public. An estimated quarter of a million people watch the race live from the banks of the river from Putney to Mortlake, around seven to nine million people on TV in the UK, and an overseas audience estimated by the Boat Race Company at around 120 million.

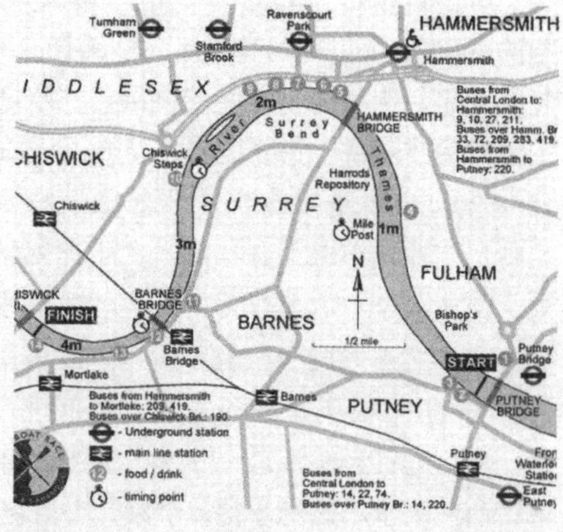

Despite being three times the length of an Olympic course, the entire event is over in just 20 minutes, a fact which should not overshadow the six months of sweat and **toil**③ which the teams endure in preparation for the big day.

There are plenty of river vantage points for spectators, many of them conveniently close to **pubs**④. A top-hat at a **rakish**⑤ angle and a half-empty bottle of expensive **champagne**⑥ might help you **wheedle**⑦ your way into some of the more **glamorous**⑧ riverside parties that accompany this event.

During the past 181 years, the race has been held for 155 times. Despite a **phenomenal**⑨ dead-heat which occurred in 1877, Cambridge won 79 times, 4 times more than Oxford. The 2009 boat race took place on 29 March at 15: 40 BST, with Oxford winning. The next race is scheduled to start on Saturday, 3 April 2010 at 4: 30 pm. Who will win this time, let's wait for the result and good luck to both Oxford and Cambridge!

---

① resume *vt.* 重新开始
② annually *adv.* 每年地
③ toil *n.* 苦工
④ pub *n.* 酒馆，客栈
⑤ rakish *adj.* 后倾的
⑥ champagne *n.* 香槟酒
⑦ wheedle *vt.* 以甜言蜜语哄骗
⑧ glamorous *adj.* 迷人的，富有魅力的
⑨ phenomenal *adj.* 奇异的，显著的

牛桥赛艇比赛

每年春天，牛津大学赛艇队和剑桥大学赛艇队都会在西伦敦的泰晤士河上进行赛艇。两个团队的成员都身着蓝色服装，剑桥是浅蓝色，而牛津是则深蓝色。

这个传统始于1829年，由分别在牛津和剑桥大学念书的两个好朋友——剑桥大学的查尔斯·梅里韦尔和牛津大学的查尔斯·华兹华斯（诗人威廉·华兹华斯的侄子）发起。那年，剑桥向牛津发起挑战，在泰晤士河畔的亨利决一胜负。第二次比赛是在1863年，比赛路线改到从威斯敏斯特到帕特尼。在接下来的几年间，关于比赛场地，两所大学总有争议。牛津比较喜欢亨利，而剑桥更倾向于伦敦。所以，剑桥在1837年和1838年就和利安得俱乐部进行了比赛。之后，牛津成立了大学赛艇俱乐部，两所大学的比赛才得以继续，并且延续至今。除了两次世界大战期间，每年，上一届比赛的输家都会向对手发起挑战，要求再次比赛。

这个活动很受欢迎，对这个活动感兴趣的不仅是两所大学的校友，它还吸引了许多公众的目光。比赛当天，多达25万观众将齐集泰晤士河从普特尼到莫特湖的河道两岸，见证这一激动人心的比赛。大约有700万到900万的英国人会在电视上收看这一比赛。据赛艇公司的估计，海外观众人数将达到1.2亿。

虽然比赛河段的长度是奥林匹克运动会比赛赛道长度的3倍，整个比赛会在20分钟内就全部结束，但这并不能抹杀队员们为了这一重要时刻所付出的为期6个月的汗水和努力。

河道旁边有很多理想的观看地点，这些地方通常离酒吧很近。一顶微倾的帽子，半杯价格不菲的香槟没准就能帮你融入和比赛同时进行的河边聚会。

在过去的181年间，比赛一共进行过155次。除了1877年出现了一次罕见的平局，剑桥一共赢了79次，比牛津要多4次。2009年的赛艇是在3月29日，英国夏令时15：40开始的，牛津获胜。2010年的比赛定于4月3日16：30进行。那么这次哪个大学会取胜呢，让我们拭目以待吧。祝牛津和剑桥好运。

Unit 10 Overseas Study
领略英伦风情

37 Odd Interview 古怪面试

Sam and Jane are talking about interviews in Oxbridge.

S: Sam　　　　J: Jane

S: Do you know that Cambridge received 14,585 **applications**① and Oxford 13,287 for entry this October?

J: Yes. But how many of them will survive the interview is still in doubt.

S: Cambridge alone rejected at interview more than 5,000 students last year who went on to get three A grades in their A levels, underlining the intensity of competition.

J: True. Interviewers in those two Universities are good at posing **eccentric**② questions.

S: They may all be academic **thoroughbreds**③, but success in the Oxbridge stakes can seem as **remote**④ as winning **the Grand National**⑤.

J: It was said that the tutors select people they want to teach ultimately.

S: The competition against other students is fierce and candidates need to differentiate themselves. "To be honest, they're competing against each other, not against the

---

① application *n.* 申请
② eccentric *adj.* 古怪的，反常的
③ thoroughbred *n.* 受过严格训练的，优秀的
④ remote *adj.* 遥远的
⑤ the Grand National 英国全国越野障碍赛马。常常被称之为世界上最盛大的障碍赛马比赛，是世界上最有名的障碍赛马比赛之一。

interviewers," said a **don**[①] in the university.

J: Yes. Nearly all applicants have excellent A-level grades, so places are increasingly awarded for original answers in interviews.

S: So it's worth actively engaging with the questions, without being rude or **confrontational**[②], rather than **tiptoeing around**[③] to avoid mistakes.

J: Some **entrants**[④] are so nervous that they even practice the interview on a daily basis with the help of their parents at home.

S: Really? Does it help?

J: It's hard to say. But a mother of a twin said that she thinks the practices are really helpful, and she even suggested parents of the applicants should help their children to practice their reaction and creative thinking.

S: That might be true. However, I also heard that **over-rehearsing**[⑤] does no good to the interview because they might lose the ability of responding naturally and **spontaneously**[⑥].

J: Yes. You really have no idea what the tutors are looking for. One of my friends who got 5 As at A-Level, was head boy, involved in Drama, **charity**[⑦] work and debating did not get into Cambridge.

S: Why?

J: Who knows why? Maybe he just didn't fit what the tutor was looking for.

S: Well, I think the teacher must also be highly pressured on this since they might have made the wrong decision.

J: Yes, I heard that next week, in an attempt to standardize its admissions **procedure**[⑧], Oxford will announce that all dons are to be put through training sessions to remind them how to interview fairly and well.

S: They just shouldn't be so **picky**[⑨].

J: They might appear to be cruel, but there are only few places, they must make the decision.

---

① don *n.* 指导老师
② confrontational *adj.* 对抗性的
③ tiptoe around 踮起脚尖在周围绕行，形容做事小心翼翼，或指故意规避问题。
④ entrant *n.* 参加竞争者
⑤ over-rehearsing *adj.* 过度演练的
⑥ spontaneously *adv.* 自发的，自主的
⑦ charity *n.* 施舍，慈善
⑧ procedure *n.* 步骤，程序
⑨ picky *adj.* 吹毛求疵的，挑剔的

S: Let me tell you an interesting story about the admissions ritual at Peterhouse, Cambridge. When a candidate entered the room, someone would kick a rugby ball towards him. If he caught it, he was in; if he drop-kicked it back, he won a scholarship.

J: That's interesting but can't be true!

S: No one suggests that happens now, but tales still **circulate**① about **baffling**② questions posed by dons.

J: They said sometimes teenagers can break down in tears.

S: How does the teacher **cope**③?

J: One of the dons said to them: "if you want to cry for another five minutes, you can." Sometimes they go away, have a cup of coffee and come back.

S: Are you kidding me?

S: 你知道吗，今年 10 月，剑桥大学收到了 14585 份入学申请，牛津收到了 13287 份。

J: 知道。但是这些申请人中有多少能通过面试还是个未知数。

S: 去年剑桥就拒绝了 5000 多名学生的申请。这些学生都是获得了 3 个 A-level 成绩的学生，这就说明了竞争有多么激烈。

J: 对啊。这两所大学的老师很爱提刁钻古怪的问题。

S: 他们可能学习都很优秀，但是能通过面试的机率就跟在英国"全国大赛马"获胜一样低。

J: 据说老师们最终只是在挑选他们想教的人。

S: 同学之间的竞争特别激烈，申请者们必须有与众不同之处才能脱颖而出。一位面试官曾讲过："老实说，他们是彼此在竞争而不是在和面试官竞争。"

J: 对。几乎所有的申请人的成绩都是非常优秀的 A-level，所以能否被录取就更加取决于他们在面试中的表现了。

S: 所以，面试者不能傲慢粗鲁，也不能畏畏缩缩的逃避犯错，而是积极地参与到问题中去。

J: 有些学生特别紧张，他们甚至在父母的帮助下，天天在家里进行面试练习。

S: 真的吗？这样有用吗？

J: 这不好说。但是有一位双胞胎的家长说，她认为这种练习十分有用，她还建议别的学生家长也在家帮助孩子们练习，以增强反应能力和创造性思维的能力。

S: 也许吧。不过我也听人说，过度的演练未必真的有好处，因为这样，学生们在面

① circulate *vi.* 流通，传播
② baffling *adj.* 令人困惑的
③ cope *vt.* 处理，竞争，对付

试中就不能很自然的反应。

J: 有道理。很难说这些老师们到底要寻找什么样的人才。我有一位朋友曾经在A-level得了5个A、担任班长、参加戏剧演出、慈善工作、也是辩论社的一员，可是他还是没被剑桥录取。

S: 为什么呢？

J: 谁知道为什么。也许只是因为他不是老师们要找的人。

S: 嗯，我觉得老师们恐怕也非常有压力，因为他们很可能会作错误的决定。

J: 是啊。我听说为了使招生程序标准化，牛津宣布下周对所有参加面试的老师进行培训，以便更好更公平地进行面试。

S: 他们实在不应该过分挑剔。

J: 看起来，这些老师是有些“残忍”，不过因为名额有限，他们不得不作出决定。

S: 我跟你讲一个有趣的故事，是关于剑桥彼得学院招生面试的。面试者一进入面试的房间，就会有人踢给他一个橄榄球，如果接到了，他就会被录取；如果把球踢了回去，就能赢得奖学金。

J: 真有意思，不过这肯定不是真的。

S: 现在这种事情肯定不会发生，不过这也说明了面试官们提出的问题有多么古怪。

J: 有人说，一些孩子面试的时候都哭了。

S: 那老师该怎么办？

J: 一位面试官跟现场大哭的学生说：“如果你还想再哭5分钟的话，请便。”有时候，他们只是暂时离开，喝杯咖啡再回来。

S: 这太夸张了！

1 But how many of them would **survive** the interview is still in doubt.

survive 意为“幸存，残存，活下来，比……活得长，经历……还存在”，既可以作及物动词，也可以作不及物动词。

➤ He survived in the desert for a week on biscuits and water.
他在沙漠中靠饼干和水维持了一个星期。

➤ Very few of these old coins survive.

这些古钱币现在已经十分罕见。

- Few buildings survived the fire.
  这次火灾中没有几座建筑物幸免于难。

- She survived her sons.
  她活得比她几个儿子都要长。

2 The competition against other students is fierce and candidates need to **differentiate** themselves.

differentiate 意为“区别，区分”。

- This company does not differentiate between men and women—everyone is paid at the same rate.
  本公司对男女员工一视同仁，大家都按相同的薪酬标准领工资。

- Can you differentiate this kind of rose from the others?
  你能把这种玫瑰与其他玫瑰品种区分开来吗?

- What differentiate these two products?
  是什么使得这两种产品有所区别?

Odd Interview

The Oxbridge interviewers are **notorious**① for asking **bizarre**② questions: What percentage of the world's water is contained in a cow? How many **aeroplanes**③ are flying above Oxford at this moment? Can a **slug**④ think? What shape is an egg? and so on.

The idea is not to elicit the correct answer, but that candidates should show clear reasoning. What does it mean to think? What "equipment" is needed to think? Do molluscs have such equipment?

The surprises may not end with the questions. Some applicants have been caught unawares by eccentric interviewers. One applicant was welcomed into the room by a scruffy

---

① notorious *adj.* 声名狼藉的，臭名昭著的
② bizarre *adj.* 奇异的
③ aeroplane *n.* 飞机
④ slug *n.* 鼻涕虫

philosophy tutor wearing no shoes. His big toe was **protruding**① through one of the many holes in his socks.

In such situations, the best hope is a stiff upper lip, although applicants may secretly wonder whether they want to be taught by such unconventional types for three or four years.

Such quirkiness, however, is rare、"I've never asked an **off-the-wall**② question in 30 years of interviewing," said one Oxford don. Tutors are free to choose their own questions, so long as they don't infringe equal opportunities.

"Applicants should be aware that it might be in the interest of commercial companies to create the impression that the admissions interview at Oxbridge colleges is 'eccentric'. This is not the case. The aim of the interview is to assess each candidate's ability and potential on an individual basis," one don said.

"What our admissions tutors are looking for is how well candidates can explain what they know, and whether they can apply their knowledge to a new problem or argue their position." A Cambridge spokesman said: "There's no need to have special training for Cambridge interviews. Indeed, applicants who are'over-rehearsed' tend to come across less well than students who are natural and **spontaneous**③."

The interview is Oxbridge's ultimate test in selecting the best students. Does it work? According to Dr Mayer, "only very rarely do we choose entrants who find themselves out of their depth". Another don estimates he has selected the right candidates in about 80% of cases. This may reassure some applicants that there is method behind the myth. Whether or not slugs think, successful applicants must show that they do.

As the only British universities in the world's top ten, Oxford and Cambridge inevitably command great attention. Both are working to **dispel**④ the mystique surrounding them that undoubtedly left some youngsters feeling too intimidated to apply in the past. Summer schools and open days, plus the wealth of information about the admissions process on their websites, all make Oxbridge more accessible than ever. But if you never apply, you'll never know.

① protrude *vt.* 突出，突伸
② off-the-wall *adj.* 荒诞的，疯狂的
③ spontaneous *adj.* 自发的，自然地，无意识的
④ dispel *vt.* 驱散，驱除

古怪的面试

牛桥的面试官提的问题稀奇古怪是出了名的，如一头牛体内水的含量占世界总水量的多少？现在有多少飞机正在飞过牛津？鼻涕虫会思考吗？鸡蛋是什么形状的？等等。

这样提问的目的并不是要找到正确的答案，而是需要申请者必须进行条理清晰的推理论证。什么叫做思考？进行思考需要什么器官？软体动物有这种器官吗？

也许除了问题之外，还有别的惊奇。一些申请者还见到了行为古怪的面试官。有一位面试者曾经遇到一位衣着邋遢的哲学教授，他连鞋都没穿，大脚趾从袜子的破洞里露出来。

在这种情况下，面试者能做的最好的事情就是保持泰然自若，尽管他们私下里也会琢磨，到底应不应该花三四年的时间从师于这种特立独行的老师。

这种离奇的问题毕竟也不多见。一位牛津的面试老师说过：“30 年来，我从来没有问过很稀奇古怪的问题。”导师们可以自由地选择自己所要提的问题，只要不违背公平的原则就行。

一位面试官说：“申请者应该清楚，这或许是商业公司出于自身利益的考虑，才会刻意制造出牛桥的面试都很古怪的印象。其实并不是这样。面试的目的是正确评估每位申请者的能力和潜质。”

“我们的导师寻找的是这样的学生，是否能够合理解释他们所知道的东西，是否能够运用已掌握的知识去解决新的问题。”剑桥大学的发言人说：“为了面试而去进行特别的培训根本没有必要。其实很多时候，那些过度排练的申请者，反而没有那些临场发挥的学生表现好。”

面试是牛桥选拔人才的最后一关。一位面试官曾说：“我们很少会选择那些力所不能及的人。”另外一名面试官说，他选对人的概率是 80%。这就说明，这种奇怪的面试背后必然有它的道理。不管鼻涕虫会不会思考，一个成功的面试者必须会思考。

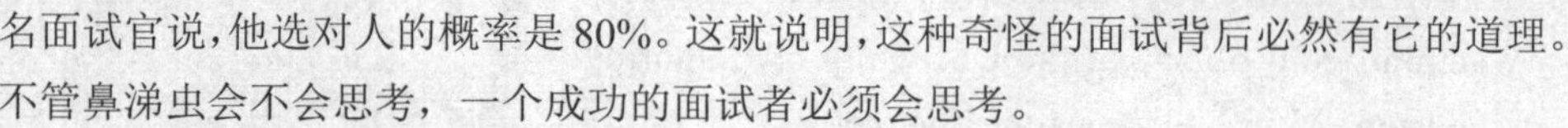

牛津大学和剑桥大学作为唯一进入世界大学排名前十的英国大学，常常会受到很多关注。因为曾让不少申请人望而生畏，它们正在努力消除自己的神秘感。现在人们可以通过很多途径来了解剑桥和牛津，比如，暑期学校、开放日，官方网站上关于录取流程的详细说明等等。如果你不试着申请的话，你永远也不会知道情况到底怎样。

38 Studying in the Library
图书馆里求学忙

焦点对话

Li Ming and Joanne are talking about the Cambridge University Library.

L: Li Ming J: Joanne

L: Hi, Joanne. I'm thinking about borrowing some books from the University Library, but you know, I am new here, so could you please tell me something about the library?

J: Of course. Some students said that it is a huge **labyrinth**①.

L: Yes. It must not be easy for a new-comer to find what he or she wants.

J: Don't worry. At the beginning of every semester, **introductory**② tours would be given by the librarian, explaining the catalogues, shelving arrangements, closed access collections and book-fetching.

L: They are really **considerate**③. But I think it will take us some time to get familiar with it.

J: True. There is an online library **floorplan**④ to help you find your way around. The library staffs are very kind; I think they will be pleased to help you.

L: That's great. Maybe it's better for me to ask the staff for help when I can't find what I'm looking for.

J: Yes. In addition, the library is the centrally-administered library of the University of Cambridge and **comprises**⑤ five separate libraries.

---

① labyrinth *n.* 迷宫
② introductory *adj.* 引导的，介绍的，开端的
③ considerate *adj.* 体贴的，考虑周到的
④ floorplan *n.* 楼层平面图
⑤ comprise *vt.* 包含，由……组成

L: Five separate libraries?

J: Yes. They are the University Library main building, which is commonly referred to simply as "the UL", the Medical Library, the Betty and Gordon Moore Library, the central Science Library and the Squire Law Library.

L: Who can use the Library?

J: All members of the University of Cambridge are welcome to use the library. Besides, academic staff and research students from other universities, private and business researchers may apply to use the library for reference.

L: Does the library charge any fee?

J: It is not free to everybody. A 10 pounds administration charge for 6 months applies to applicants from non-UK universities and the public.

L: Not expensive. I guess the library must have **covered**[①] all the subjects in human history.

J: You are right. There are many precious copies of the ancient works.

L: I heard that it is a **legal**[②] deposit library, what does this mean?

J: It means that it is entitled to claim a copy of every publication in printed form published in the UK and Ireland. Almost all of this material is claimed and can be **consulted**[③] in the library.

L: That's great!

J: It also holds **extensive**[④] collection of books, journals, maps, **microfilms**[⑤], photographs and sound recordings published overseas and has extensive special collections of rare books, **manuscripts**[⑥], and other materials.

L: It's no wonder that scholars all over the world want to come to Cambridge and meanwhile so many world-famous scholars and scientists who have made great contribution have spent part of their life studying in Cambridge.

J: Absolutely.

L: When is it open? I am afraid it is closed now.

J: Let me see. No, you still have the time. It won't be closed until 19: 00 from Monday to Friday. If it is on weekends, you should be more careful with the time. On Saturdays it will be closed at 5 pm and it is closed on Sundays.

---

① cover *vt.* 包括，涉及
② legal *adj.* 法定的，法律的，合法的
③ consult *vt.* 查阅，向……请教
④ extensive *adj.* 广泛的，广阔的，大量的
⑤ microfilm *n.* 缩微胶卷
⑥ manuscript *n.* 原稿，手稿

L: I see. I'd better hurry up now.

J: Don't forget to take your University ID Card with you. It's all you need to start using the Library.

L: I won't. Thanks for your information!

L: 嗨，乔安妮。我正打算去学校图书馆借几本书呢，但是我是新生，你能不能给我介绍一下图书馆啊?

J: 当然可以啦。有些学生说，它就像个大迷宫。

L: 是啊。对于一个初来乍到的人来说，想要找到自己想要的东西肯定不容易。

J: 不要担心。每个学期开始的时候，大学图书馆的管理员都会义务举办各类主题的图书馆使用讲座，讲解图书目录的编排，书架的摆放规则，非开放类资料和图书借取。

L: 他们想得很周到。但是我觉得，要想熟悉图书馆，还需要花费一定的时间。

J: 对。馆里还有在线图书馆楼层安排，你也可以借助这个找到正确路线。图书管理员们也都非常和气，他们都很乐意帮忙。

L: 太好了。找不到书的时候，我最好还是找他们帮忙。

J: 是啊。这个图书馆是剑桥大学的中心管理图书馆，共有 5 个分馆。

L: 5 个分馆?

J: 是啊，图书馆的主楼，通常被简称为 “UL”，医学图书馆，贝蒂和戈登·摩尔图书馆，中心科学图书馆和法学图书馆。

L: 谁可以使用这些图书馆呢?

J: 所有剑桥大学的成员都可以使用。另外，其他大学的从事科学研究的教职工或者学生，其他私人和商业机构研究员也可以申请使用剑桥的图书馆。

L: 那图书馆收费吗?

J: 图书馆并不是对每个人都免费。非英国大学的申请人和公众需要缴纳10英镑，这是半年的费用。

L: 这并不贵。我想图书馆的书籍肯定包括了人类历史上所有的学科。

J: 你说的对。图书馆里还有很多古籍。

L: 我听说它是法定书库，不知道这是什么意思?

J: 这就是说，它有权利要求所有在英国和爱尔兰出版的图书都交送一份给它。我们可以在图书馆里找到所有的这类材料，并进行使用。

L: 太棒了!

J: 图书馆里还有大量图书、期刊、地图、缩影胶片、照片和海外音像资料，更有许多的孤本，手稿和其他材料。

L: 所以，世界各地的学者都想到剑桥来，而许多闻名世界的学者和科学家都曾经在剑桥待过，就一点也不奇怪了。

J: 对啊。

L: 图书馆什么时候开，我怕它现在已经关了。

J: 我看看。还没呢，还有时间。周一到周五是晚上七点关门。但如果是周末，你就得注意点时间了。周六是晚上5点关门，周日闭馆。

L: 知道了，我得快一点了。

J: 别忘了带上学生证，这可是使用图书馆必不可少的东西。

L: 好，谢谢你告诉我这么多!

难点解析

1 But I think **it will take us some time** to get familiar with it.

take sb. some time to do sth. 意为“花费某人时间做某事”。

➢ It will take you a long time to finish this book.
读完这本书要花费你很长时间。

2 They are the University Library main building, which is commonly **referred** to simply as "the UL", the Medical Library, the Betty and Gordon Moore Library, the central Science Library and the Squire Law Library.

（1）提到，说起

➢ The scientist referred to the discovery as the most exciting new development in this field.
这个科学家提到这一发现时，说它是这个领域中最令人兴奋的新发展。

（2）参考，查阅，查看

➢ Let me just refer to my notes to find the exact figures.
请让我查阅一下笔记，看看准确的数字。

（3）有关，针对

➢ The new law does not refer to land used for farming.
那条法律并不涉及耕种土地。

（4）refer sb./sth. to sb. 指"提交给（某人或某机构）以作决定（处理）"

➢ The shop referred the complaint back to the makers of the articles.
商店把顾客的投诉转交给生产该商品的厂家。

➢ The professor referred me to an article she had written on this subject.
教授叫我查阅她写的关于这个题目的文章。

3 Besides, academic staff and research students from other universities, private and business researchers may **apply** to use the library for reference.

（1）使用，运用，应用

➢ Scientific discoveries are often applied to industrial processes.
科学上的发明通常都应用于工业生产过程。

（2）敷，涂，贴用

➢ Apply the paint evenly to both sides of the door.
给门的两面均匀地涂上漆。

（3）适用，与……直接有关

➢ This rule does not apply in your particular case.
这项规则不适用于你的具体情况。

（4）apply for 则指"提出请求，申请"

➢ I'll apply for the job today.
我今天就申请这份工作。

Cambridge University Library

Cambridge University Library is one of the oldest **institutions**① in the University of Cambridge, and for more than 600 years it has been central to the support of teaching and research at Cambridge, and a major resource for scholars around the world. It is one of the world's most important research libraries.

Though the library enjoys a history of more than 600 years, in the early days, most of the collections mainly depended on **donations**② and **legacies**③. The library began to **purchase**④ books only in 1617, and it began its claim on books provided by publishers since 1662. In 1709, the King **promulgated**⑤ the **Copyright Act**⑥ which announced that all the books published in the country should turn in a copy to the Cambridge University Library, and the amount of the collections **soared**⑦.

On just over 100 miles of shelving, it houses around 7,000,000 printed **volumes**⑧, 150,000 manuscript items, about a million maps and 400,000 musical items, as well as providing access to tens of thousands of electronic journals and databases.

Since 1710 the Library has been a legal deposit library, entitled to claim a copy of every book and periodical published in Great Britain and Ireland. Of all the libraries in Europe, the University Library has the largest collection of material on open access, with two million volumes on open shelves and immediately **accessible**⑨ to users.

The Library's special collections include thousands of medieval manuscripts such as the 5th-century Gospel text known as *Codex Bezae*; 4,500 incunabula including the *Gutenberg*

① institution *n.* 机构，制度
② donation *n.* 捐赠，捐款，捐赠物
③ legacy *n.* 遗赠，遗产
④ purchase *vt.* 购买
⑤ promulgate *vt.* 公布，传播，发表
⑥ Copyright Act 1709 年，英国的安娜女王颁布了一个法案，以保护出版商和作者的利益，后来的人们就将这部法律命名为《安娜女王法》，这是世界上第一部著作权法。
⑦ soar *vi.* 高飞
⑧ volume *n.* 卷，册
⑨ accessible *adj.* 可接近的，可进入的，可理解的

Bible[1] and a hand-coloured copy of the *Nuremberg Chronicle*; papers of scientists such as Sir Isaac Newton, Charles Darwin, Lord Kelvin and Lord Rutherford; papers of literary and political figures including Lord Acton, Lord Randolph Churchill, Sir Robert Walpole, Stanley Baldwin, Arthur Schnitzler and Stefan Heym; business archives of Jardine Matheson & Company and Vickers plc; the collections of the Royal Greenwich Observatory, the Royal Commonwealth Society, and the British and Foreign Bible Society.

The Library's policy is to provide the widest possible access to its collections, both by making its catalogues available online and by **digitising**[2] a growing range of materials. All of these are available freely to the world via the Internet.

剑桥图书馆

剑桥图书馆是剑桥大学历史上最为悠久的机构之一，在长达600年的时间里，它都是剑桥大学教学和科研的核心，是世界各地的学者们求知的宝地。同时，它也是世界上最重要的科研图书馆之一。

尽管有着600余年的历史，其早期的馆藏几乎完全靠捐赠或遗赠。图书馆从1617年开始采购图书,1662年开始收藏出版商呈缴的样本。1709年英国颁布版权法，正式规定凡本国出版的图书都要免费缴送该馆，从而使馆藏迅速增加。

在仅100余米的书架上，就摆放着大约700万册图书，15万册手抄本，100万张地图，40万份音乐剧本，还有成千上万的电子期刊和数据库。

自1710年来，剑桥的图书馆就是国家的法定书库之一，所有在英国或爱尔兰出版的图书或杂志都必须免费送缴该馆一份。欧洲所有的图书馆中，剑桥图书馆的开放存取材料是最多的，大约有200万册图书都属于开放性的资料，供读者随时查阅。

剑桥图书馆的特别典藏中有上千份中世纪的手稿，如公元5世纪的伯撒抄本《福音书》；4500余册古本，其中包括《古腾堡圣经》，手绘本《纽伦堡编年史》；多位科学家如牛顿、达尔文、开尔文、卢瑟福等等的手稿和论著；文学家和政治家如艾克顿公爵、伦道夫公爵、罗伯特·沃波尔、斯坦利·鲍尔温、阿尔图尔·施尼茨勒和史蒂芬·海姆的论著；怡和洋行及威格士公共有限公司的商业档案；皇家格林威治天文台，皇家联邦社团，英外社交圣经集团的相关资料等等。

图书馆的政策就是通过目录在线化和日益丰富藏书的数字化，为读者提供最大限度查阅资料的方便。通过网络，世界各地均可免费共享这些资源。

---

① Gutenberg Bible 古腾堡圣经（另译谷登堡圣经，也叫做四十二行圣经）是《圣经》拉丁文公认翻译的印刷品，由同名人古腾堡于1454年到1455年在德国美因兹采用活字印刷术印刷的。

② digitize *vt.* 数字化

39 Cycling in Cambridge
校园单车行

焦点对话

Mike is new in Cambridge. He and Ellen are talking about Ellen's new bike.

M: Mike   E: Ellen

M: Hi, Ellen! Is this your new bike?

E: Yes, I bought it only yesterday.

M: It's cool! May I have a try?

E: Of course. Don't forget to ride on the left.

M: Oh, I think it'll take me some time to get used to it. You know, in my country, we should drive, ride and walk on the right.

E: Well, it could be dangerous if you break the rules.

M: OK, I think I'd better try on your bike when I get more familiar with the traffic **regulations**① here. Why do so many people **commute**② by bike in Cambridge?

E: You see, Cambridge City is small and flat, besides, the colleges of Cambridge University scatter in every corner of the city. Riding a bike between lectures is quick and **convenient**③.

M: And it is almost the most **environment-friendly**④ way of commute.

E: That's right. Since riding a bike is the most common way to commute in this city, there are a lot of regulations about riding.

---

① regulation *n.* 规则，规章
② commute *vt.* 通勤，来往返回于
③ convenient *adj.* 方便的
④ environment-friendly *adj.* 有利于环境的

M: For example?

E: For example, people under 18 or above 60 should wear a **helmet**[①] when they ride, and your bike should be equipped with two lights, with one in the front and the other in the back.

M: We don't have this kind of regulations in our country.

E: It's a little bit troublesome but it's for the sake of safety.

M: I agree. I noticed that people just leave their bikes **propped against a wall**[②] and some of them are even unlocked, thus I'm wondering is it because that there is no bike crime here?

E: No, it's far from the case. People sometimes just take their bikes casually and Cambridge is the UK's bike crime capital.

M: You must be careful with your bike.

E: I will. If you're interested in biking, you can join the CUCC. That's the Cambridge University Cycling Club.

M: I'd like to, but I'm not very skilled in cycling.

E: It doesn't matter. CUCC has a wide variety of events for members of all abilities. Membership is **available**[③] for all types of students and university staff.

M: Really? Can you tell me more about the club, for example, the history of it?

E: Of course. The club came into being in 1874 with 11 members; within five years this figure was in excess of 260 and included all members of the University from undergraduates to Fellows.

M: How popular it is! Is there any competition held by the club?

E: Yes. Within two months of its formation, the **Dark Blue Bicycle Club**[④] requested the first inter-varsity race. This **inaugural**[⑤] race was held on the 18th June 1874, and consisted of an 80 mile course between Oxford and Cambridge. Cambridge won, taking both the first and second places.

M: Wow, Cambridge is really good at cycling.

---

① helmet *n.* 头盔

② propped against a wall 把车靠在墙上。英国的自行车不像中国的自行车一样有支架，所以不能随地停稳，要靠在栅栏、墙、树或电线杆上。有的甚至在石板上凿出一个窄窄的长形深槽，深槽里刚好能放进去自行车的前轮子，起到支持作用。

③ available *adj.* 可利用的，有效的

④ Dark Blue Bicycle Club 深蓝自行车俱乐部，这里指的是牛津的俱乐部。牛津和剑桥均以蓝色作为自己学校的标志，各不相让，只好以颜色深浅来区别，所以，通常人们把剑桥队员称为浅蓝对，而把牛津队员称为深蓝队。

⑤ inaugural *adj.* 就职的，开幕的

E: Yes, but sometimes Oxford won the match. The club went **from strength to strength**[1] through the 1880s, with amateur racing **flourishing**[2].

M: OK, thanks for your information. I will join the club and maybe someday I will be the winner of the **amateur**[3] race.

E: Great. There are few easier ways to get fit and healthy than by enjoying a leisurely cycle ride instead of catching the bus or getting in the car.

M: 嗨，爱德华！这是你新买的自行车吗?

E: 是啊，昨天刚刚买的。

M: 太漂亮了，我能试试吗?

E: 当然可以啦。别忘了，要靠左行。

M: 嗯，我想我还需要一定时间来适应这个规则。你是知道的，在我们国家，不管开车，骑车还是走路都要靠右行。

E: 如果你不遵守交通规则，就容易发生危险。

M: 好的，我想我还是等熟悉这里的交通规则以后再来试骑你的车吧。为什么剑桥有那么多人都以自行车作为交通工具呢?

E: 剑桥市面积不大，而且地势平坦。此外，剑桥大学的各个学院分布在城市的每个角落，骑自行车往来于课堂之间十分方便快捷。

M: 骑车几乎是最有利于环保的交通方式了。

E: 对。因为骑车在剑桥是最为普遍的一种交通方式，关于自行车的规定也很多。

M: 比如说?

E: 比如说，18 岁以下，60 岁以上的人骑车出行都要佩戴头盔。 每辆自行车都必须配备前后两盏灯。

M: 在我们国家就没有这样的规定。

E: 这有点麻烦，但也是为了安全着想。

M: 我完全同意。我注意到，这里的人经常随便把车靠在墙上，有些车甚至都不上锁，所以，我在想，是不是这里都没有人偷车?

E: 不，事实并不是这样。有些时候，人们只是比较随意罢了。而且剑桥市是全英国

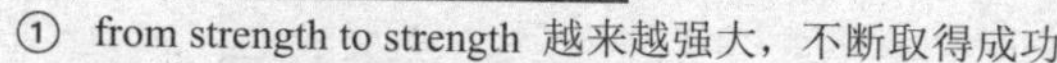

① from strength to strength 越来越强大，不断取得成功
② flourishing *adj.* 繁茂的，盛行的
③ amateur *n.* 业余爱好者

丢车最多的城市之一。

M: 你也一定得注意你的自行车。

E: 我会的。如果你对骑车感兴趣，你也可以加入剑桥的自行车俱乐部啊。

M: 我也想，只是我并不是很擅长骑车。

E: 没关系，俱乐部有各种各样的活动，成员们可以根据自身的情况进行选择。所有的学生和教职员工都有参加这个俱乐部的资格。

M: 真的吗？你可不可以给我介绍一下这个俱乐部啊，比如它的历史什么的。

E: 当然啦。这个俱乐部成立于 1874 年，当时只有 11 位成员。5 年之内，成员人数就增长到了 260 人，包括大学里各类人士，既有本科生又有研究员。

M: 它真的很受欢迎啊！俱乐部举行过什么比赛吗？

E: 举行过。在它成立两个月内，深蓝自行车俱乐部就向它发起了第一次大学对抗赛。这次比赛在 1874 年 6 月 18 日举行，赛道是牛津到剑桥之间的一条 80 米的路。剑桥赢了，第一名和第二名都由剑桥的学生取得。

M: 哇，剑桥人自行车骑得真不错。

E: 是，但是牛津有时也会赢得比赛。整个 19 世纪 80 年代，这个俱乐部变得越来越强大，业余爱好者比赛盛行。

M: 好的，谢谢你告诉我这些。我也要加入这个俱乐部，没准有一天我也会成为业余爱好者比赛的冠军呢。

E: 太好了。既简单，又有利于健康的运动莫过于悠闲地骑骑自行车了，这比坐公交或者开车都要好得多。

1 For example, people who under 18 or above 60 should wear a helmet when they ride, and your bike should **be equipped with** two lights, with one in the front and the other in the back.

（1）装备，配备，后面可接介词 with 或 for

- We can't afford to equip the army properly.
  我们无力使军队得到适当的装备。
- They equipped themselves with a pair of sharp axes and set off for the forest.
  他们带上两把锋利的斧子便朝森林走去。

（2）使有能力，使胜任，使有准备

➢ Your education will equip you for your future life.
你（所受）的教育将使你能适应今后的生活。

➢ Having anticipated the problems, I was well equipped to deal with the situation.
由于预先考虑到了这些问题，我有充分准备去处理局势。

2 It's a little bit troublesome but it's **for the sake of** safety.

（1）for the sake of 意为“为……的好处着想，为……起见”。

➢ He's going to live by the coast for the sake of his health.
他为了自己的健康，打算到海滨地区去住。

➢ I'm only doing it for your sake; I don't care about it myself.
我只是为你着想才做这事，我自己倒是无所谓。

➢ I'm not talking just for talking's sake; this is important!
我不是说说而已，我说的事情很重要！

（2）for God's / Christ's / goodness / heaven's / pity's sake 意为“看在上帝份上，千万……”，或者是表达一种气愤的语气。

➢ For goodness sake don't tell him!
千万别告诉他！

➢ What's the matter now, for God's sake?
老天啊，到底出了什么事？

3 I'd like to, but I'm not very **skilled** in cycling.

skilled 意为“有技巧的，需要技能的，（技能）熟练的”，常与介词 in 和 at 搭配。

➢ We need skilled workers skilled in welding for this job; it's a highly skilled job.
我们需要熟练的焊工做这项工作，这是需要高超技能的一项工作。

Cycling in Cambridge

Everywhere you turn in Cambridge there are people on bikes. The city has the highest level of cycling in the country. This is perhaps no surprise. The city is after all naturally suited for getting around by bike.

It is no **exaggeration**① to describe Cambridge as being as flat as the **proverbial**② pancake. The most significant inclines are railway bridges and crossings of the Cam. Only once you leave the city limits will you find anything that can be called a hill.

Cambridge's famous university is of course another factor in the popularity of cycling here. Colleges can be **dotted**③ anywhere within a three kilometer radius of the city centre. Forget the **stereotype**④ of students being hard up and thus not able to afford cars. The simple truth is that bikes are the quickest, easiest and most straight forward way to get between lectures, the library and the rowing club.

Besides, Cambridge City is very small, and a cycling ride within 40 minutes can **virtually**⑤ bring you to any corner of the city. As students of Cambridge from different parts of UK and the world scatter in various colleges, which are located in various communities or blocks of the city, they usually have to travel long distances in order to attend classes or lectures. Thus cycle naturally becomes the major mode of transportation here, for which someone even named Cambridge the "Cycle City". For this reason, Cambridge has a **distinguishing**⑥ feature from other cities—apart from the **conventional**⑦ two traffic lanes on the road, it has separate cycle routes.

The narrow cycle routes are just next to the motor ways, without any segregation. The speed of cars are unbelievably fast to the Chinese, even a **lumpish**⑧ coach can travel at a speed above 100 km per hour on the general lanes of traffic. To many foreign students, cycling in Cambridge can be the most dangerous thing in the world.

But it's far from just the students who cycle in Cambridge. So do the school kids, the

① exaggeration *n.* 夸大之词
② proverbial *adj.* 众所周知的
③ dot *vt.* 加上点，点缀于
④ stereotype *n.* 陈腔滥调，老套
⑤ virtually *adv.* 事实上，实际上
⑥ distinguishing *adj.* 有区别的，突出的
⑦ conventional *adj.* 常见的，惯例的
⑧ lumpish *adj.* 笨重的，笨拙的

pensioners and the **layabouts**[①]. As for all the workers in the city: apparently one in four commutes by bike. You see them **amble**[②] by in their business suits, their builder's overalls and their nurse's uniforms. On a **balmy**[③] summer evening, it's not unusual to see ladies pedalling out in summery frocks, gents riding down the street in bow ties. **Racquets**[④] in hands, folks ride out to the sports centre.

Cycling in Cambridge is not necessarily an activity in itself. In fact it's very much an aspect of everyday life.

校园单车行

在剑桥，你随处可以看到骑自行车的人。剑桥是全国骑自行车出行人口最多的城市。这也没有什么值得奇怪的，这座城市非常适合骑自行车出行。

说剑桥地势如平底锅一样毫不夸张。坡度最明显的地方是铁路桥和横跨剑河的桥梁。只有你离开了市区，才能见到一些小山丘。

剑桥市有著名的大学当然是骑车人口众多的另外一个原因。距市中心 3 公里范围内，分布着剑桥的各个学院。不要以为学生们是缺钱，买不起汽车。其实，这仅仅是因为骑自行车来往于课堂，图书馆和划船俱乐部之间最为方便快捷。

此外，剑桥市非常小，骑自行车 40 分钟之内就到达城市的任何一个地方。由于剑桥大学的学生很多来自英国各地、世界各地，散落地住在各个学院；而各个系分布在城市的各个街区，上课、听讲座经常要跑到很远的地方，自行车自然而然成为了这里的主要交通工具，有人甚至把剑桥叫“自行车城”。所以，不同于其他城市，剑桥在本来就只有两条车道的路上还要给自行车留出单独车道。

窄窄的自行车道和机动车道紧挨着，之间没有任何隔离装置。汽车的速度在中国是难以想象的，连最笨重的长途汽车在普通车道上的行驶速度都达到 100 公里 / 小时以上；在很多外国学生看来，在剑桥骑车是世界上最危险的事。

在剑桥，骑车的不仅仅是学生。上学的小孩，老人和闲来无事的人都骑自行车。全城的上班族约有 1/4 都骑自行车。你可以看到骑车的人有的一身正装，有的穿着工作服，还有的穿着护士服。在宣人的夏日夜晚，经常可以在街上看到穿连衣裙的女士或是打领结的男士骑着自行车穿梭往来。还有些人会带上球拍，去运动中心打球。

骑车在剑桥不能被称为一项运动。实际上，它已经成为了人们日常生活的一部分。

---

① layabout *n.* 懒汉，游荡的人
② amble *vi.* 缓行
③ balmy *adj.* 温和的，芳香的
④ racquet *n.* 球拍

40 Various Museums 多彩博物馆

焦点对话

Sofia is making a weekend plan and she goes to Dave for advice.

S: Sofia　　D: Dave

S: I am thinking about hanging out this weekend with a friend, which place do you suggest?

D: If you are interested, I strongly recommend the museums in University of Cambridge.

S: I heard that there are altogether seven museums in Cambridge. Do you know what they are?

D: Fitzwilliam Museum, Museum of **Archaeology**① and **Anthropology**②, Museum of **Zoology**③, Museum of Classical Archaeology, Whipple Museum of the History of Science, and…let me see…The Sedgwick Museum of Earth Sciences, Museum of the Scott Polar Research Institute.

S: The collections in each of them can be told from their names. I think the last one you mentioned just now is about polar research? I'd like to have a tour around it. I've heard about it before.

D: Yes, Museum of the Scott Polar Research Institute. But unfortunately, when I went there last week, it was closed for **renovation**④ and it won't be open until June.

S: What a pity! I've always wanted to have a look at the Antarctic gallery and the Arctic gallery.

D: I am very interested in them, too. The Antarctic gallery displayed permanent exhibits of material from several of the "Heroic Age" Antarctic expeditions from Britain.

---

① archaeology *n.* 考古学
② anthropology *n.* 人类学，人类学研究
③ zoology *n.* 动物学
④ renovation *n.* 翻修，修理，改革

S: In particular Captain Scott's expeditions. Besides, Roald Amundsen's flag from the South Pole is an item of particular interest.

D: Antarctic Treaty details, basic Antarctic geology, **philatelic**[1] items and polar medals were also displayed, alongside models of several **expeditionary**[2] ships, and a selection of other polar material.

S: Compared to those, I am more interested in examples of polar transport equipment: **sledges**[3], skis, snow shoes, and clothing, both ancient and modern, especially the ancient equipment.

D: And what interested me most is the exhibition of British Arctic exploration during the 19th century in the Arctic gallery.

S: That interests me very much, too. **Ivory**[4] items from **walruses**[5], sperm whales, **narwhal**[6], and even mammoths are displayed there.

D: True, and Inuit **artefacts**[7] and a display of **scrimshaw**[8] were some of its specialties. The grandfather of the modern **snow-scooter**[9], now a widely used transport device in both polar regions, was also exhibited. Maybe we can go there together months later.

S: Good idea. Since this museum has been closed, where did you go?

D: I went to the Museum of Zoology. I can assure you that it is a wonderful place to go. It happened that when we arrived, the Cambridge Science Festival was held in the museum.

S: Really? You're lucky! Is it still available if I go there this weekend?

D: I am afraid not. Generally, it lasts for a week or so. Don't be disappointed. The museum is great. It is home to a huge variety of recent and fossil animals and rivals those of the major university museums world-wide.

---

① philatelic *adj.* 集邮的
② expeditionary *adj.* 远征的，讨伐的
③ sledge *n.* 雪橇
④ ivory *adj.* 象牙制的，象牙色的
⑤ walrus *n.* 海象
⑥ narwhal *n.* 独角鲸
⑦ artifact *n.* 手工艺制品，人工制品
⑧ scrimshaw *n.* 贝雕工艺品
⑨ snow-scooter *n.* 雪上滑板车

S: That's great! I will go and have a look this weekend. Thanks a lot!

S: 我在考虑这周末和朋友出去玩，你有什么好去处推荐吗?

D: 如果你有兴趣的话，我强烈建议你们去剑桥大学的博物馆。

S: 我听所剑桥一共有 7 个博物馆，你知道它们分别是什么吗?

D: 费兹威廉博物馆、考古与人类学博物馆、动物学博物馆、古典考古博物馆、惠普科学历史博物馆，还有，让我想想……塞德威克地球科学博物馆和史考特北极研究所博物馆等。

S: 听这些博物馆的名字就大概知道馆藏的内容了。你最后一个提到的是关于极地考察的吗? 我想去参观一下这个，我之前就听说过它。

D: 是的。史考特北极研究所博物馆。但不幸的是，我们上周去那里的时候，它因为要整修而闭馆了，直到 7 月才会开。

S: 太可惜了！我一直想去看看里面的南极馆和北极馆。

D: 我对这个也特别感兴趣。南极馆一直都在展示“英雄年代”几次始于英国的南极探险。

S: 特别是史考特船长的探险。此外，罗尔德·亚孟森带回来的曾插到南极点的旗帜，最为引人注目。

D: 南极条约的详细条款，南极洲的基本地形，邮票和极地奖牌也在展出，另外还有其他几艘探险船的模型和一些极地物质。

S: 和这些相比，我对极地旅行装备的展览更有兴趣：雪橇、滑雪板、外套，既有过去的也有现代的，我对过去的装备尤其感兴趣。

D: 我最感兴趣的是北极馆关于 19 世纪英国北极探险的展示。

S: 我也对那个感兴趣。用海象、抹香鲸、独角鲸，甚至猛犸象的牙齿做成的器具也都在那展示。

D: 对啊。最有特色的，莫过于因纽特人的手工制品和贝雕品了。现代雪上单脚滑行车的“始祖”也在展示之列，现在在两极地区得到了广泛使用。再过几个月，我们可以一起来参观。

S: 好主意！既然这个博物馆关门了，你们去哪里了呢?

D: 我们去了动物学博物馆。我跟你说，这绝对是个好地方。我们去的时候，正好赶上剑桥科技节。

S: 真的吗? 你们太幸运了！我这周末去的话，还来得及吗?

D: 恐怕来不及了，通常这个科技节都只持续一周时间。不要伤心，这个博物馆真的很不错。里面大量的现代的和远古时期物种可以和世界上著名的大学博物馆媲美。

S: 太棒了，我这周末就去看看。非常感谢！

1 I am thinking about **hanging out** this weekend with a friend, which place do you suggest?

hang out 意为“居住，闲荡，厮混”。

➢ He hangs out in Green Street.
他住在格林大街。

另外，与 hang 有关的词组还有：hang over(不愉快的事情)逼近，威胁着；hang together 同心协力，保持团结；hang up 挂断电话；hang onto 继续保留；hang back 退缩，踟蹰不前等等。

2 If you are interested, I strongly **recommend** the museums in University of Cambridge.

(1) 推荐，介绍，与介词 for, as, to 连用

➢ They recommended her for the job.
他们推荐她做这项工作。

(2) 劝告，建议

➢ I recommend caution in dealing with this matter.
我建议慎重处理此事。

(3)（性质）使（某人、某事）有吸引力

➢ This hotel has nothing to recommend it except cheapness.
这家旅店除了便宜之外就没有什么可取之处了。

3 It is home to a huge variety of recent and fossil animals and **rivals** those of the major university museums world-wide.

rival 作动词，意为“与……匹敌，比得上，媲美”。

➢ Ships can't rival aircraft for speed.
船只在速度上无法同飞机相比。

- As a tourist centre, it rivals anywhere in Europe.
  作为旅游的中心，它不亚于欧洲的任何一个地方。
- I guess Linda can't rival Lucy and become the champion in the model competition.
  我想琳达不能在模特大赛中打败露茜，获得冠军。

Various Museums

Museums are a vital part of a world-famous university, which are often run by a university, **typically**① founded to aid teaching and research within the university. In the University of Cambridge, there are altogether seven such museums—Fitzwilliam Museum, Museum of Archaeology and Anthropology, Museum of Zoology, Museum of Classical Archaeology, Whipple Museum of the History of Science, The Sedgwick Museum of Earth Sciences, Museum of the Scott Polar Research Institute. Only few museums of the same kind can rival the collections in those museums in the world.

Among all of those, Fitzwilliam Museum is perhaps the most famous one. Praised by some as Britain's Best Museum and Gallery, Fitzwilliam Museum houses world-class collections of works of art and **antiquities**② **spanning**③ centuries and civilizations. Everyone who comes here often could not wait to see the manuscript of Einstein. As stated by the University itself, " Like the University itself, the Fitzwilliam Museum is part of the national heritage, but, much more, it is part of a living and continuing culture which it is our **statutory**④ duty to **transmit**⑤".

Museum of Archaeology and Anthropology offers a **feast**⑥ of images and ideas. *The Guardian* has even said that it holds "the

① typically *adv.* 代表性地，作为特色地
② antiquity *n.* 文物，古代遗物
③ span *vt.* 跨越
④ statutory *n.* 法定的
⑤ transmit *vt.* 传达，传送
⑥ feast *n.* 节日，筵席，宴会

discoveries of some of the most remarkable explorers and scholars of their time". You can see in it world-class collections of **Oceanic**①, Asian, African and native American art — canoes, sculptures, masks, and textiles — and major archaeological discoveries, ranging from the earliest stone tools, discovered by Louis Leakey in Olduvai Gorge, to British finds from Roman and medieval periods. Today the Museum remains a base for wide-ranging archaeological and anthropological research.

The Museum of Classical Archaeology is one of the few **surviving**② collections of plaster casts of Greek and Roman sculpture in the world. The collection of about four hundred and fifty casts is open to the public and housed in a purpose-built Cast Gallery on the first floor of the Classics Faculty. Although nothing here is an original, nearly all the well-known works from the Classical world can be seen together under one roof.

The other museums are **unmentioned**③ here not because of their insignificance but the length of the article; they all played an important part in either studies or researches within and out of the university. You can have a general idea of their collections from the names. In addition, Kettles Yard, The University Library, Botanic Garden, though not entitled "museum", are worth a visit.

多彩博物馆

在一所世界闻名的大学里，博物馆是必不可少的。这样的博物馆通常由大学自己经营，其设立通常是为了辅助大学的教学和研究。剑桥大学就共有 7 座这样的博物馆——费兹威廉博物馆、考古与人类学博物馆、动物学博物馆、古典考古博物馆、惠普科学历史博物馆、塞德威克地球科学博物馆、史考特北极研究所博物馆等。这些博物馆的藏品之多，在世界上鲜有同类的博物馆能与之匹敌。

在这些博物馆中，费兹威廉博物馆最负盛名。馆中有很多世界一流的藏品，其中包括诸多各个文明时期和不同世纪的艺术真品和珍稀文物。 每一个来到这里的人都迫不及待要去亲眼一睹爱因斯坦的数学手稿。 正如剑桥大学校方所说：“和剑桥一样，

① oceanic *adj.* 大洋洲的
② surviving *adj.* 继续存在的，依然健在的
③ unmentioned *adj.* 未提到的，未说起的

费兹威廉博物馆是国家遗产的一部分。但它更是鲜活生动而又延绵不绝的文化的一部分，传承这种文化，我们义不容辞。”

参观考古与人类学博物馆绝对是一场视觉与思想的盛宴。英国《卫报》曾经说它藏有“当时世界上最为著名的探险家和学者的发现”。来自大洋洲、亚洲、非洲和美国本土的世界一流艺术作品——独木舟、雕刻、面具和纺织品——还有考古学史上最重要的发现，从路易斯·李基在奥杜威峡谷发现的早期石器，到从罗马时期到中世纪的英国考古发现应有尽有。现在这所博物馆仍然是考古学和人类学研究的重要基地之一。

古典考古博物馆是世界上少数收藏有古希腊和古罗马石膏铸体的博物馆之一。馆里收藏的450余尊石膏雕塑都是对外开放的，古典区一楼还特意建造了一个石膏展览厅，以陈列这些物品。尽管这里的物品都不是真品，但是能在同一个地方就饱览所有闻名世界的经典作品也十分难得。

这里没有提到其他的博物馆，并不是因为它们不重要。在剑桥校内外人士的学习和研究中，它们都起着非常重要的作用。因为篇幅有限，这里就不多作介绍了。根据名字，读者就能对它们的馆藏内容略知一二。除了这些博物馆之外，壶园、大学图书馆和植物园这些不叫博物馆的“博物馆”也是非常值得一去的地方。